Place, Craft and N

For over four decades, Ruskin Mill Trust has worked with young people with special educational needs and behavioural issues who learn traditional crafts and organic farming as part of an integrated curriculum of therapeutic education, overcoming barriers to learning and re-engaging with the wider world. This accessible and inspiring book showcases how an appreciation of place, traditional crafts, farming and transformative education offers a wider route to human well-being for all. The authors outline the different fields of the "Practical Skills Therapeutic Education" method, which includes developing practical skills, learning the ecology of the farm and understanding therapeutic education, holistic care, health and self-leadership.

Taking the reader on a tour of Ruskin Mill's many extraordinary provisions across Britain, and going deeper in conversation with its founder, Aonghus Gordon, this book is an outstanding story of creative thinking in an age of narrow focus on classrooms and written examinations, presenting a transformative perspective on education and care. Being grounded in work supporting young people with complex additional needs, it provides a rare insight into the work of one of the world's leading charities working with neurodiversity.

With its non-specialist language, *Place, Craft and Neurodiversity* offers ideas and resources for work in different areas of education and therapy. It will inspire parents, educators and care workers around the globe.

Aonghus Gordon OBE (for cultural heritage and education) is the founder and CEO of Ruskin Mill Trust. He was awarded an honorary doctorate by the University of Huddersfield for his work.

Laurence Cox is Professor of Sociology at the National University of Ireland, Maynooth.

"Under the outstanding leadership of Aonghus Gordon, Ruskin Mill has set a superb example of selfless service in the field of holistic education. This stunningly inspiring and immensely powerful story of Ruskin Mill gives us the highest hope for a better future for humanity".

Satish Kumar, *Founder, Schumacher College and Editor Emeritus of "Resurgence & Ecologist"*

"This book is a powerful reminder of the importance of the relationship of place to our physical and mental health and our overall sense of wellbeing. The Ruskin Mill approach reminds us to imagine what this can mean for us in practice."

Patrick Holden, *Founder & CEO, Sustainable Food Trust*

Place, Craft and Neurodiversity

Re-imagining Potential through Education at Ruskin Mill

Aonghus Gordon and Laurence Cox

Routledge
Taylor & Francis Group

LONDON AND NEW YORK

Cover image by Oliver Carnaby

First published 2024
by Routledge
4 Park Square, Milton Park, Abingdon, Oxon OX14 4RN

and by Routledge
605 Third Avenue, New York, NY 10158

Routledge is an imprint of the Taylor & Francis Group, an informa business

Open access funded by Ruskin Mill Trust.

British Library Cataloguing-in-Publication Data
A catalogue record for this book is available from the British Library

Library of Congress Cataloging-in-Publication Data
Names: Gordon, Aonghus, 1955- author. | Cox, Laurence, author.
Title: Place, craft and neurodiversity : re-imagining potential through education at Ruskin Mill / Aonghus Gordon and Laurence Cox.
Description: First edition. | New York : Routledge, 2024. | Includes bibliographical references and index. | Identifiers: LCCN 2023040136 (print) | LCCN 2023040137 (ebook) | ISBN 9781032421773 (hbk) | ISBN 9781032421759 (pbk) | ISBN 9781003361541 (ebk)
Subjects: LCSH: Ruskin Mill Trust. | Special education--Great Britain. | People with disabilities--Education--Great Britain. | Handicraft--Therapeutic use--Great Britain. | Organic farming--Great Britain. | Art therapy--Great Britain. | Occupational therapy--Great Britain. | Group psychotherapy--Great Britain.
Classification: LCC LC3986.G7 G67 2024 (print) | LCC LC3986.G7 (ebook) | DDC 371.90941--dc23/eng/20231117
LC record available at https://lccn.loc.gov/2023040136
LC ebook record available at https://lccn.loc.gov/2023040137

ISBN: 9781032421773 (hbk)
ISBN: 9781032421759 (pbk)
ISBN: 9781003361541 (ebk)

DOI: 10.4324/9781003361541

Typeset in ITC Galliard Pro
by KnowledgeWorks Global Ltd.

Printed in Great Britain by Bell and Bain Ltd, Glasgow

This book is dedicated to the parents and carers who move heaven and earth for their children's education.

Contents

Foreword

By Dr Stefan Geider

Dr Stefan Geider MD, GP is Chair of Camphill Estates and Chair of Camphill Wellbeing Trust

The year was 1982. The place was Camphill School Aberdeen in the granite-grey North-East of Scotland. The person was a young volunteer from a small village in the Rhine Valley of Southern Germany eager for new experiences. The work was living and working alongside young people with learning disabilities. The impact of place, people and the therapeutic practices of Camphill was life-changing.

I know this because I was that young volunteer. What I learned and experienced during my first four-year encounter with Camphill and its integrated approach to health, education and care for people with disabilities and other support needs determined the direction of my life and formed its purpose.

Ten years later, in 1996, having completed an extended medical training encompassing anthroposophic medicine at the newly founded University of Witten/Herdecke, Germany, I returned to Aberdeen to continue my life's work.

Since then, and for the past 27 years, I have worked as an NHS GP with a special interest in learning disabilities and have also practised the extended AnthroHealth approach (based on anthroposophic medicine) with a wide range of patients. Throughout I have been intimately connected with the therapeutic work of the Camphill organisations, particularly in the North-East of Scotland, living within one of their communities for over seven years.

I first met Aonghus and his evolving therapeutic educational approach over 20 years ago. His thinking and practices had similarities to the Camphill approach with which I was so familiar. Both Camphill and Ruskin Mill Trust aim to create life-changing experiences for people with learning disabilities and other challenges by integrating education, health and care supported by positive relationships and therapeutic environments.

Aonghus has since progressed, refined and consolidated the methodology he initially developed at the Ruskin Mill Trust organisations and successfully embedded his approach – now known as Practical Skills Therapeutic Education (PSTE) – into all the Ruskin Mill organisations. By so doing, Aonghus has helped create a cohesion throughout the various organisations, equipping and enabling them to respond successfully to the complex and ever-changing challenges facing providers in this educational sector. Most remarkably he has done this while remaining true to his own identity and his inspirational sources: John Ruskin, William Morris and Rudolf Steiner.

This book for the first time articulates, for a wide readership, the principles and practices on which the PSTE approach is based. As with all successful therapeutic educational models, PSTE has a coherent underpinning theoretical framework which has been developed and tested by Aonghus through 40-plus years of practical experience working alongside young adults with a range of additional support needs. This practice-based approach resonates strongly with my own 40 years of professional experience of applying Camphill's integrated health, education and social care approach.

The format of the book is reader-friendly – enabling a quick overview of the whole PSTE method before dipping into its various aspects in the individual chapters. The way in which the content of each chapter is presented engages interest throughout – striking a helpful balance between theory and practice, amply illustrated with practical examples and enriched by personal insights from Aonghus himself. The refreshing, easy-to-read style is accessible to a wide readership.

I can fully recommend this book to all whose lives are touched by those with additional support needs or who want an introduction to the Ruskin Mill approach.

For family, carers, friends: this book offers an insight into why your loved ones benefit from the Ruskin Mill approach and might spark some ideas for helpful activities to try at home.

For professionals working in special needs education, social care, therapy or medicine: this book offers inspiration, ideas and models for practice that may serve as a catalyst to enrich or transform your current work.

I not only enjoyed reading this book but gained new perspectives on Aonghus's work and the Ruskin Mill methodology. I look forward to further exploring these in my own work to create something anew.

Like Aonghus I too believe that "a fulfilled human life is one which we actively co-create, becoming more and more able to be authentic owners of our own lives while taking account of others and the planet".

This book offers some signposts along the way.

Preface: Why Ruskin Mill Matters

This is not only a book about caring for young people with learning difficulties and differences. It is also a book about being human, and human flourishing in general.

Place, Craft and Neurodiversity draws on a particular, and very demanding, experience: Ruskin Mill Trust's 40 years of using traditional crafts and biodynamic/organic farming to help transform the lives of some of the most vulnerable young people in Britain, people with learning differences and difficulties that may be compounded by different forms of disadvantage or experiences of trauma. Some may be on the autistic spectrum or have AD(H) D, some exhibit behaviour that challenges and some have complex additional needs of other kinds.[1]

Ruskin Mill's approach has developed out of a practical response to these needs, drawing on the work of John Ruskin, William Morris and Rudolf Steiner but worked out in specific contexts and shared across the Trust when a particular approach has proven itself to be effective. At the same time, the method parallels much of what is now, four decades later, becoming widely recognised in research and best practice, not only in "special educational needs" but for everyone:

- The connection to nature matters, for our health and mental health.
- Working with our hands, developing practical skills, is regenerative and transformative.
- We do not live suspended in mid-air, but inhabit specific places with their own histories, whose particular qualities shape our lives within them.
- Neurodiversity – the rich variety of different kinds of human minds and hearts – is not the situation of a few but our common condition of *diversity*, and it is important to create education and care that meet each person's particular needs.
- Care, and medicine, need to speak to the whole human being.
- Finally, a fulfilled human life is one which we actively co-create, becoming more able to be actors in our own lives while taking account of others and the planet.

Taken together, these different dimensions of Ruskin Mill's method have proven to be transformative in the lives of many young people with complex

additional needs of many kinds, who have moved from an inability to engage
with a world that has often failed them, through mastering practical skills whose
results they can see, to being able to give back to others and the community.

They also underpin a remarkable approach to staff training and development in which staff face the same kinds of challenges they will help students
with, as the resistance they encounter in working with the material world com-
pels not just the acquisition of practical skills and understanding but also the
overcoming of emotional barriers: from hands, to head, to heart. We think the
method and its results may be of interest to a wider audience still, of people
seeking to change themselves and their world.

The effectiveness of the method has been acknowledged in many different
ways and places: by the parents and guardians who push for their children's
admission; by the young people themselves during and even more significantly
after their stay; by the local authorities or tribunals that direct funds to support
their education, health and care plans at Ruskin Mill; by donors, volunteers
and Trustees who support its non-profit activities; by the Trust's continued
capacity for growth; by many different inspection bodies; by international interest and requests for assistance from the US, India, Malaysia or China; most
recently by the awards of an OBE and an honorary doctorate from the University of Huddersfield to its founder, Aonghus Gordon.

However, this book is not a manual for professionals working in the area
or an overview of research in the field. A key aspect of the Trust's own staff
training is the understanding that what is beneficial for the young people in
its care is also helpful for the staff who work with them. Each may face their
own very specific challenges, but the wider questions of what constitutes a
fuller human life, what enables development and transformation and how we
can become genuinely freer individuals, contributing to the world around us –
"self-generated conscious action" as it is called at Ruskin Mill – are not fundamentally different.

This book goes a step further. It presents the different dimensions of Ruskin Mill's method in ways that will speak to parents and to some young people;
that may be helpful to professionals and researchers; and that we hope will
inspire related initiatives in other areas. In doing this, it starts from the specifics of what has been found to work and offers these as a wider contribution to
everyone's thinking about what it means to be human and how we can support
transformation.

Practical Skills Therapeutic Education and a good way of life

When people visit Ruskin Mill's colleges, garden schools, RISE provisions and
other locations, a common response is "I wish my child could come here" –
irrespective of whether that child has particular learning or social challenges.
This is often followed after a time by "I wish I could have gone here".

It is central to Ruskin Mill Trust's model that "people with complex additional needs" are not fundamentally different; in fact staff need to understand

and transform themselves if they are to genuinely help students. There are many flavours of being human – this is what the term "neurodiversity" points towards – and the specifics of what an individual needs may be different. For example, someone who for whatever reason has missed out on a particular developmental stage may need to "re-step" the process in an age-appropriate way. However, staff also have their own wounds to work with – as do we all – and what is good for human beings is shared, even if there may be different paths in that direction. This is one reason why Practical Skills Therapeutic Education (PSTE) has proven to work for many different specific challenges, for different age groups and in different cultures.

The other is that it speaks to the whole human being in the world. It does not just offer "connection" with people and nature – which we widely recognise as being transformative in many ways – but more specifically *engagement*, an active and practical process of mutual transformation. By shaping raw material and working the land, we change ourselves.

Moreover, it identifies a need for this active engagement across the whole spectrum of human experience, rather than artificially separating out a single element as equally effective for everyone. Thus, it offers a model where we understand our own situation; we engage transformatively with the physical matter of the world and with the growing processes of plants and animals; we engage with the fundamental human relationships of *learning* and *teaching*; we pay attention to a form of care which enables greater freedom; we diagnose where change needs to happen in ourselves; and we take courage for ourselves and for others.

The Ruskin Mill method

What is now called Practical Skills Therapeutic Education was not developed as a scheme on paper which was then imposed on other people. Rather, it emerged organically, starting from the very specific needs of particular young people. At the very beginning, for example, teenagers in a special school were regularly putting chairs through windows. Engaging them in practical outdoors activity – rebuilding an old mill wheel – proved emotionally absorbing, stretched their skills hugely and offered a glimpse of a different kind of future.

Over time, with very different groups of participants, it became clear that practical skills – in craft and landwork – were powerful tools, not to train young people as future farmers or artisans, although that also happens, but as a form of education which is deeply *therapeutic:* geared not only to the acquisition of knowledge or skills but also to the transformation of the whole human being.

The method's articulation as "PSTE" only came about in its third decade, as Ruskin Mill's continued development meant that intensive investment was needed in training, education and research both to embed the method thoroughly in the staff body and to take it forward on the basis of what practitioners were learning.

Taken together, the seven fields of the method provide staff with an over-view of areas in which they can both support and positively challenge pupils, students and post-education participants. They also provide a checklist for areas in which staff can engage in personal development to help them support others better. This book suggests that the method also offers a wider model of what a full human life consists of and how we can transform ourselves. Each chapter introduces one of these fields.

About this book

This book aims to show, not tell. Each chapter starts by inviting the reader to share something of the experience of visiting one of Ruskin Mill's many dif-ferent provisions – an old Cotswold mill valley, a re-imagined metalworks in Sheffield, a Scottish woodland, a garden school in Bristol – as concretely as we can. Depending on the season and the path you take, these are some of the things you might see and hear, touch or smell, and some of what you might see happening. This section of the chapter builds on the "genius loci walks" that the Trust offers visitors as the best way of coming to understand its work.

The second section of each chapter steps back from this to answer some of the questions that are often raised by this kind of visit, in everyday language: responses to "why do you do this?" Each chapter focusses on one of the seven fields of PSTE, building up an overview of the different aspects of the method in as clear and accessible a way as possible.

The third section goes deeper; drawing on interviews with the Trust's founder Aonghus Gordon, they unpack some of the wider questions and chal-lenges involved in the work of the Trust, combining a depth of reflection honed by four decades of ground-breaking work in the area with the flow of everyday conversation and reflection on some of the moments that led to the development of the Ruskin Mill method.

This book could have been written in many different ways, but three choices in particular need mentioning. One is that it does not attempt to duplicate Ruskin Mill's own internal training material: this is not a manual or a how-to book which would only be of interest to people already working in the field. Similarly, we have not tried to duplicate the research effort mentioned above, but rather to present the method of PSTE for a wide audience, with references kept to a minimum.

Lastly, we have chosen not to place the book's emphasis on the sometimes very severe challenges and difficulties faced by the young people at Ruskin Mill. As noted in Chapter 7, for people who aren't familiar with these difficul-ties, this can lead to an overly sentimental response ("that's so awful!") which makes people objects of pity and does not help practically. Conversely, the young people themselves, their parents and guardians and those who work with them already have a very clear sense of just how hard things can be and do not need to have this reinforced. What they may need, and what this book at-tempts to provide, is a practical sense of hope, of what may make a difference.

The book is shaped by the process of writing it. When we started, Laurence was a sympathetic outsider, an academic researcher with an interest in radical initiatives for cultural change, familiar with care work and Steiner education but new to Ruskin Mill. Over time he visited the different provisions profiled in this book and gained a deeper understanding of the method through talking to staff as well as doing a series of in-depth interviews with Aonghus Gordon about different aspects of the method. Aonghus and Helen Kippax, Vice-Chair of the Trust, carved time out from their intensive schedules to work through a draft of the text with Laurence, and senior staff also gave up their time to give very helpful feedback.

We hope this book will be helpful to the parents and guardians of young people struggling to find their place in the world, as well as to some of those young people themselves if they like reading books like this. It also aims to be useful to craft practitioners, organic and biodynamic farmers, therapeutic educators, carers and other professionals working in the different areas touched by the method.

Beyond this, the book is intended to share what has been learned and developed over 40 years in Ruskin Mill Trust with the wider world. We hope it will benefit some readers who find this method helps them to transform their own lives in different areas and make their own contribution, as well as inspire other initiatives for cultural transformation.

Note

1 Language in this area is changing very fast, and Ruskin Mill's usage is also changing. We hope it is clear that the language used in this book is intended to convey respect. It is also important to note that usage varies from country to country as well as between different institutional sectors. In England and Wales, "special educational needs" is an official category, and where used the phrase refers to this.

Acknowledgements

Our thanks go above all to Helen Kippax for her vision, encouragement and persistence around this book. Helen was the patron of this book's process: she stood steadfast in understanding its importance and encouraging Aonghus to complete the task of conveying the insights, methods and the story of Ruskin Mill Trust to the world, his colleagues and students.

Anna Daniels and Anna Mitchell made the book possible through finding time for Aonghus to meet with Laurence, making sure printouts of drafts were available, and in many other practical ways. Thank you both.

Very many thanks to Matt Briggs, Constantin Court, Berni Courts, Renatus Derbidge, Francesca Meynell, Sofie Rasmussen, Simon Reakes, the late Sue Reed, Sue Smee, Órfhlaith Tuohy, Richard Tucker and Julie Woods who commented on different chapters of this book.

Thank you also to the many Ruskin Mill staff and others who helped this book in many ways, with conversations about their own practice, help with practicalities, organising visits, selecting photos and otherwise. This book is a tribute to your work:

Judy Bailey, Jamie Bradford, Janine Christley, Michael Collins, Samantha Courtney, Andrea Damico, Alan Ellsmore, Paul Garnault, Colin George, Keith Griffiths, Vivian Griffiths, Chris Helliwell, Lone Helliwell, Chloe Hindmarsh, Roger Holloway, Angie Iversen, Marti Jachimczyk, Elisabeth Johnson, Gill Nah, John Ó Laoidh, Chiara Borelli Paker, Ricardo Pereira, Darshan Robson, Richard Thatcher, Richard Turley, Paul Turner, Peter van Vliet, Laura Wallwork and Anna Willoughby.

Our apologies to anyone we've forgotten.

1 The spirit of place

Walking through the Horsley Valley

The Horsley Valley is a couple of hours' walk from the Slad Valley that Laurie Lee immortalised in *Cider with Rosie* (2002), two of the "five valleys" that converge on the Gloucestershire town of Stroud. It lies a bit north of Thomas Hardy's Wessex, and to the southern end of JRR Tolkien's imagined Shire (centred on Worcestershire and Shropshire). This places it at the heart of a certain vision of the English countryside as lived-in and farmed on a human scale.

As you walk out of the pretty Cotswold town of Nailsworth, above its old stone roofs, you turn down along the Old Bristol Road, built in 1800 as a toll road. Past houses and mill buildings, you come out under trees and cross a stream, walking up to the busy space of Ruskin Mill and its surrounding cottages and outbuildings.

You enter the Mill through a beautifully carved wooden door into a gallery space, often hosting exhibitions of art and craft made by the young people studying here or by visiting artists. This was once the basement of a 16th-century corn mill, rebuilt as a textile mill in the 1820s. In the 20th century it was home to many activities, including stiffening leather, cider-pressing and ink-making, before it fell derelict.

In the early 1980s, the basement floor was relaid as part of a creative social project, and three different layers of older paving were found. The new floor was laid in a zodiac pattern using limestone and sandstone, clay tiles and granite cobbles.

Going up the staircase, you are in the old entrance space. To the left is a stained-glass workshop, where windows from Gloucester cathedral are regularly restored. If you turn right, you find yourself outside once more, facing the millpond, with water running through one of the strangely beautiful "flowform" features that are everywhere in this valley.

Walking upstream, you travel alongside the small lake that is the old millpond. The far bank rises steeply, a forest of straight tall trees. This whole valley is a haven of biodiversity – over 50 species of birds have been recorded here. The land is worked using the principles of biodynamics, the original form of organic farming, in which the whole farm is seen as a single, interconnected

DOI: 10.4324/9781003361541-1

Figure 1.1 Re-inhabiting place: Ruskin Mill today

organism. At any time of year, from bedraggled winter through sparkling summer to pressing apples in autumn, the valley teems with life.

At the far end of the lake, you walk through the market garden, where paths and streams crisscross among rows of lettuce and clucking chickens, trellises and polytunnels for fruit and vegetables. As it has been for centuries, this is a lively, working landscape. On the opposite hillside are ancient weavers' cottages clustered together in terraces with stone walls, woodpiles, tiny patches of green, steep steps and paths. Students and staff are busy here, but the rights of way and other paths that once brought mill workers from the valley sides down to the mills are still open and beloved by strollers. Students with autism in particular are often seen as needing a controlled space without new faces, but here the work itself – and skilled staff – create a safe container.

The main valley path takes a turn to the left, up and over a Monet-inspired bridge and into a space of reeds and ponds, as the Nailsworth Stream spreads out. Here the land has returned to something closer to how it was before the Huguenots drained it – a better space to fish or hunt in than to build houses, and indeed the villages traditionally sit along the spring line, higher up the valley sides.

The names too are telling. Very commonly in England rivers have some of the oldest placenames, often Celtic where the villages along them have Anglo-Saxon or later names. Here though, where the older dwellings sat high above them, the waterways of the Five Valleys are (re)named after the villages: the Nailsworth Stream, Painswick Stream, Ruscombe Brook and Slad Brook. Only the River Frome (fine or brisk) keeps its Celtic name.

Craft workshops sit on the forest slopes to the left, and ahead is Horsley Mill, now the college's main administration space. As you pass the courtyard, there is a dramatic piece of Celtic knotwork surrounded by craft tools, carved in stone by student Andrew Geary, who went on to become a master stonecarver.

Figure 1.2 Supporting outdoors work: the green woodwork building at Ruskin Mill

At one time, there were nearly 200 mills in Nailsworth and the neighbouring Stroud valleys. But when coal replaced water power, these mills couldn't compete with the Pennines, even though the millowners built a canal to bring coal from the Forest of Dean as far as Stroud and, later, a railway from Stroud to Nailsworth – this latter now a cycle track through the woods.

Though Horsley's mill wheel has long since vanished, water still owns this space. It runs through flowforms into pools and bubbles up in springs once used as fridges to keep butter and milk bottles cool in summers past. Just past the mill are the pools of the revived fish farm, once again teeming with alevins, fry and parr – the wonderful names of the brown trout's life cycle – along with fully grown trout breaking the surface.

Small wonder that in its earlier incarnation as a fish farm, kids from the weavers' cottages came to poach here: today the poachers are more likely to be otters and birds. There have been fish ponds in this valley since an 11th-century Norman priory made its own. At the long feeder pool above, you can sometimes see a kingfisher as more than just a flash of iridescent blue caught out of the corner of the eye – at a quiet time you might see it perching and dipping for a few minutes before it spots you and vanishes.

Past the fish farm, the rules are reversed: rather than permissive paths passing through Ruskin Mill College's land, the right of way goes through an inhabited landscape up the narrow valley bottom. Here the path becomes almost a ledge, especially when bicycles pass you. To its side the stream runs clear over glittering pebbles, a natural paddle-way for children in summer and a good place to find watercress.

At the hamlet of Washpool you cross a tarmacked road that runs steeply up on both sides – to the left around a hairpin turn that regularly traps GPS-led delivery vans as surely as pixies might have led locals astray on dark nights in the past. This is Barton End Lane, part of the ancient route from Avening to the village of Horsley and beyond to Nympsfield by the Neolithic barrow and down to the old Severn ford at Newnham.

From earth to air

Past the road and you are under trees, coming into the forest and seeing a green man statue carved out of living wood where the path forks. Up to the left, wooden steps take you up into the forest banks previously only seen from across the valley. Suddenly the floor is covered in the rich brown of fallen leaves in autumn and winter, the green of wild garlic in spring or the white of its flowers in early summer, and the trees are all around you. The steep angle of the path speaks to the straight, tall trees that reach up past each other in search of the light. The wild garlic – along with wood anemones, primroses and bluebells – is an indicator species, telling us that this is semi-natural woodland, going back many centuries. Small-leaved lime trees, also indicating ancient woodland, were widespread after the ice age but are now rare in Britain.

This is Park Wood, still managed today on a ten-year cycle, similar to traditional forestry. Each year students and staff work one tenth of it, coppicing for charcoal, felling for green woodwork and to clear spaces where sunlight can enable young trees to grow, so that the whole forest doesn't reach old age at once and be devastated by a major storm. As elsewhere in the Cotswolds, these edges are too steep for tillage but ideal for a mixed-use woodland. These woods have been a working landscape since the Bronze Age: in 1262 Horsley had 14 carpenters, 12 saddle tree makers, 11 sawyers, two timber dealers, two chair makers and a glasswright, probably burning beech charcoal. Villagers had rights to gather firewood and to run geese and pigs in the wood, paid for in poultry.

Suddenly the light changes as the path breaks out of the woods and into the lower end of Gables Farm, beside the reconstructed Iron Age forge and the spiral curves of the Woodland Kitchen that feeds staff and students working up here. Between the two is the Festival Field, an open grassy top used for seasonal festivals, and more recently for a specially commissioned *Arthur* play (Chapter 3). It has also played host to two Neurodiversity Conferences, joint events with the Hay Festival where autism advocates and artists with autism, professionals and researchers met students and staff – as well as many visitors with autism or with children on the spectrum.

The grass that grows on these upland limestone fields has fed grazing animals for many centuries, back before the medieval wool trade that built the great wool churches of this region and gave the Chancellor of the Exchequer the Woolsack to sit on. When the Romans came, the Celtic Dobunni tribe were already running their herds on these uplands. The neighbouring uplands of Minchinhampton and Rodborough Commons, grazed since antiquity, are Sites of Special Scientific Interest, with flora shaped by this history.

Further back still, these hills and valleys were home to woolly rhinos and mammoth, herds of muskox, bison and horse. Hunter-gatherers left their microliths on the uplands 5,000 and 6,000 years before Christ, and Neolithic farmers built spectacular tombs on the Cotswold Edge nearby. An ancient path ran along the top of the scarp. Today, Ruskin Mill students work with sheep and cows, pigs, goats and donkeys, as well as the beehives scattered throughout the land.

Past a first collection of barns stands the Field Centre, the heart of Ruskin Mill's research and higher education. It is an extraordinary building: the grassy roof is shaped like an interplay of doves' wings, with a glass dome in the centre allowing the sun to illuminate the building. As you sit in meetings, the valley falls away below you and buzzards hover at your eye level.

Inside, the walls are coloured layers of rammed earth, taken from Ruskin Mill Trust's various provisions around the island, with the local limestone on top and the Horsley Valley clay at the bottom. Wooden pillars cut from the valley's beech trees support a central ring of wood, which in turn supports the curved wooden beams supporting the roof.

A spherical blown-glass flask of water turned red by gold nanoparticles sits suspended in the sunlight from the beams of the dome. In the floor below, a hole like a well leads down to the Moon Chamber, a pillared space surrounding a silver flowform set above the fissured limestone. Digging down into the foundations, workers broke into a narrow cleft in the rock, which leads off into darkness but not silence: once in a while a toad appears in the chamber, which must be connected to narrow passages leading out somewhere on the slopes below – when the wind presses against the hillside, you can feel it on your face in the chamber.

Beyond the Field Centre are – unsurprisingly – more fields, farm buildings again and an orchard before you reach the student-run farm shop, in turn nestled behind the pub on the Old Bath Road, built in the 1780s as a toll road across the dry, high ridges. Travelling from here on the road that zigzags down the Cotswold Edge, the Severn and the Forest of Dean can be seen, and, in clear light, the mountains of Wales beyond.

Meeting the "spirit of the place"

Much of the background information above is drawn from the "genius loci" surveys that Dr Margaret Colquhoun carried out with Ruskin Mill Trust's staff in 1994 and 2006, and a more recent one in 2018. These surveys are an important early step when Ruskin Mill Trust establishes itself in a new location: a process of discovering where it is, and what might be appropriate for that location. They can also be thought of as a way of making first contact with a place, and, later, of renewing the encounter with that place.

The *genius loci* or spirit of place is a concept familiar from the first written records of Celtic religion here: altars and other inscriptions from Roman-occupied Britain. The Italian peninsula that Rome conquered was already a multi-lingual and multi-cultural area, and such dedications were not unusual there. As the legions conquered new areas of Europe, its soldiers, themselves drawn from across the Empire and beyond, would often make dedications – and, no doubt, offerings – to an unspecified *genius loci*, the deity of a spring, hill or wood.

As the Celtic upper classes learned Latin and sought to assimilate, they too would sponsor inscriptions, sometimes naming a specific deity. From this process too, we have the familiar process of equating local deities with Roman ones: sometimes with the tutelary deity of a particular tribe, but sometimes with the spirit of a place. Famously, after the introduction of Christianity a number of such deities remained venerated as local saints.

Thus, for example, the hot spring at nearby *Aquae Sulis*, Bath, had its own deity, *Sulis*, equated with the empire's goddess of wisdom as *Sulis Minerva*. She was addressed in over 100 leaden curse tablets thrown into the spring, which acted as a form of religious lawsuit: the goddess was asked to inflict suffering on a thief until they returned items stolen, often from the baths themselves.

As a concept, this "spirit of place" points us towards the recognition that if at one level the human being is universal – capable of communication and understanding, collaboration and cooperation across vast geographical differences and even time – this universality always expresses itself in specifics. We are situated and contextual beings, existing in relationship with the world and people as we encounter them in a particular time and place, rather than in the abstract; as poet Hugh MacDiarmid wrote, "The universal *is* the particular".

This does not mean that we cannot change or move, or that these particular locations are not themselves subject to deep historical change. Nailsworth, with its Anglo-Saxon placename and surrounded by remnants of the Norman aristocracy, sits below the vast upland earthworks on Minchinhampton Common, probably dug by the Dobunni before the Romans came.

In the first decades after that invasion, it lay to the west of the Fosse Way from Exeter to Lincoln, which marked the boundary of the earliest conquest, perhaps with a ditch (*fossa*). As you drive along that route, now the A429 from Cirencester through Stow-on-the-Wold and Moreton-in-Marsh, the western Cotswolds to your left were then still "barbarian" territory, with the more easily tamed lowlands to the right.

Two miles away, at Woodchester's Roman villa – not uncovered for over 50 years – is Europe's second-largest Orpheus mosaic, in a British style with animals parading around the legendary musician, facing outwards. As the Romans pushed further west, they erected a statue of Mercury, today in the British Museum, over an Iron Age shrine near Uley, itself probably replacing earlier standing stones; the Roman temple was replaced in time by a timber church.

Not far away, where the Cotswold Edge looks out westwards across the Severn to the Forest of Dean, the Wye Valley and the Black Mountains of Wales, are the Neolithic long barrows at Nympsfield and Uley, indicators of a yet longer history, which could be extended further to the Mesolithic footprints preserved in the mud of the Severn estuary and indeed to the very different landscapes before and after the ice.

"Place" is not fixed, any more than "community" is, but we are shaped by how we interact with who we encounter and where we are. So if the phrase "genius loci survey" might sound strange, the meaning underpinning it is not. Its close attention to the specifics of place – to geology and geography, to prehistory and history, to placenames and language, to the changing patterns of agriculture and craft, culture and creativity – has become central in recent decades to the best forms of nature and travel writing, in the work of authors like Robert Macfarlane (2012) or Tim Robinson (2007), but with roots going back to the Romantics (Nassar, 2022) and in particular to JW von Goethe's natural science work (Chapter 6).

This attention to complex specifics serves as an antidote to the flattening and impoverishment that comes when our lives are reduced to money and consumption, to an education in arbitrary content for the sake of our subsequent income, to working at meaningless jobs and to culture reduced to the status of commodities.

The concept of "genius loci" is widely used in gardening, landscape design and architecture, as a way of underlining the importance of recognising *where* we are and thinking about what we do in relation to that:

Consult the genius of the place in all;
That tells the waters to rise, or fall;
Or helps th'ambitious hill the heav'ns to scale,
Or scoops in circling theatres the vale;
Calls in the country, catches opening glades,
Joins willing woods, and varies shades from shades,
Now breaks, or now directs, th'intending lines;
Paints as you plant, and, as you work, designs.
    (Alexander Pope, *Epistle to Burlington*, 1731)

Being here, now

You walk up *these* Cotswold slopes that, from a distance, stand out as stark as cliffs and close up resolve themselves into steep, almost 45% angles: they are tough on the legs unless you stay in practice. If you are away on flatter ground for a week, you can maybe still climb them without difficulty; but if you are away for two weeks, all the running up and down stairs in the world does not compensate and your legs have to learn them again. They are different from the slopes of gritstone mountains like much of the Pennines, which make for long heavy slogs uphill over peat: the Cotswolds are an ancient seabed fossilised into limestone, which erodes spectacularly under rainwater to produce these often dry but sharp slopes, with grassy uplands and claggy mud on top.

As the Ice Age receded, water that once flowed south and east towards the Thames seems to have been captured by sudden flows of meltwater and diverted west and north towards the Severn. Such flows sometimes cut out bits of the Cotswold plateau, creating spectacular outlier hills facing the edge. In the Five Valleys, the water dug steep-sided valleys with lines of clay in the bottoms and springs bubbling out of the limestone, exposing different layers of limestone and clay from top to bottom, each layer of limestone with its own shellfish fossils. Your leg muscles feel the nature of that limestone, which is also locally variable: most obviously in colour, from gold to silver-grey as you travel around these hills, while the clay goes from red to brown.

The land is bewildering to an outsider: the big fields are not in the plains but on top of the plateau, together with grassy spaces that feel like the sea and open out to even further vistas, across the Severn into the Forest of Dean and the Black Mountains. Meanwhile the valleys are confusing, hard to make sense of and navigate. Their steepness means that often to go from A to B you need to retreat down one valley and up another – a mirror image of travelling around coastal peninsulas.

You walk through *these* five valleys: they are still so damp that hanging washing outside makes little difference much of the year. The first farmers found these valley bottoms filled with swamps and streams, alder and willow, and drained parts for pasture and crops, but kept their villages along the spring lines and the sheep paths along the top. By Domesday there were 251 corn mills in the district, including one where today's Ruskin Mill stands, meaning the creation of millraces and ponds. Water was also needed to wash out the colours used to dye wool (red madder, blue woad).

In the 17th and 18th centuries, refugee Huguenot weavers took the process of working with water further. These valleys once held the world's greatest concentration of mills – for a short time, until coal displaced water power and the canal (now being restored by volunteers), built to bring coal from the Forest of Dean, was not enough to compensate for the closeness of mills and mines in the Pennines.

In the early 19th century, the recession that followed the Napoleonic wars and the decline of the mills made this a place of emigration; but they left behind them the complex interplay of houses and market gardens, mill paths and buildings, water and trees we have seen earlier, an intricate weaving of ways of walking and ways of being. That same soft limestone meant that the poor could live in cheap stone buildings, so that here you can still see the vernacular architecture of the early modern world – not just the lord's manor and the church – preserved in stone in some villages.

The combination of pretty cottages and the landscape of small farming in turn attracted Victorian tourists at the same time, and for the same reason, that Thomas Hardy and Laurie Lee lamented the passing of an older way of life. The Cotswolds are quintessentially "English" *because* of this history: because there was a space for tourism, for romantic literature – and, later, for the Arts and Crafts movement, for Waldorf kindergartens, and eventually for the alternatives and creatives, coexisting uneasily not only with the local working class around the area's surviving light industry but also with the second-homers and city retirees who have driven property prices beyond the reach of many locals.

For the children of that working class or the children of organic farmers, for writers and artists who settle here or retirees who want to contribute, for migrants from beyond southern England or tourists visiting the farmers' market, and for the constant flow of visitors to Ruskin Mill – the questions of how to live in this place and who we live in it with are also questions about who we want to be.

The genius loci at Ruskin Mill

In Ruskin Mill's practice, these questions are formalised into the process of enquiry that is the genius loci survey. The process looks like this:

1 Collecting the information: mineral, plant, animal and human
2 Bringing the parts into the whole
3 Finding the essence
4 Who are you?
5 May we have permission to re-create?
6 Transforming the past as the future emerges
7 Manifesting the intention

Hence a starting point is simply to discover whatever can be known about the geology and geography of a location; its flora and fauna and their ecology; and the many ways in which human beings have lived with and in this situation, particularly of course how they have worked with the other dimensions: where they lived, how they farmed etc. This naturally moves away from collecting isolated facts to an understanding of ecological relationships and how we practically inhabit, are shaped by, and transform our natural environment.

Up on the tops of the ridges, sheep have their own rhythms and needs, and in turn enable work with wool – carding, spinning, dyeing, felting, weaving. On the slopes, trees need planting, coppicing and felling, in turn enabling green woodwork and charcoal making among many other things. In the valley, clay and stone enable pottery and stonecarving.

This more holistic, relational vision encourages us to seek patterns, meaning and an essence that we can grasp – what is it that makes this area what it is? From a conventional viewpoint this may sound like wishful thinking, and we may laugh at the idea of an essence – but of course the particularity of any given place is precisely that. As another Romantic thinker observed, concrete reality is "a rich totality of many determinations [forms of causation] and relations". It is in the relationships that we can call "ecological" in this sense of interrelationship that reality actually manifests.

And, importantly, as human beings we grasp it as such, as "here", as "place". And if we do not do so – if we experience ourselves as existing in a bland or banal world of interchangeable and fundamentally uninteresting spaces, our eyes simply focussed on a screen, on our careers or whatever – we are impoverished in turn. To misquote Philip Larkin, where can we live but places? For the vast majority of our species' history – whether as foragers, as farmers, as craftspeople or in networks of human connection – place has meaning to us. The question "Who are you?" is then a way to bring out this relationship emotionally rather than hide it; to consciously put ourselves in relationship with place and ask what that encounter is like.

Ruskin Mill staff next seek permission to recreate. They might ask how the different components of the land enhance the student's experience; why the craft and farming curriculum should have particular activities or how Ruskin Mill itself has shaped the valley. The genius loci survey in a new location helps to identify what might be appropriate emphases in farming and craftwork in this location: what the place offers, and what the history tells.

In an old metalworks in Sheffield, Freeman College's signature craft is metalwork, not least the cutlery that has long been associated with Sheffield. At Stourbridge, the Glasshouse – in Royal Doulton's old glassworks – has glassblowing and glass cutting, in the heart of the Glass Quarter. At Ruskin Mill College, Gables Farm has sheep and other animals, and works from that through shearing, cleaning, carding, dyeing and spinning towards crafts like felt-making and weaving. These forms of farming and craft speak not only to a place but also to the people in that place: after the passing of those industries as major commercial enterprises, the people – or rather their grandchildren and great-grandchildren – are often left there, without work and with little transmitted memory of how people once lived here. The re-imagining of these buildings and heritage (Ruskin Mill Trust, 2019) was a primary motivation for Aonghus Gordon's OBE.

Not all Ruskin students come from the immediate locality, any more than the people who worked in these factories were always local. Indeed, the dislocation felt by so many people in much of England is in part a product of how early and widespread the enclosures were, proletarianising a once rural workforce, and how rapidly manufacturing shifted jobs and centres of production. It is not only the Stroud valleys which represent an image of rural prettiness layered over what is in effect an early industrial brownfield site: the same can be said, for example, of the White Peak in Derbyshire, where mill pools enhance now-quiet rural valleys and walkers and cyclists use the tracks of a now-vanished railway. Change is constant. Yet if young people can re-engage with one place, they can then learn to re-engage with others.

Transforming the brownfield pasts of specific locations, new possible futures emerge. Ruskin Mill College's present-day role was not yet obvious when local unemployed people started on the project renovating the disused mill, or later on when students with learning difficulties came to work with the craftspeople who came to the mill. And new futures are of course also emerging for those students – and indeed for craftspeople, moving in their turn from being primarily artists or recreating old crafts to being primarily therapeutic educators, using their crafts not alone for their beauty or history but for the benefit of the young people in their workshops.

These intentions, then, finally, need to manifest – in an ongoing process of seeking to encounter the genius loci and respond creatively to the situation we find. Landscape, literally, does not exist without us, because we are not in wilderness but in land that has been worked for millennia and which still today is reshaped through our responses to what it offers: possibilities of water and food; an encounter with birds, animals and plants; shelter and leisure; education and therapy. How do we inhabit *this* place?

How this helps young people

For these reasons, the genius loci or spirit of place forms the first field of Ruskin Mill's seven fields of practice. Knowing, deeply and in multiple dimensions, where we are is a fundamental and necessary step towards a fully human life, which does not mean that we can only know one place or one community, or that that place is fixed in aspic. Why does this matter to young people?

Renovating Ruskin Mill was a very physical, practical task for local people recruited from the Stroud dole queue in the 1980s. From that point to the 2013 building of the Field Centre as a purpose-built expression of Ruskin Mill Trust's many different provisions and activities, there has always been a process of practical discovery, shared by students and staff. What was this mill, this factory, this farm? Or rather, what different things has it been? When did it come here, how was it remade over time, how was it shaped by the wider place and how did it help shape it? What materials and possibilities are here, now, that could be meaningful to students, and what needs to be done to bring those potentialities into being?

One way of talking about this is in terms of helping bring young people down to earth, helping them to arrive fully in the physical and interpersonal worlds that have been a challenge for so many of them. Some arrive at Ruskin Mill living in a world of screens, not as a way of relaxing but as the only world where they have some degree of control, understanding and presence – as successful gamers, mastering the imagined worlds of celebrities, but still only moving fingers on glass, unable to fully inhabit their own physical movements, their speech with others or shared physical action.

From this starting place, the elemental realities of the valley are visceral ones: the exposed uplands bring wide vistas, exposure to wind and bitter cold when working in the fields in winter, appreciation for the warmth of sheep and cow bodies, a lifting of the heart when the skies change. The woods are quiet, reflective, non-intrusive spaces: some students need to start simply by spending time in the woods with a calm staff member, not yet even working but just succeeding in sharing the space without becoming overwhelmed. The market garden, in a deep valley, can be baking hot in summer and clear and cold in winter. Each space has its own qualities.

What for other young people might be a manageable add-on to otherwise well-functioning lives is something else for those with complex additional needs, in one of the first such generations not to live in a society where physical labour, craft and farming were respected and widespread activities. Ruskin Mill's "Practical Skills Therapeutic Education" (PSTE) does not aim to create new generations of farmers and craftspeople, though some students do go on to make a living in this way. Rather it seeks to offer those who have been damaged by a society that has left them behind the opportunity to experience a lived-in world of meaningful work with peers.

Figure 1.3 Each space has its own qualities: in the trout pond

"From seed to table", or from sheep to slipper, from sand to cutting the blown glass, or from the metal billet and pieces of Blue John to selling the silver spoon, the spirit of place helps to shape a meaningful narrative which is not arbitrary but can be discovered in the place itself and what it affords by way of opportunities.

It is quite an achievement for the urban student to come into a space like this and understand how it works, to see not just the process of seed to table but also how it works across time and space. To inhabit this space and time physically can be transformative in itself.

The affordances of this situation start from locating oneself within the specific mineral, plant, animal and human realities of a particular place and of finding ways of engaging with that, using not only one's finger on a screen but one's whole body in three dimensions, through collaborating with others in transforming the particular material realities found there, and moving from the barriers to education created by histories of personal and generational trauma, via supportive apprenticeship around a meaningful task, towards giving back to the wider community.

Another way of putting this is to say that Ruskin Mill's students are reinhabiting relationships which in some sense already exist, but out of sight. Their physical movements are of course present but often constrained in various ways. They communicate, with their bodies and words, but often in damaging ways. They are surrounded by other people but are often the objects of stigma or abuse. In very concrete ways, engaging with the spirit of place can help to change this.

The buildings Ruskin Mill operates in once had potential. So too did the young people there, before that potential was taken from them – whether by how society has treated their particular needs, or in the wider sense by how the worlds in which some might once have had happy and fulfilled lives have been undermined by economic and political change, so that skilled and specialist supports are needed to help find what their potential can now be.

Conversation with Aonghus Gordon

How genius loci came to Ruskin Mill

Before starting Ruskin Mill in 1981, I had travelled extensively and was always interested in what generated places of human settlement, and why certain things happened in certain places. For example, is Stonehenge built where it is because it couldn't be built anywhere else? Is there anything particular about a place in which a world-class building is conceived and created? The same goes for Venice: what is the background to a situation where an independent state builds itself out of the silt of the lagoon and can then maintain itself and keep renewing itself for a thousand years?

This question interested me, so I travelled extensively to the locations of sacred buildings and sites. Later on, I put a history of art programme together with students, in which we went to particular centres of culture: Ephesus, Knossos, Florence, the Pyramids or the paintings of the Tretyakov gallery in Moscow, where the icons were considered to have a social power of regeneration.

My interest was in visiting what I thought of as the places where certain transitions took place in consciousness – often in connection with youth. It became clear that some places afforded the potential for particular capacities to be developed in human development.

So place was central to my question "Could this take place anywhere else?" Very often a certain ritual has a geological context, a biological one, and sometimes it might require a specific latitude. I was aware of this when Ruskin Mill started, but I didn't yet fully appreciate that I should apply this interest to the place where I was working. It took time to realise that we hadn't really investigated the location of our educational work and to ask whether it was significant that what was ostensibly a centre for cultural development was happening *there*. I did know that it was significant that we were doing it in a derelict building.

Learning to appreciate place

I then got involved in an exhibition and a publication on the dying forests of Europe. In the 1980s the issue concerning the pollution from British power stations causing acid rain and damaging continental and Scandinavian forests, and the pollution from the Soviet Union into the Eastern bloc's forests, was topical. This is when Jochen Bockemühl's (1986) book *Dying Forests* appeared, along with an exhibition that highlighted the consequences of our lack of reflection on forests from a number of perspectives.

What Bockemühl did was to introduce a Goethean method of appreciating place, as a consequence of the evolution of consciousness. I realised that what he'd discovered in this book was totally relevant to Ruskin Mill's need to be fully aware of the value of place, which was starting to become an interest for me and others: we were not just a market garden and a building, but an ecology.

At this point Ruskin Mill had a market garden, a shop and a café, and we were looking beyond that into the fish farm, which wasn't yet ours, nor was Gables Farm or Park Wood. The exhibition became part of the Nailsworth Festival, and Bockemühl came to give a talk. At this time there was a growing environmental awareness; the Green movement was fully active, and his talk drew over 250 people from Nailsworth and Stroud. The spirit of the time and the spirit of dying forests resonated in the Festival. The exhibition also went to Westonbirt Arboretum where it was seen by thousands of people.

Bockemühl then ran a weekend workshop following his talk. Participants studied trees, opening up their perception of what is a healthy tree, and what is a tree under stress. We were taught to observe the health of nature, particularly the trees. But we can only see health by training our observation and including the wildlife, the grass, the geology, the water – every aspect. It wasn't that everything was unhealthy, but our perception wasn't fully integrated.

So Bockemühl taught us to see in a developmental and inclusive way. This left a significant impact: learn to see, and learn to observe health. Interestingly, the land where he did this workshop was later put on the market, and the Trust was fortunate to have a backer who enabled its purchase. In fact wherever he did this workshop outside, that land would come up for sale. I then realised that maybe he'd released something through this workshop and in a way provided a new spirit of potential renewal. Maybe the land was trapped and with the 40 people at his workshops appreciating the landscape, something became more fluid.

The background to Bockemühl's work lies in what we call Goethean science, a form of investigation through collaborative action research, in this case participating in the valley. At that point, the fish farm had already gone on sale and we bought it. Later on, Dr Margaret Colquhoun undertook a collaborative action enquiry with around 30 staff. This spanned the period from the last Ice Age to the current post-industrial period in human history, animal and plant history. We looked at the post-glacial period in the Cotswolds and how the early people's migration through this landscape emerged: where were the tracks, the sacred places? You can map it out, how the Dobunni then inhabited the hilltops; how the Romans, Saxons, Normans and Huguenots came to leave their imprint. The team began to develop an insight into the multiple layers of culture, initiative, economy and the sacred in Nailsworth and the Five Valleys.

The animal audit included the discovery of mammoth tusks in Stonehouse; there were bears and wolves. Using different lenses we could appreciate what the landscape may have looked like with animals that are now extinct, of the 13th-century Cotswolds, or the industrial and contemporary Cotswolds.

This exhibition was drawn and presented by Dilly Williams, who's still the genius loci visual presenter for each of the Trust's sites. That process is both collaborative and iterative and offers you a chance to participate in building an understanding by appreciating the mineral, plant, animal and human histories.

This was put into a public context in the Zodiac Room, and it had a vision of transformation. The process invites you to understand what you are involved in, both past and present, but also to ask permission to recreate what is there. Finding the spirit of the place and giving it a name created the conditions to invite students into the re-creation of the valley, along with their own personal biographies.

Finding the wound of the place

In looking at human history, we can sometimes discover heroic instances where generosity is equally matched by what you could call the wound of the place. There has been a history that has not necessarily developed in an appropriate way. You can obviously see that within the context of human history, because we leave our shadows on places. But you can also see this situation with significant disruptions in the woodlands of the Horsley Valley. The deer have become unbalanced and they start migrating into areas that aren't really ideal for them, so they start to nibble the bark of the ash trees in winter because of hunger. This doesn't necessarily destroy the tree, but it heals itself and buries the wound within its bark in the spring.

In Park Wood you can see very interesting histories of trees being attacked like this: after a number of years there is no visible evidence of the wound. It is deeply embedded, and the memory can't be seen on the surface of the tree. Various student histories also have buried wounds like this within them.

What you begin to see when you start looking into this form of understanding is that the whole of nature is actually compromised by events, and has various challenges to overcome that need to be addressed. You begin to use your eyes in such a way to realise that maybe nature needs some caretaking from human beings: with a transdisciplinary holistic approach, we can find the right intervention for nature to remain in balance, even though humans may have caused the initial problem. And when you look into the biographies of the students and those situations that they come with, you realise that they too have suffered different levels of hurt. They have buried those wounds deeply, but they live on as trauma in the muscles of those young people.

In further researching the wound, you begin to do what I call finding the double, the motif of the location, whether in the tree, the animal or the human. So, for example, in coppicing we have a chance to cut trees down for legitimate reasons and turn them into charcoal. Then we can start looking into the rings of the tree, which reveal that the life of the tree is not a logical sequence of events. It's full of obstructions, as with the example of the deer. In fact it's amazing that certain trees actually survive some of the obstructions that they have had to endure. A good forester will point that out, without necessarily naming the parallel in the lives of students. But their self-knowledge of their own biographical journey can be put into a narrative in which life is a struggle and there are both setbacks and opportunities for recovery. These stories can be very powerful if they're captured in the right way.

So by being open and deeply sensitive to the natural order, we can bring the biography of the student's journey into the ecological journey, let's say, of a coppice. Or we can bring it into the journey of a donkey that might have suffered multiple abusive situations, but is now responsible for grazing a little green pasture that enables quietness and balance, and the donkey will allow itself to be touched by another student, stroked and cleaned.

Biography of place, biography of people

This is what I mean by the biography of the place and the biography of the students. If you don't go into the place in a developmental, as I call it "morphological", way to see how things evolved – not necessarily in a harmonious way – then you might miss the melding of the two. There are many examples, such as a predatory situation with one young man whose biography was such that his mother was terrified that he might commit harm, and she then sought out a placement in Ruskin Mill.

He had an untamed nature: I recall introducing him to the life cycle of the pike, which is one of the most predatory animals in water, because he was interested in fishing. Pike use their teeth to capture and subjugate: they are inward-facing, and once bitten it's very hard to release them. So his biography was met by the context of the valley, because pike existed in some of the ponds that the Huguenots created in the Stroud valleys.

He undertook a study into the life cycle of the pike and in doing that awoke in some respects to how his own urban biography related to the valley and the pike in particular. In studying how the pike hunt, he began to awaken to the recklessness of some of his peers, and himself, on the streets of Coventry. And as he discovered more details, he had the shocking realisation that his own conduct mimicked the pike.

That was a profound moment for him, and out of that parallel he awakened a new inner ethic and as a result generated a sense of shame. He avoided a potential prison career and later on visited me with his wife and three wonderful children. They sat around the table and there was a real sense of dignity in the family. He informed me that both he and his partner were airport security guards. You could hardly make it up!

And behind this young man's awakening was an utter commitment from his mother to find a new path. That enabled me to work in tandem with her: this couldn't have been achieved if she hadn't been there.

The need to ask permission

Now if we think about the genius loci: when I started this with about 25 colleagues, we went through a very precise process. However, there were certain
limitations, in that asking everybody to contribute without them having a
degree of understanding of financial resources can become a difficult situation.
In the end, the ideas have to be subject to the resource situation, if you're going to involve 25 people in a process of re-envisioning the valley. What was
interesting in the case of Horsley Valley is that we realised at a certain point
that we needed to ask permission, in the same way that you have to ask the
student's permission as to whether they really want to do this.

It's a tough choice for students to come into the Ruskin Mill programme,
because it moves from one modality of learning into a totally new one, in that
it's practical. The good news from the student's perspective is that if you don't
want to pick up the tool, you can't do anything. And until you're willing to
pick up the tool, we actually can't do anything for you, because there is no
other entry point. So by picking up the tool the student has given you permission to work with their obstructed biography.

In the case of the valley, how you might take the potential in its history
and grow it really depends on whether that discovery of potential is congruent with the needs of the student. If you can match the need of the student
with the potential of the valley, then you remake the valley through a joint
biographic process: the student's biography shakes hands with the valley's.

That process is based around what the student needs to do, such as keep
pike or a donkey, or undertake coppicing as part of understanding time. Or
they might do some leather tanning work as a response to what happens when
the cowhides come back from the slaughterhouse: do we waste those skins,
in that we don't take them back to be used in the college, or do we set up a
very simple tanning process where the students can make, for example, leather
drums or a leather belt?

Harvesting curriculum from place

So the biography of the location gives you an insight as to how you can harvest various practical curricula, because they were performed in that place at a
certain time. Ruskin Mill was once a leather stiffener works, making the inside
soles for army shoes, and in fact when Ruskin Mill set itself up the first knock
at the door was from a leatherworker, who made leather bags and trained our
students to make leather products such as belts and wallets.

So the past can still be recalled by awakening your consciousness to what
took place in certain locations at certain times – the built environment or the
natural environment. There's this alchemy of fusion between the past and the
present. But there's one further component that needs to enter it, which is
the educational relevance of the activity, whether it still has traction. And the
genius loci provides an authentic context for growing a new curriculum of

engagement through understanding the past, but the future has to be connected with the developmental needs of the students. So you are given permission to rebuild the past into the future through the needs of the student.

This is where that co-relationship of biographies creates a new and very powerful vision of transformation. Now what you find is that wherever you go similar crafts tend to show up, because they are so primary to the history of economy and locality. For example, you can't really go anywhere in England without discovering wool and sheep, cloth and textiles. That's great, because over time what you discover is that one of the most valuable things that students can do is to meet an animal in various capacities.

Working with wool can come before befriending the sheep: the products from the animal can be touched so that the student knows about sheepness before they are involved in the lambing. Of course once they have met the sheep, that enhances their work with the wool. They meet the journey within the life cycle of sheep, wool and cloth. This process can engage students – not all students, but many students – in processes that help them think.

For example, learning to string a loom is a sophisticated and intellectually demanding activity; it isn't for everyone. It demands agile thought processes: the pre-cognising of pattern is built into threading the loom. We are engaging a visual mathematics. There are certain students who love the idea of doing this, and certain students who wouldn't know what you were talking about, so you have to enter it in different aspects.

So what the genius loci provides is Ruskin Mill's Field Two, which is practical skills, craftwork. The practical skills entry point is built in a healthy and authentic way based on what you already know about the locality, because you can rediscover its locality if you look for it. Pottery, for example, was historically done not in the Horsley Valley, but four miles down the valley in Stonehouse. The lias clay seam, the blue clay, emerges below the fuller's earth, on the border of the Jurassic limestone. You can dig directly into this clay which is older than the limestone, and that clay on the valley floor is a highly prized material. And what we've done is work with our clay and then formulate a clay curriculum by working pottery, which is authentic to the wider place.

Now given the water in these valleys, the pioneer plants were very specific in the recovery of the area after the Ice Age. Willow is one of these. It was cultivated in the Horsley Valley at one point for baskets, many of which collected apples from all the orchards which lined the valley sides but have since disappeared. So when you realise that willows were grown extensively here, you can look and ask "has willow any relevance for today?" Well, its ecological responsibility in enabling water to be accommodated in the right way is crucial. But its value to the student, in having to arrange the chaos of 15 strands of willow to make the base of a basket, gives rise to a re-ordering of mental capacity, a mind clearance exercise.

So when you put the educational element and the practical element into the genius loci, you can begin to see our Field Three, biodynamic farming. The landscape, the garden and the farm emerge. This is how the environmental structure encompasses the knowledge of growing willow as part of the location's ecology due to the water, but also for therapeutic education, which is Field Four. How do the students' senses become further polished, enhanced or developed? If you ask a student to organise all the strands of willow that are required to make a wastepaper basket in a sequentially ordered way, they have to use a high quality of gaze, focus and thoughtful reflection, because

Figure 1.4 Working with complexity: a student-made basket at Ruskin Mill College

their actions show up in the weave of the willow strands, so you are actually developing certain personal capacities.

And what's interesting is that the students love doing it! There is no great necessity to corral students into basket-making workshops. There are exceptions, but they're the minority. So the foundation of Field One, genius loci, is one of the unique elements of Ruskin Mill. This evolved in time, and its legitimacy comes from giving what's created out of the place a renewed voice.

You're also looking to do something similar in the developmental offer for students: how do you find their renewed voice? And there is a marriage between the curriculum that is found through the genius loci in nature, in buildings and in the history of the place, with the fundamental developmental needs of a specific adolescent boy or girl of 16, when they come into the college. What are the things that they enjoy doing? How do you offer guided choice in their activities so that they are already in a process of change and development, in which the next level of demands grows out of their first entry to work and skill?

Equally, how do they overcome their barriers to learning? These are highly developed. Because of this, the genius loci is at the forefront of any initiative that the Trust wishes to develop for the students' future. When we look at what we've actually done in genius loci surveys, we've essentially observed human beings and their footprint on the earth, the materials of the animals over time, the materials of plants, stone, clay and metals to meet their primary needs. There's a descending element of resource management and use from those three zones of life, so this survey, this cut into time and location, is a vertical discipline.

The double of the place

Inevitably some past activities of mining, transforming, exploiting have left their legacy, often to the detriment of the places where they have happened – not necessarily out of ill-will, but following an economic need. Naming this is very powerful and gives clarity about the impact of past injustice or injury to the living world of nature, particularly when the material then enters the production line and can create an additional challenge in human relationships.

The genius loci shows up past leadership, past organisational challenges and hurt, which can be called the double of the place. If you can name what is still damaged, you can also become aware from an organisational perspective how students can be part of the renewal of the place itself, transforming the integration of animals, plants and materials through an integrated thoughtfulness, an ecology of practice.

We could look at this further: many of the Ruskin Mill Trust colleges occupy the sites of iconic industrial processes. In the Horsley Valley, when the Huguenots came in the 17th and 18th centuries, they did something called "spring capture". They re-routed the flows of water by rodding the spring lines to ensure the maximum flow of water to drive cloth production. This filled their millponds overnight to store the water they needed. So in a sense they were taking water from others for themselves. They had no option, because their management of water and their production of cloth was dependent on the storage capacity of their millponds. By maximising storage capacity and flow rate, they reached economics of scale and power that enabled a particular size of waterwheel and level of production and placed them in advantageous positions.

This sort of process gave rise to certain ways of thinking about who owns what, and some legal concepts were perfected around disputes on water rights. The idea that you could own or have power over water led to new considerations around commodifying natural resources for personal gain. This has now unfortunately become accepted currency with our current private ownership of water companies, and has led to a number of ecological tragedies. It had its origins, however, in disputes between millowners: so these mills were centres in which certain types of thinking were developed.

The commodification of natural resources through personal or company ownership led to significant social inequalities: they are increasingly owned by the few. This situation gave rise to what John Ruskin saw as the "illth" (rather than health) of Britain, which vulnerable people like our students are victims of, leaving them in economic and cultural poverty. The communities associated with some of the iconic production processes that once took place in Ruskin Mill's various locations can be said to be still shrouded in the after-images of this legacy.

This is not so much about the resource of water in itself, but about the type of thinking that has become acceptable. You could argue that the millowners were among the first people to initiate that type of commodification of resources; this is not only the double, but also a wound. So if you are initiating educational ideas, then the question of how you can address that demands new thinking: how can you transform the thought and action into cultural regeneration?

What became clear through the genius loci process was the importance of transforming that legacy by making it open to the public. They were invited through permissive pathways into the valley, as they too needed to be participants in the transformation process. As people walk their dogs past the streams and lakes, they become the endorsers and third-party supporters of the cultural changes which the students are part of, learn and gain qualifications from.

One of the key things that I realised very early on was that if the original millowners had initiated this private commodification of water in legal disputes, then I'm now a millowner on behalf of the Trust. What is my new responsibility in this situation? To allow people access to appreciate water, plants, methods of integration gave rise to a form of social medicine through understanding the genius loci. In this way the double is transformed, by the students' own challenge to transform themselves.

Reigniting the spark

But this is also no different than actually allowing the medicine of clay and willow to become a sensory opportunity to address student challenges. As an educationalist, I found myself having to generate ideas to resolve some very complex educational, therapeutic, socio-political and economic issues. I had to try and define what was in the DNA of Ruskin Mill Trust's offer to young people.

My teacher training did not focus on "special educational needs", but with those who were falling out of the regular education system. What I soon discovered is that the education system that I worked in in the 1980s was attuned to people with average and higher academic potential. What I began to define is that that wasn't my task or the task of Ruskin Mill. This led to some serious rethinking of the purpose of education and how it should be distributed to all. It was all too easy to label a group "Class X" and treat it as an awkward addendum to the main process of schooling. In my situation, those young people became the central focus of interest, research and action.

This took me to work in a special school, and I was soon introduced to the "two-inch file", which was required reading in working with students who everybody had given up on. The two-inch file was a shameful legacy of professional bodies, and often the family home, not managing the developmental path successfully into adolescence. It was a legacy of failure and incredibly sad to read.

But from past experience I'd had the opportunity of working with "Class X". The success of placing the learning context outside, in a three-dimensional setting, proved transformational for the pupils, but it led to some challenges for me: the pupils voted with their feet that this class was the one they all wanted to come to. I was still a student teacher and found myself assailed by statements that I was undermining the authority of the school, as the pupils were not learning within what was supposed to be the school's context for learning. At 23, this was a wake-up call for me, but at the time I didn't know that this would be my future path for innovating.

What the file showed was that whatever anybody tried with a particular student, they seemed to fail. They couldn't see that they needed to start from another entry point, because the entry point they were imagining was the type of thinking that had let the kid down. So what was the new type of thinking that needed to be introduced? The quality that I arrived at was that you needed to start with the idea of blowing on the ember again, to reignite the young people's spark. The flame had been extinguished but the embers were still warm.

The pupils wanted to learn, and made progress. I realised that it was unlikely that I could work within the regular educational system, because the ideas I had from observing the pupils meant that their learning needed to be freed from a sedentary into a moving, kinaesthetic, process. That took me into a whole new area of the philosophy of education. And I began to realise that really what Ruskin Mill did, and could do quite well, was to re-imagine that which had had potential, because the flame was out.

Stepping back to finding the ember, and not demanding that it just ignite out of its own accord, was a journey into re-stepping to the point of obstruction in pupils' biographies. Many of the reports in the two-inch file also undertook this path backwards, but didn't give clear indications for additional or alternative methods for learning.

Re-stepping back to the ember often meant recognising that the young person had been traumatised at an early age, even as young as two, and found themselves stuck in a revolving door, unable to make progress until this was resolved. Re-stepping at Ruskin Mill to identify the point of obstruction re-awoke and ignited the spark. In Ruskin Mill Trust, we describe this as re-imagining potential.

So our specific skill is to reignite the ember, the moment when they "had potential", while the situation of "has potential" is the job of regular education. In applying Rudolf Steiner's insights to education, there's a well-understood principle that many obstructions in learning are the result of certain primary processes in early childhood not being fully developed, so that various exercises and modalities of intervention to pull that situation forward become available through imagining the potential of each situation.

As someone who was interested in why people don't learn, it was natural for me to understand the idea of a second, third, fourth, fifth, 20th chance. In a way that's what I'm really involved in.

My view is that that in the end, nobody can be left behind. I've never met a child or young person who can't contribute to the world.

Finding the right entry point

This inner commitment to each child drives me into having to be relentless about how you approach a biography that is often full of rejection and needs a pathway to achieve and participate. Our task is to find the platform onto which each child can make a step. It often means understanding the primordial elements in very early childhood learning processes, for example in learning to read the script of children's drawings. Very often when we do this, we are given permission to develop a pathway forward.

When an event has taken place in time and things are not going as they could, you have to re-calibrate those processes that give the foundations for learning. We had different entry points for different students. There was an entry through the relationship with nature; there was the relationship through the semi-enclosed production process of the workshop; and there was the entry through a trusting relationship with a mentor. Another entry point that emerged was service, either in a shop or café or in working directly with people.

The garden, shop and café formed one of the earliest curriculum offers for students in the early 1980s. They brought a whole kaleidoscope of separate activities into a continuous flow. Now they had all been developed at Ruskin

Mill before the students arrived. The shop was given to Ruskin Mill as a going concern because someone wished to move away and they wanted to see it in the community, and the café was already an independent business. Through what we now call the seed to table curriculum, students joined up their experience into knowledge and understanding of these separate activities and the interrelationships of how to grow, harvest and serve. This early discovery in providing the joy in learning has been rolled out in every school and college and integrated into the student journey.

There is always work to be done; innovation and insights have to be drawn from the work on the ground, never abstracted, always absorbed, observed and following that move into reflective practice. Therapeutic education involves a discipline that is built into its processes rather than external. Taking a question from each day and awakening in the morning with insight is a necessity for innovation.

You could borrow something that's already been tried and tested – there are some brilliant prototypes. But you might then wish to go into another domain and develop another paradigmatic entry point. For example, maybe I want to research the thought that human freedom is sacrosanct. That might centre on giving volition to overcoming impediments to young adults themselves, with guidance.

Reflecting as an educational design thinker, it is crucially important to have the processes separate in time so as to free oneself into stepping outside and inside to the challenges. It is similarly essential not to be leant on by students or staff, but to help them find the skills so that they themselves gain capacity for autonomy and are free from dependence, including dependence on yourself. Any projection of dependence only dulls one's capacity for relentless innovation. That's a tall order, but that is one of the choices I made. So you could argue that one of the objectives in education is to become free of yourself as a needy person, in both discreet and obvious ways.

This also includes having the capacity for a handshake, to co-create the future with all concerned, being in the moment where the spirit touches everyone. You then have to ask who are the freedom fighters who drive a method for independent judgements and give you opportunities, not only of borrowing an idea but also of developing it.

Braiding the fields

There are choices that have to be made. In the Ruskin Mill case, I borrowed extensively from Steiner's educational insights. He provides a treasure trove of new thoughts and entry points. I don't draw from him exclusively because there are many aspects of his work that needed to be anglicised. The English perspective is a great interest of mine, not because of any nationalism but because there's a complex legacy there that is unresolved. So I also drew from

Ruskin's incisive perception about the difficult condition of England in the last century and the type of thinking that was needed for trans-disciplinary insights.

Between Steiner's and Ruskin's insights, a distinctive amalgam emerged. Into this came the important work of William Morris, who redesigned the entire aesthetic of the time with one drawn from nature and handwork. Leo Tolstoy, Mahatma Gandhi and Bertrand Russell all saw Morris as a genius and a key critic of his time. These three inspirations form the foundation of the Trust's approach. All three come from a new and much needed perspective, of reverence and compassion, as an embedded principle in their work and action.

So the thinking that we harness from these figures is a developmental, morphological type of thinking where you understand patterns of relationships. You see which patterns appear to generate health, which ones show up in healthier situations. Other patterns might be hangovers, or they might be habits that can't be given up.

And then certain patterns are evolutionary – they themselves create new forms. So the type of thinking that lives in Field One, genius loci, gives the need to then find Field Two, the crafts of that place. Field Two requires Field Three, farming, and you have a curriculum. One gives the other the launching pad. You have to understand the different dimensions of Field One – the mineral, plant, animal and human dimensions of place – and then incorporate those areas back into the whole again. Then we work practically with that whole, which gives us Field Two. Then you have to provide a sustainable context which is Field Three, the landscape as a whole organism. So Field One gives you the possibility for using the syllabus and Fields Two and Three are the curriculum. And Field Four, therapeutic education, is how we apply all this, why we do one thing and not another with any given student.

There is quite a lot of work to do in understanding the fact that each field builds on the other. I've often described them in sequence, which is difficult because it looks logical, but it's relational. I think that the challenge is to overcome the training that we've all been given, which is to put everything into separate silos, rather than try to move out of specificity and back into relational cooperation. That's not just a Ruskin Mill problem. That's a societal issue that everybody is battling against.

But I do believe that we're overcoming it increasingly effectively in what we call the student study (Chapter 6), where specific aspects of a student are observed objectively to build up a picture so that we move from opinion to insight into the question of "how do we help you?" This is a Goethean observation process, where you look at the subject and attempt to displace simple opinion. It's reasonably effective if you do it with a team of at least six, because you often then have your own insight validated more than once amongst your colleagues, but they might describe it in a different way. What you begin to hear is a repetition of feeling, even if you couldn't articulate it, being voiced by your colleagues. That entry into the different dimensions of a student should be done in a dispassionate research context.

Figure 1.5 Place, farm and craft: teasing wool at Ruskin Mill

Seeing like an artist

The challenge is how to bring the parts back into the whole, how to re-braid it so that you have a picture of what could emerge. In the genius loci survey, the next question in relation to the landscape is "who are you?", which can be challenging because it endows the place with being-ness. Some people drop out at this point, because we are asking a question of what people might see as an inanimate situation. It can be a challenging question. A poet or an artist wouldn't necessarily find it challenging, but if you are trained in a scientific medium, how can you consider such a thought?

You have seen the trees but not the wood, you have failed to see the ecology of the depth of inter-participatory relationships. When people see it, the poets describe it in their language and the artists paint it. So educationalists need to learn to get to where the artists and poets are, which is that we have a being, a young person in front of us. That's not too difficult, but we need to link that being into the context of participatory learning. This requires imagination, in Ruskin Mill as in the wider society. But we're going in the right direction, because our induction programme for staff starts with opening up those questions.

Thinking from practice

If we trace the development of the Trust: as a practitioner-based process it tends to reflect after doing, or while performing. It doesn't start from an idea: it starts from action, but there is an architecture of intention. These thoughts can be found in our charitable objects, in the vision, value and methods, and are then enriched through Steiner's insights.

The concept of seven fields emerged from practice. We started with a craft activity and a piece of land, and then we built from that and became more conscious. You begin to see that as events unfolded, there were developments in time. Some areas became named. Nobody started with the idea that there were going to be seven fields. It was 25 years later when action research started to name these critical elements that were either resourced, strategised or taken for granted in our practice. As they were being named in action research, the developmental sequence became apparent, so there are no absolutes about it.

There are different perspectives as to whether you let's say put Field Three (farming) after Two (practical skills) or Two after Three. However, there are some pre-givens to the seven fields, which probably need some explanation. How does "the inspiration of Rudolf Steiner" show itself in a contemporary way, not just taking a syllabus and a curriculum and putting it into operation? That is not how the Trust started.

Instead, there were young people who needed to engage, who to a certain extent were in the last-chance saloon. Their funding was coming to an end and they only had a couple of years to find their place. They weren't going to accept a formal way of learning, so that wasn't even possible to implement. They all had "spiky profiles": they were two, 15 and 20 years old, all in one being.

Going deeper

For our staff too, understanding and naming the seven fields of our method can be challenging after 20 years of practice, if you then say, "thank you for your work; you've been working in Field Three". Or "you've been working in Field Two and this is the pedagogy behind it".

However, through action research you can see that all seven fields were in place in the first couple of years. As a conscious order and sequence, we identified the seven fields in my Master's research as being implicit in practice; this is what we were drawing from. The Trust has then had to learn to separate them out, research each domain, and find methods to re-embody all the seven fields in a conscious creation.

For the staff, the order of fields gave us an authority to train our therapeutic educators systematically. For the students we can't order this – we have to find a personal entry point. With the staff, we undertook their own re-stepping of identifying where they were, what they were doing now and what they still needed to do as they recognised their own self-limitations, if they feel they are in league with the earth or if they are still fighting it.

Each of the seven fields of the Trust's method, Practical Skills Therapeutic Education, has an architecture of human development behind it. In Field One we separate and assimilate mineral, plant, animal and human and attempt to find the essence of the place. This builds and contributes to our curriculum offer. In Field Two we guide the students into performance of what we might call lawful movement, movement in keeping with the requirements of the material world and the affordances of their own bodies. They make items of civility, things that people recognise and use, and become skilful in space through developing their spatial awareness. This is particularly delivered through green woodwork on the pole lathe and glassmaking.

In Field Three we have the conscious design of a farm entity. Each component works in an integrational way. The farmer is the conductor of the farm organism: the food and the life forces resound. Young people become part and parcel of the farm and co-manage the mineral, plants, animal and human in a conscious design. In Field Four, therapeutic education, we bring insight into the phases of human development, and we recognise the students' 12 senses, all the capacities to be alert and pro-active.

In Field Five we have the seven care qualities that ensure that the student has autonomy over their functions and their interior – breathing, warming, digesting etc. In Field Six we work on the constitutional challenges that the student presents, drawing particularly on speech, language and movement. In Field Seven we support the capacity for their self-management and self-leadership in the world.

From practice to understanding

In all of these concepts, the insight comes afterwards as you name it, but the practice comes first. You might say to a green woodworker or a glass blower, "I need you to research the three planes of space", because in the research that's emerging we need to explore what happens with ADHD when you perform practical skills. The ADHD dissipates into performance and a new muscle memory is being built.

Then you have to say "OK, so what's going on here?" You do a bit more research and you find that *Being Human* by Karl König (1989) gives an explanation, which is that you are developing focus out of gaze. That means that you are more effective in comprehending the world, rather than being in opposition to the world, because you have the faculty to absorb it. As a result of grasping you have spatial developments, particularly horizontal capacities as well as sagittal ones, so when the student is rolling the glass over the steel plate, they come to understand the importance of proportion and moving it right and left in front of their rib cage, which is where they're breathing while they grasp.

Figure 1.6 In process: working with goats at Coleg Ty'r Eithin

From a Steiner educational perspective this is the place of interiorisation, the life of the soul, breathing. Then you begin to see a kind of functionality that has been picked up by researchers as well as educationalists and practitioners like König, who says that we have to learn to grasp. Then physically grasping leads to an interiorisation of that as a capacity, to hold something inwardly as well as outwardly. This inward holding is a morphology of the outer holding. That's a spiritual perspective. So when the green woodworker or the glassworker meets this, they are being confronted with another explanation for why their practical craft has gone from being something everybody does to being the most powerful education we have; there is a problem if they don't understand that.

There are three stages here. There's the practitioner, being a bloody good glass blower and wood turner. Then there's the next level upstream from there, which is "This is why kids learn", and then there's the next level behind that again for our young people, which is how to inhabit space if you've been knocked off your perch. You have to return in this idea of human development to what enabled you to stand up as an infant, which maybe you didn't fully learn because you were beaten into standing up. So here's another chance.

The acceleration into that insight comes from a spiritual idea about the morphology of human development. If you feel you didn't need that, but you just want to be a craft practitioner, that's fine, but you won't be invited necessarily in the organisational context to help with redesigning the future. I think in five years there'll be a team who know what they're doing and why. That team is emerging but hasn't quite formed yet. We have a team responsible for researching the different fields and how we practise them, so that we are still articulating our practice and subjecting it to research.

An overview of Ruskin Mill

Ruskin Mill Trust is one of the UK's largest independent non-profits (registered charities) in special needs education, working with young people with autism and other learning difficulties. It uses practical craft and land activities in outdoor learning environments and renovated historic buildings as tools for therapeutic education, meaning that the central purpose is the pupils' and students' development; 85% of leavers also achieve vocational qualifications. A rich curriculum of craftwork, farming, life skills, performing arts, therapies and social enterprises support young people to re-imagine their own potential.

The Trust holds that everyone has the potential to shape their own future through meaningful relationships with universe, earth and people. Its method, outlined in this book, seeks to enable each learner to further develop their capacity for self-generated conscious action, whether they are a young person in the Trust's care or a staff member.

Ruskin Mill currently has around 1,200 staff working with young people with learning difficulties and differences, physical health issues and social challenges of various kinds. Starting from re-imagining the potential of specific buildings and places (Chapter 1), the Trust's various provisions (schools, colleges, adult spaces) use traditional crafts (Chapter 2) and biodynamic farming (Chapter 3) as forms of therapeutic education (Chapter 4). The Trust's young people are often in residential care (Chapter 5) and in need of additional therapeutic and medical contributions (Chapter 6), while the staff working with them also need to consider their own self-leadership (Chapter 7).

While this book sometimes uses terms such as autism, learning differences and difficulties, behaviour that challenges and so on, Ruskin Mill works with each young person as an individual, on the basis of the needs they or an advocate have identified. In England, local authorities have legal obligations to provide for the specific needs of young people with "Education, Health and Care Plans" (EHCPs). This, and related procedures in Wales, funds a continual stream of students. Alongside this, Ruskin Mill's work meets with goodwill from a wide range of different directions, leading to collaborations and donations enabling the further development and expansion of the project.

The many places of Ruskin Mill

Thus, the original Ruskin Mill, today's Ruskin Mill College (Chapter 1), was slowly renovated between 1982 and 2000. The initial project was for the building to be a centre for cultural development, with workshops for master craftspeople and designers, scope for training and study and a café. By 1986 the café created the need for land that could provide food; a couple of students who were social leaders within a group of five brought the plants to the café, prepared them and then served them at a salad bar. The Trust was able to buy the neighbouring Horsley mill and two farms in the Horsley Valley between 1994 and 2000 and to inaugurate the Field Centre (Chapter 7) in 2013.

Between 2000 and 2010 the Webb Corbett glass factory in Stourbridge (Chapter 2) was gradually transformed into the Glasshouse, combining the college with an arts and heritage centre and workshops for craftspeople. In Sheffield, Freeman College (Chapter 6) was opened in 2005, renovating the Sterling Works cutlery factory and the neighbouring Butcher Works and reviving the Merlin Theatre, followed by Brantwood Specialist School.

Between 2015 and 2018, the derelict Standard Works in Birmingham's Jewellery Quarter became Argent College, with the Hive café and bakery. Argent's rooftop microgarden is an innovative solution to the need to make land-based activities available to all students. Often these are available on-site; in other cases a city provision will have its own attached smallholding a short distance away: High Riggs market garden for Freeman; Valehead Farm for Glasshouse; Eyam outdoor classroom for Brantwood school.

The process of growth and development continues, in each case seeking to encounter the needs and potential expressed in a particular place: in Wales, the bilingual Coleg Plas Dwbl in Clynderwen, Ty'r Eithin near Swansea and the Trigonos workshop and retreat centre in Nantlle; in Scotland, Pishwanton's RISE centre for older participants emerged (Chapter 3). The Clervaux provision near Darlington (Chapter 3), Grace Garden School (Chapter 4) and the forthcoming Helios Centre in Bristol have all recently joined the Trust. In 2017, the Trust started operating Sunfield Specialist School (soon to be re-imagined as Sunfield Garden School) in the Clent Hills of Worcestershire. Founded in 1930 and visited by Gandhi, Sunfield was co-founded by Ita Wegman, a close collaborator of Rudolf Steiner and co-founder of Weleda; it was also the origin of the Nordoff-Robbins school of music therapy which is internationally known.

This list – including five colleges (for students in the 16–25 age group), four schools (for pupils from 6 to 19) and two RISE provisions (for participants over 18) – will almost certainly soon be out of date as the Trust develops and grows. The following chapters visit some of these provisions, and others are shown in photographs.

Ruskin Mill's provisions are open to the wider world in various ways. Some, like the Horsley Valley, have permissive pathways enabling the public and visitors from around the world to walk through the valley space. Where possible, provisions include cafés or shops selling food and craft items produced by the young people, offering an opportunity for students to gain a range of real-world skills (Chapter 5). A range of cultural events, exhibitions, talks and workshops are also often available at the larger provisions, supporting closer engagement with the wider community. Finally, courses in different aspects of PSTE are offered to the public as well as staff members and offer a unique opportunity to engage with the method.

Seven fields

The spirit of place identifies what is unique to where we stand in the world. In the Trust's educational work, we work with the landscape, its flora and fauna, and the long history of human activity to develop forms of craft and farming that are appropriate to the location, renovating and repurposing heritage buildings and connecting with the holders of traditional skills. More generally, this book asks, who are we? Where do we stand in the world, physically and in other ways? What does this ask of us?

Practical skills: Craft and landwork involve learning new, skilled physical activities. These support young people's cognitive, emotional and physical development and tie to executive functioning (how we come to be an effective individual acting in the world). Physical materials (mineral, plant and animal) are sourced from a specific place, reworked with our hands and transformed into something that others recognise and value, helping to reconnect with the earth, the self and the wider community. In the process we can become more reflective and creative and resolve past developmental issues.

Ecology of the farm: Physical engagement with the outdoors offers many benefits, starting from the immediate experience itself. Young people at Ruskin Mill come to experience connection across time – through the cycles of the farming year and the different stages of crops and animals. The different aspects of the "farm as an organism" are also interconnected, enabling young people to practically grasp how to live with complexity. Finally, the encounter with specific animals can also be transformative in many different ways.

Therapeutic education: Ruskin Mill doesn't train young people to become farmers or craftspeople for career reasons in most cases, but rather because farming and craft activities are beneficial in themselves in many ways. Staff practitioners meet the students as therapeutic educators, using the vehicle of the craft or landwork to help the learner develop. Often what is crucial is to understand the different phases of human development, and in particular to notice when particular steps have been missed for whatever reason, so that young people can be invited to "re-step" these in an age-appropriate way.

Holistic care: The supported environment of Ruskin Mill's farms, craft workshops, residential provisions and elsewhere aim to care for all aspects of the young person. Seven care qualities help staff to think about the different dimensions of students' and pupils' needs: daily and yearly rhythms, physical and emotional warmth, good and appropriate nourishment, trust in themselves and others, a constant environment, a world of many kinds of culture and scope for recreation. Care and support across these different dimensions creates a context enabling flourishing, development and human freedom.

Health and the whole human being: Ruskin Mill's young people often face several challenges simultaneously in their daily lives, which might be described in many ways: neurodivergence, autism, behaviour that challenges, physical dis/abilities, poor health and other terms. It is fundamental to the Trust's approach to see the young person and not simply a label or category but also to integrate the many forms of care they may need in a way that works for a particular young person. Thus, students are supported by doctors, nurses and therapists working collaboratively with practitioners and support staff. In the student study, these many different perspectives are brought together to try to see the person in all their richness.

Transformative (self-)leadership: Ruskin Mill's ultimate aim for young people is for them to be able to engage in self-generated conscious action. This means being able to experience an adult's freedom as far as possible, choosing for themselves what to do and how to go about doing it, aware of the challenges and the benefits for self and other. They aren't frozen and unable to act, or simply driven by uncontrolled reactions to their own emotions, other people and the environment. Staff in turn role model how to bring the different parts of ourselves together and develop a healthy ego, setting our own course through life; what transforms staff will also benefit young people and provides a way of thinking about human freedom for self and other.

Practical skills therapeutic education is robust

The Ruskin Mill model has been powerfully tested, in many ways. Firstly, the challenges of providing an education that can transform young people's lives are underlined by the institutional processes involved. Students often arrive at Ruskin Mill with a two-inch-thick file documenting the ways in which some conventional approaches have failed to help with their differences and difficulties. What motivates local authorities – often on the steps of a tribunal – to approve the greater costs of its rich education, health and care experience is that Ruskin Mill's approach can work where others don't fully deliver. All of this means that if a student arrives at Ruskin Mill, there is a very formal agreement that they need nothing less. They are therefore people with high levels of need that aren't being met elsewhere: and over the years PSTE has a recognised track record of being able to help people in this situation.

Secondly, this is a highly regulated area, made more complex by the different regulatory arrangements for different age groups and types of vulnerability, for residential and non-residential students, and in England, Scotland and Wales. The result is that Ruskin Mill Trust has to meet the scrutiny of up to 14 different agencies inspecting educational provision, residential care and so on. It has to continually demonstrate good practice and beneficial outcomes and justify its approach.

Despite this, it thrives and keeps growing, with new centres continually being added. Its model is financially successful and attracts significant capital donations beyond this: from the Department for Education, the Education Funding Agency, the Heritage Lottery Fund, the Learning and Skills Council and Advantage West Midlands among others, as well as gifts of property from Sunfield Children's Home, Tintagel House, the Catherine Grace Trust and the Responsive Earth Trust among others.

Most recently, its experience during Covid-19 lockdowns was telling: while most educational and care establishments across the country closed their doors, went online or provided minimal levels of provision, Ruskin Mill simply accentuated its already-substantial outdoors provision and carried on working with the young people in its care. The educational fallout so often highlighted in relation to conventional systems failed to materialise; here was one group of young people who were not cut off from their peers and pathways.

Finally, Ruskin Mill punches well above its weight as a medium-sized NGO in terms of staff training, further education and research: its practice and thinking is constantly placed under internal and external scrutiny. For over a decade and a half, it has delivered or co-delivered Master's courses, with dissertations centring action research into different aspects of the method and the results fed back into staff training. Action research by practitioners is also part of its lower level internal training courses.

Meanwhile senior staff are supported to carry out PhDs in several different universities exploring the method through a range of academic disciplines, while the Trust also employs associate researchers to carry out research into the underpinnings of the method and is funding independent researchers to look at Trust outcomes: its Centre for Research is based at four different provisions in England, Scotland and Wales. The Trust's research is made publicly available through its two research journals, occasional publications, conferences and exhibitions.

Bibliography

Berberich, C., Campbell, N., & Robert Hudson, R. (Eds.) (2015). *Affective landscapes in literature, art and everyday life: Memory, place and the senses*. Ashgate.

Bockemühl, J. (1986). *Dying forests: A crisis in consciousness*. Hawthorn.

Brook, I. (1998). Goethean science as a way to read landscape. *Landscape Research*, *23*(1), 51–69.

Day, C. (2002). *Spirit and place*. Taylor and Francis.

König, K. (1989). *Being human: Diagnosis in curative education*. Anthroposophic Press and Camphill Press. (Original German publication 1983-4).

Lee, L. (2002). *Cider with Rosie*. Vintage. (Original publication 1959).

Macfarlane, R. (2012). *The old ways: A journey on foot*. Penguin.

Nassar, D. (2022). *Romantic empiricism: Nature, art, and ecology from Herder to Humboldt*. Oxford University Press.

Reed, S. (2017). *Creative Journeys: Enlivening Geographic Locations through Artistic Practice* [Doctoral thesis, University of Derby.] https://www.proquest.com/openview/6c037a3cfae1ac1690fcd6f9b40e2272/1.pdf?pq-origsite=gscholar&cbl=2026366&diss=y

Robinson, T. (2007). *Connemara: Listening to the wind*. Penguin Ireland.

Ruskin Mill Trust. (2019). *Vital beauty: Re-imagining the buildings of Ruskin Mill Trust*. Ruskin Mill Trust.

Ruskin Mill website: https://rmt.org/

2   Practical skills

Visiting the Glasshouse

At first sight, Stourbridge in the Black Country – so named for the smoke in the 19th-century air and the nearby coal seams – is about as far from the rural beauty of the Cotswolds as you can get. A 1960s ring road, complete with underpasses, circles tightly around the town centre, traffic thundering past as you walk from the station to what optimistic marketers have dubbed the Glass Quarter – although the days of large-scale production are gone and not adequately compensated for either by the small boutique producers of the area or by tourism.

Here, on the "Crystal Mile", there were once more than 200 glass-related firms employing 2,000 workers, the heart of the industry in Britain and producing the majority of Britain's crystal glass – made with lead oxide to increase sparkle and ease of cutting. The canal brought in raw materials such as sand to melt into glass, fireclay for the furnaces and coal for fuel, and took the finished glass out. Production peaked as late as the 1980s before succumbing to the globalisation of the Thatcher years.

As with Nailsworth's Huguenots, this industry was founded by immigrants from Bohemia and Lorraine in the 17th century. The Coalbourne Hill glassworks was built in 1691 as one of the earliest industrial glass sites in northwestern Europe. It passed through many hands, and many changes, finishing up with Royal Doulton from 1969 on.

Revitalisation

Ruskin Mill acquired the mostly vacant site in 2000, keeping on five of the last remaining glassworkers to hand on their skills. Many of the local students are themselves from families who worked in the glass industry, working in a material with powerful local resonances. Students and staff helped with the archaeological work during redevelopment, finding several glass cones, including one of the original 1691 furnaces, as well as artefacts from earlier centuries. When a new bronze bell was cast for the college, locals queued up to throw in unwanted silver and gold jewellery for this revived site.

DOI: 10.4324/9781003361541-2

Approaching from the outside, your entrance point is not institutional but a delicate tracery of metal curves in air and space, tracing how the planet Venus moves as seen from the Earth, and meeting at coloured glass roundels. These gates are designed to offer students an invitation to enter rather than a sense of enclosure.

Moving inwards, the courtyard in the old centre now houses a large flow-form made from recycled television screens, plants and benches. One old glasshouse has become an arts and heritage centre with a vast auditorium where glass once cooled, a theatre and display space – it hosts the British Glass Biennale (see Chapter 6) and exhibitions such as the 2018 "Experience Colour", a stunning scientific and artistic exploration of Goethe's work on colour. As well as the working glass spaces, classrooms and offices, the site also hosts around 20 different glass studios and a café run by students.

From 2019 to 2022 the "Voices from the Cones" project run by Ruskin Mill, Dudley Museum Service, Stourbridge Glass Museum and Dudley Council worked with oral history interviews with former glassworkers to produce a combined song cycle by Dan Whitehouse and narrative by poet/storyteller John Edgar, reminiscent of Ewan MacColl's "radio ballads". Performed as a live show for the community and at the International Festival of Glass, it has now been published as an album (Whitehouse & Edgar, 2022). The project brings the experience and feelings of work and community to life; the final song, "Hands heart head", points to the re-imagination of potential represented by the Glasshouse.

Figure 2.1 Re-imagining post-industrial spaces: the courtyard at Glasshouse College during the International Festival of Glass 2019

Blowing hot glass

When you step into the hot glass workshop, it hits you immediately: the heat from the furnaces and the hot glass, the sound of roaring gas, the crackling sound of glass cooling. The wider workshop has space to move and talk, to hang protective gear, to store finished pieces – but there is no doubt where the centre of attention lies.

When the furnace is opened, the molten glass is there, resting in its basin as a sinkful of liquid at a terrifying temperature. You take up a long, heavy metal rod and lower it into what looks like water but doesn't behave like water, or anything else, really. If you rotate the rod at the right speed, glass adheres to it, only a little bit like runny honey on a teaspoon.

You have to keep turning the rod or the glass sags on one side – and then you have to swing the long rod round to where you want to work it, keeping the rolling steady on the bench, and at the right speed, staying aware of others and obstacles. This takes not just strength, but the right kinds of movements – there is a way to grasp and a way to roll that spares your arms and keeps the curves of the glass even – together with an intense focus on this point of great heat, and the time pressure of the glass cooling and becoming unworkable.

If it is hard to write this clearly or make sense of it while reading, it is even harder to do the first time: you have to watch, and then learn to feel it while doing. It takes courage, not just for the heat, but for the risk of getting it wrong in front of others, and care for those others while you move the molten glass on the end of its rod. You need to bring yourself to the point where you are willing to blow into a tube with hot glass at the other end or hold the molten glass with just a pad of wet newspaper as you shape it. This requires a lot of trust – particularly from young people whose pasts have often been deeply traumatic.

A world of its own

The shapes that glass can take are only limited by your own skill: you can roll it into the shape of a paperweight, adding sprinkles of colour, or blow it into a mould for a vase, or twist a piece someone else is holding with pincers into an icicle. As it cools, its colour changes, it hardens and its flow slows down. There is sheer magic in seeing this extraordinary material – once just sand – change.

Later, when you drink a glass of water, a banal household object, which you might have used thousands of times before, suddenly appears extraordinary, in a magical re-visioning of something we take for granted. The everyday world is *made* – it does not just appear, shrinkwrapped in a shop or in a delivery box. Even mechanised, the process that brings it to our hand draws on the skilled hands, arms and brains of many generations.

It is a testament to generations of glass craftsmanship that students can be shown anything at all that might work the first time with this weird, fiery stuff – and no surprise that it takes years to master the skill, building up from one kind of item to another and developing a real sense of the material, the tools, the actions and the tasks. A first taster like the session described above – a couple of hours in a small group with a tutor – shows how much practice would be needed with each task to develop real skill in the movements and the processes.

There is a whole world to master: the furnace, the glory-hole for reheating glass, the lehr to cool it down without cracking, the marver to roll it on, the hand-held board to press against it, the rod, the steps to stand on so you can blow down the blowing iron into the mould, the "chair" you sit on to roll – and all this in the first session.

The tutor, Roger Holloway, is a big quiet man, who worked for 24 years in Stuart Crystal, five of them as an apprentice ("an extra 50p a week!") until the factory closed. He's now been at Glasshouse College for nearly as long. He is a very reassuring presence, showing rather than telling, saying just the minimum needed. Learning to work hot glass with him, you feel genuinely held: you have to trust that he knows what he's doing and find your own confidence. And, later, the extraordinary sense of achievement that comes from making your own first piece of glass.

It is remarkable, in a world of risk assessments and nervous managers, how a single craft tutor with one assistant can hold three students with all their specific issues – and young adult energy – in the workplace. And yet this is how it has been in this space for generations, with those other young people, and their own specifics and the pressures they were under. And looking around

Figure 2.2 Learning the craft: pouring glass at Glasshouse College

you see some extraordinary student pieces: bowls as thin as porcelain, or a snake made in hot glass.

Transformation through relationship with the material world

A craft curriculum growing out of place

Each of Ruskin Mill Trust's provisions has a "signature craft", given by its location. At Ruskin Mill College, in a land that for centuries was dominated by flocks of sheep and textile mills, that craft is based on wool: more specifically, for therapeutic and educational reasons, working with felt. In Sheffield, it is metal work. In Stourbridge, of course, it is glass – not only because of three centuries of glass blowing and cutting in the factory but also because the town grew as the centre of the glass industry out of its location on the Stour, near the raw materials of the craft. The sand from under the Glasshouse makes a bottle green glass.

Any craft has to grow out of the materials offered by a particular place, whether in its animals, its plants or its geology. Textile crafts such as felt, weaving, leatherwork or silk making are all based on the animal kingdom. The plant realm affords possibilities for green woodwork (with unseasoned timber), weaving willow, papermaking and more. Geology enables stoneworking, pottery, metal work and of course glass. Young people can make these connections practically as they care for sheep, work in the woods or dig out clay, working forwards from place to material, from material to craft, and from craft to a useful and meaningful object: a spoon, a coathook, a pair of slippers, a vase, a chair.

Iron from plants

At one point, Ruskin Mill took students to Clearwell Caves in the Forest of Dean, a site of mining for 5,000 years where there are still Freeminers with the traditional right to do so. There they found iron, made charcoal from the woods and went through the whole process of smelting, beating iron out of the slag and so on. They felled timber to make handles for their knife or axe blades and made scabbards from animal hides.

When the science curriculum was being developed, students visited Sweden with their Iron Age forge teacher. They encountered a Sámi teacher who gave them access to a very different process of mining iron. In March, just before the ice melts in northern Sweden, the water has been very still and the plant life attracts the iron oxide that saturates the water.

Students collected large quantities of pondweed, dried it and burned it. They then hammered the ash, leaving nodules of iron that could be smelted, until they were able to forge a knife. Handles would be made from knotted birch burrs and sheaths from reindeer skin – the three kingdoms of mineral, vegetable and animal.

Such moments of creation have a magical quality, transforming not only the material but also the student in the process.

What do we actually enjoy doing?

Once upon a time, not so very long ago, skilled manual work was a central part of working life in Britain. While the older crafts of a farming world, from blacksmithing to hedge-laying, and the "handicrafts", from knitting to doll-making, ceased being practical necessities of daily life for most people over the long process of industrialisation, becoming instead leisure activities or forms of therapy, the new workplaces were dominated by the skilled hand and the machine. Shipbuilding and ships themselves, car factories, engineering, mines and metalwork, clothing and printing – if the education system failed to value the skills of the hand and the eye, the workplace often recognised their value.

Notoriously, the late 20th century saw a collapse in these activities in Britain, an extreme version of a pattern felt elsewhere in the global North. "Rust-belts", empty factories, "brownfield" sites, dying towns, mass unemployment, intergenerational poverty – these are familiar features of the last half-century, in which the prestige of celebrity and image, media and marketing, managers and PowerPoints have apparently eclipsed any sense of a meaningful and socially valued relationship between human beings, the skilled hand and the material world that we live in, reshape and use.

And yet, and yet … when you ask people what they most value and enjoy doing, so much of it consists of precisely this. Growing flowers or vegetables, cooking and baking, mending things and improving their houses, making music, tinkering with bikes or cars – these are not obscure or minority pleasures but rather things that people do far beyond what the simple calculus of time or money would suggest. We readily recognise and enjoy the skilled physical encounter with the material world outside ourselves.

It is only in very limited contexts and in recent history that significant numbers of people other than, perhaps, the idle rich have *not* had to master at least some skills in building or cooking, farming or fixing things, making clothes or caring for others. If industrial employers sometimes spoke of un-skilled hands, most of those hands had many different skills in at least some parts of their lives. This is one reason why – even as skilled manual labour declined *as a form of paid employment* – arts and crafts movements developed, and people sought new ways to revitalise this encounter outside of the socially sanctioned workplace. Ruskin Mill's work connects to a much wider contemporary rethinking of the importance of practical skill and craft (e.g. Crawford, 2009; Korn, 2017; Marchand, 2022; Rogowski, 2017; Sennett, 2009).

Socially meaningful work

Crucial to Ruskin Mill's practice is making socially meaningful items. Any given community has an understanding of what is required of a glass, a butter knife, a stool, a slipper, a loaf of bread: there may be variation and experiment, but people will either accept and use an item, or not. This means that the community is the designer, and the craftsperson ultimately relates to this design.

From the young person's point of view, this can have several levels of meaning. Is what they make recognisably useful to them? Can a student residence use place mats they have felted, for example? Will other people eat the food they cook? If they give a spoon they have made to a family member, will it sit politely on a shelf or appear in the sugar bowl? And if they offer what they have made for sale, will people buy their vase, their pot, their knife?

Figure 2.3 A socially meaningful item: Freeman College student with his jug

Items that pass these tests are genuine items of service: they are meaningful in the everyday life of a particular community, and so they shape the crafts that produce them. The craftsperson in turn is transformed by their engagement with the requirements of the community's design. They step into other people's needs and their everyday lives: and if their items are accepted, they too are accepted as making a real contribution in practice.

The material as teacher

The truly unskilled hand, the eye that has not been trained to focus on any precise task, the body that does not know how to hold itself for necessary work, the mind that is unused to dealing with a material reality outside itself – these have only become widespread on a global scale in the last few decades, as the fast food and fast fashion industries, planned obsolescence and objects produced to be thrown away rather than fixed have come to dominate many people's lives.

In skilled work, the material is our teacher: it stands outside us and requires us to understand it as glass and heat, soil and seasons, water and pipes, to master the means of working with it – the furnace or the oven, the glass pincers or the spanner, the soldering iron or the oar – and to remake ourselves to deal with it. We need to develop new kinds of strength or precision, of confidence in the process or tolerance for frustration, a new physical balance or a new sensitivity in our taste.

Together with the emphasis on making socially meaningful items, this means that the learner is not engaging primarily with an adult presenting arbitrary tasks: authority is delegated to the material. The focus can shift to the item being produced, the skill of wielding the tool, the resistance of the material and the emotional challenges of engaging with these; and the young person can learn directly through this process.

An extensive body of psychological and neurological research underlines the value of practical skills for the development of brain structure, cognition, executive functioning and mental as well as physical health (see the review by Sigman, 2023).

Re-inhabiting the body

It can sound very odd to talk about how we inhabit our bodies as a physical activity. Musicians, athletes, actors, jockeys or dancers may already be very conscious of this, but most of us are not very aware of what we do with our bodies except when it becomes an effort or when we start to suffer from lower back pain, carpal tunnel syndrome and the other ailments of modern life and are forced to take it seriously.

Spend time around young people with learning differences and difficulties or behaviour that challenges, though, and you begin to notice the variety of ways in which human beings have learned to inhabit their bodies, and some of the problems that can arise. A key concept in the Trust's work is the need for re-stepping: where a particular learning process, in early years or teenage life, has been interrupted or gone through under traumatic circumstances, people can mislearn it in damaging ways. The challenge is then to return to that learning process in a new context, re-step and go through the learning once more.

The craft workshop can bring such things to the surface, including in people who think of themselves as normal. Felt-making, for example, involves massaging wet fibres back and forth across a padded surface as they change from wet wool to matted felt: some people find this brings up the feelings of disgust that others might feel around, say, holding a slug. Another example: forges are often dark, small enclosed spaces dominated by intense heat and the noise of hammering, where you need to stand close to danger and to others. Not everyone can do this easily.

Holding ourselves

We might think of "three dimensions" as a purely passive, visual or even mathematical way of grasping reality. But in craftwork they are central domains of activity – and, for those who have struggled in this area, healing. We not only exist within these dimensions, but we *move* within them – and much of craftwork consists of the skilful application of controlled effort using these dimensions. What movements do I have to make in order to keep rolling the rod with the hot glass from one side to the other, steadily, so that it does not start to sag, for example? It might sound simple on paper – but the first time we try to do it, it may prove to be anything but.

There is a frontal dimension – ahead of us, what we can see, grasp or step into; behind us, perhaps a tutor, an assistant, or a wall – and we are all familiar with the different ways people sit (slouched or hunched) or stand (bending forward, leaning back). The sagittal dimension (from *sagittarius*, an archer) includes our balance between left and right. We might see people who tend to hold themselves one way or another – but most craft activities are "sided", with different hands doing different things, to such an extent that archaeologists can identify traces in people's bones, including archers. Finally, the horizontal dimension – up and down – is an obvious aspect of the exercise of effort in particular: how do I chop wood, lean into the rolling pin, fix a lightbulb above my head while perched on a ladder?

Karl König, founder of the Camphill movement of communities involving co-living with people with learning differences, identified focus, grasp and step as key elements of what a craft asks of us. We need to focus our gaze, and through that our mind and our bodily activities, on the task: never cut bread, or hammer nails, without looking! This asks us to combine the frontal dimension of our face, with its widely spaced eyes, with the sagittal left-right dimension that enables judging position and distance.

And that task is literally "in hand" – held in a skilled combination of the sagittal and the horizontal. The skilled holding of a chisel to the lathe, of a guitar neck or of carding tools is fundamental to getting the job right and helps us reorganise our physical effort around this. That involves a characteristic step – how we plant our whole body, in all three dimensions, whether the task involves standing still or, as often in farming, moving.

Focus, grasp and step are very different for blowing a glass vase or in whittling wood, in making a felt slipper or in hammering hot iron; and a skilled tutor can often see whether the learner has "got it" without looking at the tool or the material itself. The material, and the tools, give us feedback directly, and with time and support we can come to hold ourselves – and not just the tool – differently. Put another way, we do not just make the item we are working on: we (re)shape ourselves, and this is part of what it means to be human.

The wider purpose is to develop a personal compass of orientation which is not just physical. The student comes into dimension with focus, grasp and step, but in the process they also develop their cognitive, emotional and social

Figure 2.4 Working in the three planes of space: Argent College student working on
the shaving horse

capacities – and in turn their capacity for self-generated conscious action. This curriculum was developed over time at Ruskin Mill, through a long process of responding to the needs of young people and the concrete situation.

Conversation with Aonghus Gordon

The first practical task in renovating Ruskin Mill – this derelict place that had once had potential – was to create an art form that would give it a signature. The building was full of rubbish, up to the ceiling in some places, and as we were digging it out we found flagstones in the current gallery. We found a buried baker's oven, with square ceramic pan tiles on its floor, and kept those. There was also a deposit of lots of different kerbstones and granite sets of stone from when the local council had renewed the sewage line; they had just dumped the stones they took up there.

So we had all these wonderful stones, and rather than throw them out I turned them into a floor mosaic. We had these extraordinarily beautiful limestone flagstones from the Cotswolds, granite sets from the Malverns, and sandstone kerbstones from the Forest of Dean, as well as clay from the Severn Vale – all of Gloucestershire was there. I could also bring out the synergy between the silica processes of the granite and the calcium processes of the limestone, which are both very important in biodynamic farming and in Rudolf Steiner's medical theories.

Previously I had visited an ancient Egyptian zodiac floor, and I later discovered the remarkable zodiac of San Miniato del Monte in Florence, which had been laid down in 1207 and connected celestial events with their religious calendar. So I spent some time researching this and set about to try and make something that would symbolise the key elements that I believed Ruskin Mill needed to explore.

If you go down into the gallery today, you will see a mosaic depicting the contraction of the night and the expansion of day, which is the bigger artistic picture. Granite contracts and limestone expands, creating an interesting tension, so I decided to do a sun mandala in the middle of the floor and then make the journey back from that centre to the periphery.

We put a mandala of limestone in the centre with 12 radiating spokes, surrounded by 7 granite sets to represent the 7 life processes, and then 12 limestone flagstones to represent the 12 senses of the human being, which are important in Steiner education, and lastly a ring of granite. Between all these there are pentagons in sandstone, which mediates between granite and limestone – some of the sandstone is a conglomerate, so it brings everything together.

In this composition, differences merge into one and are assimilated into a new matrix, which as a potter I find very interesting. And between the symbolism of the zodiac, the sun and the moon and the symbolism of human sense and life processes, there is a bigger picture which connects the human being to the universe and the universe to the human being.

When, about 15 years later, I invited Howard Hull from the John Ruskin museum at Brantwood to give a talk about Ruskin's influence, he was blown away by the zodiac floor. He said, "I don't know who made this, but I know it's exactly what Ruskin would have appreciated". So we got something right there.

Finding volunteers

At this point our strapline was "Ruskin Mill – a centre for cultural development, design and craft workshops, training and study". I needed more volunteer help, so I went down to the dole queue where there were some very capable young people. I intercepted a couple of them and said "I'm Aonghus and I'm doing some voluntary work on this project called Ruskin Mill. Would you like to help me out and I'll give you lunch and your bus money?" And the amazing thing was that about one in four said yes.

So they cleaned and scraped the room. Some of them were good at maths, and I gave them the job of drawing out some of the triangles, which I then cut with an angle grinder. They cut out some of the pentagons and did the measurements with me, setting it all out on a cement background. Some of the young people also liked chipping and grinding, so there are still markings in the room of some quite creative rechiselling of the stone surfaces.

Now when the zodiac was nearly finished, I didn't know what to put in the centre, but someone gave me a meteorite that had fallen in Thailand and said "This should be in the centre, because this is where it all comes from".

And then when it was completed, it was used for about three or four years by a circle dance group, but people had some very peculiar ideas about the room. Some thought it was a séance room or for witchcraft, because they weren't used to seeing anything like it. I nearly covered it up with cement, because it was causing so much grief, but in the end it became an art gallery with a mosaic floor.

Making things happen

At the same time, we were renovating the rest of Ruskin Mill, which was a very interesting experience. If we needed something, I only had to let enough people know about it and somehow things would happen. For example, there was no staircase up to the level above the zodiac floor. I was down below working on the floor and a colleague, who later became a beekeeper, put his head down from above and said "Hi Aonghus, when are you putting the staircase in?"

I said "Well, I don't have one". "Ah. Well, I work at a printer's in Gloucester and they just chucked out a staircase. Shall I have a look?" So three days later he picked it up, drove it down and it just fitted.

Or about four months later, I'd invited some Stroud musicians to sing some of their new songs, which were very much about the environment, and the place was packed. A lady called Lorna St Auburn, who was a friend of the musicians, came up to me and said "I gather you might be looking for some money. How much do you want? I've just set up a bank". She came from a wealthy family in Cornwall and she had liquidated her assets in order to lend money to new spiritually based projects.

I only needed £2,000, which was enough to set workshops up in 1983–84. Two of the young people who had come to work on the zodiac didn't want to leave, so I told them that I was setting up workshops on the floor above, and if they wanted to take up a craft I'd help them to become apprentices. They said yes, and after their apprenticeships, they rented workshop space and became independent craftspeople.

The grant enabled me to renovate the building and have craftspeople move in. I rented them spaces to pay off the loan, so the craftwork came in the form of social enterprises. We had hoped to find work for the craftspeople through an architect, following William Morris' intention to bring the arts and crafts back into architecture, but unfortunately people who were commissioning bespoke buildings disdained spending money on arts as part of that.

But what did happen was that people who visited the café would commission work from the craftspeople. The artist was incredibly successful with portraits; blacksmithing was popular, and the leatherworker was outstanding. The felt-maker had trained at Konya in Turkey, making dervish-style felt hats which were incredibly beautiful.

I had personal connections to some of them. The jeweller was my wife Sabrina, the photographer was my brother Alisdair, and I had been to school with the textile maker and the first potter. The artist, Kay Wedgbury, was almost the conscience of Nailsworth. We had Johannes Steuck, who made stained glass and mosaics. We also had a patchwork quilt maker, an ecological water engineer, a boat builder and a café – the place was packed.

Working at a school

That whole process took about four or five years. In the meantime I started working two days a week as a potter at a local school. It was a residential Waldorf special school, with bright kids between 10 and 16 who were emotionally and socially deprived. They didn't necessarily have learning difficulties, although there were consequences from deprivation, such as ADHD, trauma or a history of physical abuse. They were cocky, clever, antisocial and defiant: quite difficult young people for many adults.

The school was Steiner based, but in an old-fashioned way, with very formal teaching. There were a lot of assumptions around what children needed, rather than a strategy of leading children who didn't want to learn to learning. But we found that I never had any behavioural problems with them in my workshop, in fact the opposite: they were so quiet that I couldn't grasp the gap between what could happen in the courtyard and how they were in the pottery lessons. There was never any throwing of clay, for example.

The water wheel

As what was happening in those pottery workshops became known I was asked questions, and soon I was invited onto the board of management, and advising on how to handle certain behaviours. So when things got difficult, I would take some of the more challenging boys and girls down to Ruskin Mill on Saturdays and work with them on renovation.

I got them working on renovating the mill's waterwheel with me and another teacher. That was a massive metalwork project. We laid it all out on the bank, with the two cheeks of the waterwheel to left and right and the hub parts in the middle. We spent nearly two years just grinding, welding and pitching metal. Then we assembled the bearings and the spokes.

We studied hydrology, social history, physics, chemistry and engineering. Each subject was taught in the context of the whole around the waterwheel: the task formed the curriculum, and the curriculum had to be understood around the wheel having to work.

When we had it all reassembled, I heard a rumour that there was a church near Hereford that wanted to get rid of its generator, so I went up there and got it and connected it up. We couldn't find the gearing needed to transmit the power from the waterwheel to the generator, but I'd brought in a local guy called Bill Benton. He was something of a genius bodger, joiner and engineer. Bill saw a gearwheel on a flatback, going to a scrap merchant. He stopped the truck, bought it there and then brought it back to the Mill and it just fitted. We got it to work, boiled a kettle and lit the basement. So we also got a generator project out of it. And students were involved in all these processes. It was quite magical.

Figure 2.5 A curriculum from place: the restored water wheel at Ruskin Mill

Developing a craft curriculum

After all this I went back to the school and offered to set up an independent
course at Ruskin Mill for the 16- to 18-year-olds to resolve their behavioural
issues. They turned it down initially, which was quite wounding, and I went
back to my main work. But six months later they came back to me and asked
if I was still interested in that idea. I was ready to bargain with them, but they
accepted everything I asked for, which was to have no interference with the
curriculum design and no extra charges for the students.

Now at this point Ruskin Mill was a buzzing craft centre, but the architecture idea wasn't working. So I contracted time from the craftspeople there –
two hours here, a morning there – and they were paid well. I set up a timetable
and found one or two other interesting people.

I built a seminar room to do English and Russian literature and to write
poetry. I found a green eco-warrior woman who could teach them maths
through meteorology. We set up a meteorological station and I made links
with the glider club in Nympsfield, a few miles away. So every so often the students would go gliding with a trained pilot. They would measure the clouds,
the air pressure and so on and take photographs as they ascended. She consolidated all the maths and translated it into a graph and then they would write
about it with the literature teacher.

So literacy and numeracy were incorporated at a core level, but the students
had no idea that they were doing it. Their progress was amazing, and one of
the first students I tested it out with, Kim Robinson, still comes down from
Hull to see me. He did leatherwork, photography, blacksmithing and some
work in the café.

Seed to table

At this point I was offered an organic greengrocer's that had started in Uley,
just down the road. The people who ran it were moving to Ireland and they
didn't want to close it down. So the whole business, and its reputation, came
down to where the herbalist is today, just in front of the main entrance. I built
a little shop in about a week and the greengrocer's went in there. The maths
teacher had some time, and I employed her to run the shop, which offered
students another level of vocational numeracy and social skills.

Now we had the task of linking up the vegetable growing which was happening in the little market garden at the other end of the lake with the shop
and the café. This is what became the seed to table curriculum.

By this point we had the core of Ruskin Mill: the crafts; literature, arts and
culture; the social relationships of the café and the retail element of the shop;
the primary growing of food. It was based on the development of the human
being and the development of the earth. At this point what we offered was
called the Living Earth Training Course, and in a sense the core foundation of
the curriculum has remained since then. Of course, then we had to work out
what those ideas meant in practice.

Growing the project

Now students who came down thrived most of the time, but to expand the project I knew that I would need external endorsement outside the school, which meant parents and the authorities. What I noticed is that what was critical was meeting a parent, particularly the mothers, and whether they trusted you. So I rearranged the student review process so that I only did it when both the mother and the social worker could come. The mothers acted as champions for their children, and they talked about what the students needed.

From then on it just expanded exponentially. There were social workers sitting in the reviews with the parents, and it was a totally transparent situation. The kids would say "I want another year", which I often didn't expect. Parents would say "It's the best thing since sliced bread". The social workers could see it, and local authorities would say "It's not a problem", which was amazing. And they'd say "Would you like to have this or that?" and so I could grow it.

Things took off after I'd established five students successfully. I'd started with one student, gone to two and three, and in the fourth year I went to five, so it was quite slow. But I had established the Living Earth Training Course and I had agreed with the school that I could go directly to the social workers and vice versa without going through the school. They had no idea of the consequences of that!

From craft to materials

So from this point on, the project grew through delivering craft activities, social enterprise in the shop and the café, and landwork. And then I discovered that it was critical to the craft that the clay needed to come from the ground locally. The fleeces needed to come from the goats or sheep we were working with, and the leather from our animals if possible.

When the garden was up and running, I opened up a new facility in Horsley and employed someone to look after sheep and goats there. We got the milk from the goats into the shop; we took the skins from the goats, tanned it, did leatherwork and made drums; we dug clay and made pots. So we had the seed to table curriculum established.

Now when the students were involved in harvesting the primary materials for their crafts, they had a deeper level of ownership and knowledge. You could say that there was a re-stepping in time to the period before the Industrial Revolution, or you could say that this was a deeper therapeutic approach.

In Steiner education there is a pedagogical tool called re-stepping, where the curriculum is scaffolded on some of the significant developments in human history, encountering what they meant in a practical way. We were able to do that, and I could see what it offered these young people. It gave them legitimacy and primary knowledge of what they were doing. They weren't *believing* anything: they understood it through practice, as self-discovery.

That was necessary because these students often had no constraints, whether socially, intellectually or emotionally. But if you offered them containment within the day and across the week, they could move into some very interesting ways of doing things. You might teach them a discipline, but before you'd turned your back they'd already changed it and were doing it their own way – sometimes with negative effects but more often positively. And all of this happened within seven or eight years.

Discovering a pattern

The processes by which all this developed were quite fluid ones. The journey of discovery was partly led by students, who usually told me what helped them, not by saying "This is nice" but through how they engaged with different activities. There was an underlying intuition, certainly, but I then had to discover myself what it meant.

One important inspiration was Ivan Illich's (2018, orig. 1971) book *Deschooling Society*. I knew enough about John Ruskin to know that he liked industrial buildings. I knew enough about William Morris to know that he liked doing things by hand and was a genius at craftwork. And Steiner education offered a structure to innovate against.

I also knew that I didn't need a curriculum, which is quite a radical idea. But having been to a Steiner school I knew you could improve the curriculum, and my experience with students was that Illich was 100% right to say "Get them out of the classroom". So in those first five to seven years a lot of things came together, and when they worked they became established practice. There was no roadmap; we had to find the route ourselves. And what we ultimately relied on was the confirmation and advocacy we found at the end of each year from students, parents and social workers.

The benefits of crafts

One thing I noticed about craftwork is that students became silent in leatherwork, metalwork and pottery, but they became verbally active and quite transparent when they were working with textiles. So what happened in the space around textiles, if the tutor was open, was that students would tell their own stories and all their secrets, and it would never leave that room. The tutor was totally confidential.

So by accident I had found a therapeutic environment in textile work, which meant that we didn't need additional assistance from counsellors at that point. But we did need storytellers, and I employed them at Ruskin Mill. That led to interesting tensions, because stories are so biographically powerful and their pictures of human development are so strong, and it turned out that storytellers are often therapists. But my request to them was to focus on the story, rather than trying to be therapists, because craft gave us other ways into that. Instead, for example, I would ask a storyteller to ask the group what their story is and to give them back the big story that lives in them, but in a coherent way that could give them insights as to how they could complete those stories.

We had one remarkable student who was deeply cultured, with a prodigious memory. He knew all sorts of stories about King Arthur, and five or six different versions. One day he suggested that he would set up a story and then pass it to another student to carry on. Ofsted were visiting that day and it blew them away. The inspector said he'd never seen anything like it: "Memory skills, communication skills, empathy skills, cooperation skills – you name it, everything that I want to see in an educational context was there".

Working with violence

So we have the stories of the crafts, we have the stories from culture and history and we have re-stepping. We start from stories and then we go into a more mythological space. As the process developed and I wanted to engage the primary crafts that come directly out of the land, something shifted. We got even more challenging students, who we couldn't have helped without that shift. So when we started coppicing and I could make charcoal with the students, I could take them into the metalwork of 1,500 BC and I could start to work with quite high levels of previous violence in some of the boys.

As individuals, they didn't necessarily have a propensity for violence, but it was incited in the group context. Outside that context they were relatively safe. So, for example, some of the young men were coming with knives to the college. Astute care workers would come to me and say "He's got at least two knives under his pillow, but it's under the sheet". And I'd say, "Well, can you go when the student is at college and let me know whether the knives are still under the pillow?", because I wanted to know whether the knives were in college or not.

What we discovered was that one knife would be left under the pillow, and one was at college; they always had two knives. That's when I decided to not tackle it head-on but to tackle it indirectly, and the Iron Age forge curriculum became centred on knife making.

Now one time a mother came to me with her new partner, a senior policeman from the West End. The mother was coming to thank me for the curriculum, but her partner had never heard about this side of it. He was deeply shocked and really very angry, and we had some very heated conversation. "How can you be taking kids from London and then you make knives in this valley? This is so shocking – I've never heard anything like it. Our job is to take knives off kids". I was concerned that he'd even go and report me, but maybe the mother saved the day.

It was good to have a senior professional deeply object to what I was doing. I very rarely get deep objections, but his objection was on every level; he was completely flummoxed. He didn't get it of course, and I said "Well, if you sleep with a knife, what do you think is happening? He's absorbed the knife into his psyche as a phantom. So my reading of it is that this young man can never let his knife go until you replace it with something else, because he has a dependence on it. I'm setting up the Iron Age forge in which I pursue the most ruthless accountability around his effort to make that knife. The effort in itself will transform that need, because it is giving him new skills. I believe that I'm releasing the phantom that he is possessed by, which he now has to go to sleep with, both as a psychic quality (and the policeman didn't like that word!) and a reality".

So he said, "No, Mr Gordon, you just take the knives off them", but I said "It'll only be replaced. Knives don't replace themselves, but the phantom replaces itself, because it wants a physical manifestation". And the young man made his knife, and I would say that that released the phantom knife he was carrying and he didn't need his knife any more.

And he handed the knife over after he'd made it. He made a scabbard, making it safe because he had to give it to the craftsman. In fact he gave it to the coppice manager, because that knife could only be used really for coppicing. He had no problem with giving away his knife, and he didn't need knives beyond that point. So I didn't win the argument with that policeman, but I won in pragmatic terms, because that young man gave away his knife himself.

The transformative power of craft

So I became very interested in how the effort required in the craftwork has a transformative power on the young people, and what I concluded is that they have to become more present. In Steiner education, the purpose is to enable the individual to develop a healthy autonomy through how they organise their own ego. That means that they have ownership of themselves, including the capacity to say no to themselves from a space of freedom. That defines a high level of integrity and moral aptitude.

Now craftwork requires the student to enter into what we call the lawfulness of the material they are working with – its nature and how it works, how it responds to what you do. At the same time the student is undertaking a task which already has other people inside it: the wider community or the specific individual that you are making a pot or a knife for. You are doing it for them, but you also know that it is they who decide whether the knife is sharp, because it is they who will either use it or not. The effort involved in making craft items brings the students to a higher level of awareness in relation to other people and to the material they are working with, and that effort is a teacher in its own right.

Is the craftwork doing all the work? No, but it is like an aide-memoire, helping you gain autonomy when you meet resistance and have to focus your attention outside your self-interest, or what might be your unconscious resistance to making a greater effort.

Changing types of student

At the start, the people from the dole queue who volunteered to work with me were pretty self-motivated, otherwise they couldn't have done it; they were choosing to do so. Even so there was trouble with the authorities. One day they visited me because they'd heard I was using unemployed labour. The man who visited me challenged me and said "You should be paying these guys". I said,

"Well, they're volunteering". "Yes, but they're not allowed to do more than two days a week, and I've heard that you have some of them for more than two days. So they're going to lose their dole, and you're going to get into trouble".

And in fact there had been a couple of cases where people probably shouldn't have come, so I was being accused in order to put him in an awkward position. I said "Look, in 18 months you'll be able to read in the *Stroud News and Journal* about Ruskin Mill opening a new social enterprise centre with some of these kids, who will be renting workshops. So either you back off and let me get on with this, or I will make a fuss. But better still, come and see me in two years' time and see if I'm bullshitting you". And he backed off.

So the bureaucratic nightmare I had to go through, with planning, building control and general officialdom, set me up to be somewhat cavalier on behalf of the young people. And to be honest, I don't regret anything of that, because I wasn't just doing whatever I wanted; I was doing it for the kids. It's interesting how people do back away at that point. If you were doing it for yourself you'd have been banged up, and you'd have had to take the buildings down.

What it means to be working in a very responsive way, when you get really difficult kids and you've got to have a building, is a totally unique situation, and a bespoke relationship between the personality of the individual student and the craft. You have to respond in almost mythical ways, and that doesn't sit well with officialdom.

Now that first group were competent, lonely, socially isolated and on the scrapheap – but self-motivated. Then there was a transition from that group to students with learning difficulties. I worked with vulnerable students from a special educational needs school who came down with their teacher two afternoons a week, and at the same time I was working on Saturdays with other school pupils who had behavioural challenges, more than learning difficulties.

So over those first five years I had every profile of student. They were all verbally, practically able, but some of them were on the autistic spectrum, some had ADHD, some were "oppositional-defiant" and some of them were just bright and clever.

Working with challenges

Over the ten years that followed, I had students as difficult as anyone I see today. For political and educational reasons, I didn't define who I would or wouldn't work with as a category, so I was thrown the most difficult kids imaginable. Ruskin Mill became the place of last resort, but I didn't mind. I could never say that, because I also had the kids from the aristocracy – but because I wouldn't define who I was working with, their parents didn't know that, and so the policy worked.

I did have the last say on yes or no, but I very rarely turned a kid down, because it wasn't in my nature to do so. We worked with some very difficult and violent people, but we de-escalated everything through the craft curriculum. I identified different profiles of violence that could be accommodated with different methods and crafts.

For example, I noticed that some young men were very fascinated by knives, and sometimes they would cut themselves. So I introduced a leather curriculum, enabling them to cut skin. They stopped cutting themselves, because now they could cut skin externally, and they had an objective. Or as with that earlier story, I got them to make knives to work externally with the pathologies that were living inside them.

But in order to be able to do this, you have to personally take responsibility for the risk. You need the clarity in yourself to know that you are looking at something objective, but that you aren't seeing all of it. And therefore you have to have the courage to say "I'm going to try it". And you need to have no qualms about failure, because you will fail. That failure isn't necessarily face-to-face with the students in the workshop, but in terms of how they develop or not. And then you have to look very carefully, and learn to read what it is that they're doing.

Action research

Over these first 15 years I was doing a kind of action research, although I didn't know that it was called that. So there were students with some very complicated profiles under my scrutiny, showing me what worked and didn't work. And because I wouldn't define who I would take and who I would reject, I was thrown some very difficult students indeed. But those were the minority. I had pupils from Waldorf schools who were failing, who I gave bursaries for; there were students of middle-class parents whose children had mild learning difficulties, because in those days you could get funding to come to Ruskin Mill; there were even kids from the aristocracy; and there were kids who had been grazing from bins on the streets of Newcastle.

And what the aristocratic parents never knew is that side by side with Lady So-and-So's daughter was somebody from Middlesbrough who had probably been handling business for his mother, who was a sex worker. With three or four students in the group, all of these could work under the same umbrella, and at times there was the most extraordinary social mixture going through this healing and educational process, because it was the craft that was the unifying process. The craftwork allowed those differences to become present but also to be integrated.

There was a point where I was interested in thinking of craft as medicine, and prescribing a particular craft for a certain profile of need. We don't do that anymore, because it's too complicated a skill. Some exceptional staff members do have that capacity, but we can get better results for students in other ways, in terms of the wisdom we can build into an institution rather than an individual.

The real question is how to use the craft curriculum for a particular profile, with a particular personality issue. It's not just about whether it's leather or wood they are working with, but also about what tools are being used. What is the purpose? How much violence, for example, can be transformed in the act of cutting a piece of leather with a very sharp knife?

Or what about the brutality of a diamond/carborundum stone? It has to be held so gently over a piece of glass that you can give a very intentional tap in which the glass breaks but doesn't shatter. I've done glasswork with students for no other reason than to help them control shattering, so that they stop shattering on every level. And it works.

So every material, and every act in relation to material, can work therapeutically, for different personality, social or behavioural profiles. In detail this is very complicated, but it's not difficult to understand the broader sense of what is likely to be beneficial for a particular student with a given craft.

Figure 2.6 Focus, grasp and step: on the lathe at Clervaux

John Ruskin and the integrated human life

Ruskin Mill takes its name from the 19th-century thinker, art critic and social reformer John Ruskin (1819–1900). Ruskin is now best known for his thoughts on paintings and architecture, but these are grounded in a much wider perspective on seeing and our relationship with the natural world. These led him to champion the importance of skilled handwork, to challenge the destructive effects of the Industrial Revolution on people and the natural world and to seek to support regenerative efforts. Ruskin Mill's work draws inspiration from this (Cox et al., 2023).

Today, JMW Turner's paintings, with their powerful explorations of the qualities of light, water and weather, are too famous and beloved to need any introduction; but at the time their challenge to the conventionality of landscape painting was widely criticised. Ruskin's first book, the first volume of *Modern Painters*, defended Turner's work as seeking to be true to nature, both visually but also ethically. Ruskin's art criticism would inspire the Pre-Raphaelites (Dante Gabriel Rossetti, John Everett Millais, William Holman Hunt); via William Morris, he also had a major influence on the arts and crafts movement.

A craftsman with words in defence of the paintbrush and chisel, the 20-year-old Ruskin won the Newdigate Poetry prize, beating Arthur Hugh Clough into second place. He would go on to become a bestselling author and a celebrity public speaker, Oxford's first Slade Professor of Fine Art and eventually a public intellectual.

The importance of seeing

Ruskin's writing is deeply visual: in an age without many public art galleries, and before colour images could be reproduced in cheap books, there was no alternative. What to us can read as purple prose was also an attempt to bring the reader closer to the experience of directly seeing. In his public lectures, which were often for mass audiences, assistants would unroll vast images that he had painted by hand; these were dramatic performances like Dickens' readings, and a key part of his celebrity among working-class as well as middle-class publics.

Seeing things as they are was a central practice for Ruskin: how can a painter, or a naturalist, accurately see the world as it presents itself: the form of a feather, the play of light in a painting, the different elements of a Gothic cathedral? In some respects his approach parallels Goethe's methodology, with the concern first to grasp phenomenal reality as it is and then to inwardly grasp its essence. This is part of what underpinned his rejection of vivisection, leading to him resigning his Oxford professorship in protest: the living, whole animal in action is something other than the sum of its butchered parts. Ruskin brings the world back together, bringing consciousness into the rethinking of embodiment, a metaphor for Ruskin Mill's work with young people with autism.

More generally, in some ways, seeing has an ethical dimension. If I really try to see who this person is in front of me – a challenging student, my child in a family communication, a colleague I am in conflict with, a stranger on the street – I can start to consider who they are in that moment, what their needs are, and how I can meet them. This engaged response to specifics is quite different from an abstract and often self-justifying application of a rule. It is also, of course, something that we can bring to seeing a landscape being damaged, or becoming aware of the extent of social suffering: what can we perceive, what is happening, what is needed?

The skill of the hand

We have not only to see but also to do. Ruskin wrote that half of his understanding of the arts came from "my stern habit of doing the thing with my own hands till I know its difficulty... I make myself clear as to what the skill means, and is". He goes on to talk about learning the basics of sweeping a street, cleaning a stone staircase, shaving a board and painting wood but found bricklaying with a trowel the hardest challenge (2012, pp. 274–5).

He also discusses learning how to break stones for road-making, part of an 1874 project when he directed the young Oscar Wilde, historian Arnold Toynbee and the later co-founder of the National Trust Hardwick Drummond Rawnsley in trying to build a road between two villages in Oxfordshire. The project faced wider challenges and the project was never completed; but the attitude of practically learning how to do something and then attempting it is characteristic.

Elsewhere Ruskin wrote: "Every youth in the state … should learn to do something finely and thoroughly with his [sic] hand … Let him once learn to take a straight shaving off a plank, or draw a fine curve without faltering, or lay a brick level in its mortar; and he has learnt a multitude of matters which no lips of man could ever teach him" (1907, pp. 134–5).

This attitude stood him in good stead as a draughtsman: his drawings of flora and fauna, landscape paintings or architectural sketches, are impressive.

The underlying view is not simply one of an instrumental need to do things, or Victorian moralising about the benefit to self and others of hard work; rather, it is the specific discipline of a particular craft and the transformed knowledge of its materials and results that comes through doing. If Ruskin writes as an art or architectural critic, it is not simply from the viewpoint of the consumer, but with a deep appreciation of the process and skill of *making* well.

Handwork in an industrial society

This respect for skilled work was no doubt a key reason why Ruskin was so revered among many 19th-century working-class radicals. Engaged on their own journeys of self-education in a world which reserved these things to the children of the rich and powerful, they found in Ruskin a deep appreciation for the practical skills which they themselves had developed, and so also a space where they could make forays into the written word not unlike those he made into the world of physical craft.

Both also shared a strong opposition to the deskilling and dehumanising processes of mechanising industrialisation, the process through which knowledge and control were removed from the individual worker and relocated in the structure of the machine and the organisation of the factory. The profits generated for a few were mirrored by the impoverishment of the many through the division of labour: reduced to assembly-line workers, easily replaced if they resisted declining wages.

For Ruskin, the misery of the Industrial Revolution was paralleled by this alienation of the worker from the act of making as an insult to humanity, and both were connected to the ongoing destruction of the natural and agricultural environment. He famously objected to the railway viaduct across Monsal Dale in Derbyshire, built to serve local mills. Today, with the mills gone and the old railway track turned into a walking and cycling trail, the viaduct has been redeemed in a comparable way to Ruskin Mill's own buildings.

Ruskin Mill's homage to John Ruskin is to seek out the jewel in the process of skilled making, industrial or otherwise and use it for therapeutic development. Young people from post-industrial communities learn these skills in a different way in the buildings that once shaped those communities: the Glasshouse, mills in the Horsley Valley (Chapter 1), Freeman college in a Sheffield metalworks (Chapter 6) or Argent College in an old jewellery factory in Birmingham.

A vision of social transformation

In the face of poverty, alienation and ecological degradation, Ruskin attempted to use his own position as cultural critic not only to sound an alarm bell but crucially to encourage others to take action. His inspiration was so widespread that the students of today's Ruskin College Oxford, then a central location of working-class education, named it after him during his lifetime. Rachel Dickinson notes that his *Fors Clavigera*, monthly "letters to the workmen and labourers of Great Britain", has more of the flavour of a blog than what we imagine Victorian writing to be.

His book *Unto This Last* (1985), a critique of political economy, fell into the hands of the young Mohandas Gandhi, who read it on a train between Johannesburg and Durban in 1904. Gandhi "determined to change my life in accordance with the ideals of this book" and later translated it into Gujarati.

Ruskin would also go on to found the Guild of St George, an education trust which survives today. It attempted various pioneering agricultural and community projects, seeking to develop models for a route out of profit-centred industrialism and towards a different kind of society.

... and Ruskin Mill?

From John Ruskin, Ruskin Mill draws its concern for craft skills as a route both to self-transformation and to a different understanding of the world. It shares his critique of the human and ecological cost of industrial capitalism and his concern to develop practical models of how we can live differently, in the world and with each other. Perhaps most importantly, it finds in John Ruskin an inspiration for a life lived in and through beauty.

Bibliography

Alexander, J. (2014). *Make a chair from a tree* (3rd ed.). Lost Art Press.

Batchelor, J. (2001). *John Ruskin: No wealth but life*. Pimlico.

Cox, L., Gordon, A., & Hewison, R. (Eds.). (2023). *Ruskin today: John Ruskin for the 21st century*. Ruskin Mill Trust.

Crawford, M. B. (2009). *The case for working with your hands*. Viking.

Illich, I. (2018). *Deschooling society*. Marion Boyars. (Original publication 1971).

Jackson, K. (2018). *The worlds of John Ruskin*. Pallas Athene.

Korn, P. (2017). *Why we make things and why it matters: The education of a craftsman*. Vintage.

Marchand, T. H. J. (2022). *The pursuit of pleasurable work: Craftwork in twenty-first century England*. Berghahn.

Rogowski, G. (2017). *Handmade: Creative focus in the age of distraction*. Linden.

Ruskin, J. (1907). *Time and tide/Crown of wild olive*. George Allen. (Original publication 1867).

Ruskin, J. (1985). *Unto this last and other writings*. Penguin.

Ruskin, J. (2012). *Praeterita*. Oxford University Press. (Original publication 1885).

Sennett, R. (2009). *The craftsman*. Yale University Press.

Sigman, A. (2023). *Practically minded: The benefits and mechanisms associated with a practical skills therapeutic education*. Ruskin Mill Trust report.

Whitehouse, D., & Edgar, J. (2022). *Voices from the Cones* [album]. Bandcamp.

3 Ecology of the farm

Visiting Pishwanton and Clervaux

When you arrive at Pishwanton Wood, the first thing you hear is the sound of rooks above you, ahead and behind. The tall Scots pines hold the largest rookery in East Lothian, as well as jackdaws, mistle thrush and song thrush. The air is alive with their voices, adding an oddly rich background to all the other sounds and voices of the working day. Space, and air, are important here.

Pishwanton sits just below the dark browns and greens of the Lammermuir Hills to the south; to the north, across a ring of bright gorse, the land falls away into sheep folds. An impressive Iron Age hillfort, one of many nearby, is a reminder that this area has been rich in farming for millennia. In the distance, the land slopes downwards to the Firth of Forth and the Lomond Hills across the water echo the Lammermuirs. The site's location exposes it to sun, wind and rain – and water underfoot speaks back to the rooks above.

At the centre of the wood, the site's home space is warmly held within a wide ring of trees. The main craft building is to your right, built in stone and insulated with wool, with a low turf roof and faced by a wooden bench. Ahead of you, apple trees lead into the heart of the clearing, with currant bushes and a polytunnel beside the gate to the deer fence that surrounds the market garden. To the left is a wooden toolshed built as a project by Steiner school children; on the right, the compost heaps and chickens.

Beyond the far gate of the market garden is the herb garden, sheltered to the east by a low rise. Here an ancient stone kist burial was discovered in 1913 when a newfangled traction engine broke one of its cover stones and fell in. Each space in the clearing is distinct and meaningful, but interconnected like the rooms of a home.

A held space

Arriving here for the first time, you might not easily identify who is staff and who are participants. Pishwanton hosts Fairhill RISE centre, for adult participants whose needs and challenges are such that they need lifelong care. Unlike

DOI: 10.4324/9781003361541-3

Figure 3.1 Engaged in the work: picking marigolds for herbal tea at Pishwanton

many of Ruskin Mill's pupils and students, they do not qualify for their own individual support workers, despite their high levels of need.

And yet the space, and the work, hold them well: as you watch to the interactions, you can see that a participant and a staff member are taking turns with the lawnmower around the herb garden, or that a participant is being supported to build a chicken coop in the woodwork area. Over here is a participant taking time out after a difficult interaction; past the wood, in the Colquhoun Research Centre, a participant is watching over ducklings in a cage under a sun lamp.

The level of participant engagement is extraordinary: they might compete with one another over using the lawnmower or a ladder. What looks at first sight like two participants jostling to be first served at lunch turns out to be them collaborating with a staff member to plate up soup and salads for everyone on the site. Cooking and cleaning up are meaningful and valued tasks.

As elsewhere at Ruskin Mill, participants are not shielded from the wider world but encouraged to engage with what is necessarily a small number of new faces: a visiting researcher; a social worker come to meet one of her clients; parents and a prospective participant. Participants' capacity to engage is varied, but sitting in the craft building's dining room, a participant might come up and show a visitor the wooden "television" they've made, explaining the different steps involved: drawing and sawing, sanding and hammering.

As far as possible, participants engage independently with the wider community, not only family and professionals. This does not contradict the held nature of the space but is made possible by it. The safe environment, the familiar faces, the rhythm of activities and the warmth of human care enable them to deal better with more challenging spaces, with strangers, with less routine activities and other kinds of emotion. Freedom and care support one another.

The RISE concept

For the parents of young people with learning difficulties, there can be many different stages on their journey. If their children's differences and difficulties are such that they may never be able to live independently, the question of what happens when the parents themselves age out of being able to help is a particularly difficult one, and RISE aims to offer an answer to this.

Held on biodynamic farms, RISE provisions are no longer educational but aim to offer a full life supported by participation in community life, engagement with the outside world through social enterprises and a cycle of festivals that generate an annual rhythm, a different connection to the wider world and the meaningful activity needed for hosting events.

At Pishwanton, participants engage in small-scale farming and catering work that goes beyond self-sufficiency and enables meeting the world through social enterprise. In time, the site's signature products will come from the herb garden – herb teas, balms, aromatic distillations. Other viable products include apple juice and cabbages, the meat from rare breeds of cows, pigs or goats and sustainable birch charcoal from the woods.

Pishwanton is already a site for public events and regular courses – training in biodynamic gardening or herbalism; explorations of the cycle of the seasons; a summer camping week of excursions to nearby megalithic, Pictish, Celtic Christian and contemporary spiritual sites. RISE participants set up a temporary campsite and cater for the event. Like festivals, these events offer participants the excitement of an influx of visitors and give the regular tasks of harvesting, cooking and cleaning a greater urgency and meaning than in the everyday context. If the location seems isolated, these events reverse that and bring the wider community to Pishwanton, creating a space of diversity and collaboration.

Arthur

In 2019, before Covid and with Brexit still not yet a reality, Ruskin Mill Trust commissioned leading playwright Peter Oswald – the Globe's resident playwright for a decade, whose plays have sold out on Broadway and in London's West End – to write the play *Arthur*, engaging with the journey of self-discovery and the challenges of a changing world.

Over the following three years, students took part in a research trip to Tintagel and connected the play with their craft activities: Ruskin Mill College students created a giant willow puppet and made wooden swords and shields; Glasshouse students designed and created a wooden stage for touring.

Plas Dwbl students in southwest Wales made cloaks, while Freeman College students in Sheffield forged a metal sword.

The play made it possible to create a theatre company connecting students across the Trust, up to 50 at times, including actors, musicians and stage crew. Rehearsals and performances travelled around Britain, arriving in Pishwanton in May 2023. Here, in their own space, Pishwanton participants were at the centre of a true cultural event and could come to life preparing the venue, catering and watching the play.

James Watts, responsible for music across the Trust, tells the story of two participants with Down syndrome who saw the instruments and told him, "We want to join you". Within half an hour they were drumming with him as if they had been rehearsing together for months, fully part of the performance.

The wider space

The home space described above, surrounded by 19th- and early 20th-century plantations of Scots pine, birch trees and mixed broadleaf, is just a small part of the site's 60 acres. Through the woods, you come to the Colquhoun Research Centre, named for the Goethean scientist Dr Margaret Colquhoun, one of the initiators of the process of re-imagining the sense of place which Ruskin Mill calls genius loci (Chapter 1). She first developed what modernising farmers saw as a worthless piece of wet land into a research project over 30 years before handing it on to Ruskin Mill Trust. The cob building is beautifully warm and dry inside, with enticing niches on the first floor that can only be reached by ladder. Her research archives are in a neighbouring wooden building.

Past these buildings and the Crescent Barn, you come out of the trees to two rises, Church Mound and Little Mound, covered by unimproved, species-rich grassland with – in good weather – stunning views northwards to the Firth of Forth and beyond. This pastureland is ringed by gorse, with a steep slope down to the glacial stream valley of the wonderfully named Dumbadum Burn. On this side of the valley, the land is being left to regenerate naturally, with hawthorn scrub and species such as cherry, elder and hazel. Between the two mounds a small stream flows into the burn, with its own valley adding rowan and hawthorn to the mix.

The wet valley bottom in turn has many different habitats – rush pasture; wet woodland with alder, grey willow, sedges and other species; reed canary grass fen; floating sweet grass and watercress; a tall-grass and rush mire fen with medicinal plants, including meadowsweet, angelica, valerian and marsh marigold. On the far side of the valley, a "forgotten field" – because farm animals can't easily cross the flooded bottom – is rich with meadowflowers in season.

Climbing up again towards the entrance, a rush pasture (soft rush, crested dogtail and Yorkshire fog grass) and more species-rich grassland flank woodlands – a damper one of silver birch and downy birch with star moss underfoot, higher up adding willows (the site holds three different species), sessile oak, blackberry and honeysuckle to the mix.

Unsurprisingly, this cornucopia of flora supports many different animals and birds: badger setts, deer and hares; yellowhammers, woodcock and white-throats, together with many smaller species. A barn owl nests in the beautiful cruck barn.

The multiplicity of spaces enables a multiplicity of uses, dependent on the seasons. The home space is a constant centre for work and care, eating and socialising. The meadows and birchwood can be used in many different ways in season – pasture and festivals in the meadows, charcoal-making and other woodland crafts with the birch. The remainder of the land offers scope for summer camping and guiding visitors when it is sufficiently dry. It needs work in turn – not least, clearing gorse. Sawing, clipping, moving and burning gorse is a job well suited to working together; the tasks are relatively self-explanatory and allow for a good alternation of activities, finished off by the satisfaction of a dramatic, safely managed, fire.

Clervaux

At Pishwanton, human effort often appears as a small element at the centre of a much larger and more complex ecology, although the balance has changed many times since the first Neolithic farmers. Two and a half hours by train to the south, Clervaux RISE near Darlington seems to reverse the relationship, with the broader powers of nature enhancing a farmed landscape shaped by people, livestock and crops.

Clervaux sits at the very north of the Vale of York, with the deep brown waters of the Tees forming one boundary and the Yorkshire Dales just visible to the west. The nearest village, Croft-on-Tees, was Lewis Carroll's childhood home; a carved stone seat in the church where his father was rector is said to have inspired the Cheshire Cat's smile, while the vorpal sword that supposedly slew the local Jabberwocky (the Sockburn Worm) is presented to each newly appointed Bishop of Durham as he crosses the Croft bridge to enter his diocese.

The land's 100+ acres span the Clow Beck, which flows into the Tees at one corner of the site. Here dark glacial clay, laid down by meltwater from the Dales, is exposed, with a spring line above which underground water can sink no further – the clay is readily dug for pottery.

Floodgates protect the buildings near the road crossing; higher up the stream, the buildings of the garden school sit on an artificial terrace above possible flooding. Clow Beck changes fast, in one place undercutting a fence at a rate of about a foot a year. Just above the school is boggy woodland surrounding an oxbow lake, rich in wildlife and holding the green woodwork space. Further up is a wild field where barn owls hunt, used for adventure work with den building and fire making.

The school is also home to a forge, charcoal burner, textile workshop, pottery kiln, kitchen and gardening spaces; by the footbridge across the beck a local eco-group are keeping bees. Polytunnels enable up to three salad crops a year as well as peas, cauliflowers and shallots. Here you can see pigs turning over a weedy paddock; there, the new orchard: there are 300 trees in all, making harvesting and pressing a major seasonal event. For garden schools (see Chapter 6), the challenge is to develop a special educational curriculum that will stand up to the most robust inspections but be closely grounded in the specifics of the land and its crafts.

On the farm

Up the far bank of the stream and through the old orchard, you come to the buildings of the RISE and the Fold, a dedicated family centre also working with PSTE. Here, at the centre of the whole site, is the barn, because this is a working farm even if its purpose is not, unlike most modern farms, to make money but rather to feed and care for the people who work there. When Ruskin Mill staff arrived, walking the land, they noted the rise and the fold in the landscape as part of the genius loci survey (Chapter 1).

Cows, sheep, goats, pigs, donkeys and the remarkably fluffy Silkie chickens make for a good mix of farming tasks and relationships for the RISE participants: feeding, mucking out, milking goats, clipping sheep's and goats' feet, collecting and counting eggs all need doing and help to develop a sense of connection and responsibility with a social enterprise qualification. The animals are circulated around the site according to grazing needs but with an eye to what is most beneficial to participants. (The process of meat production

Figure 3.2 With donkeys at Clervaux

is transparent to participants on site, but – following the food and nutrition policy – meat raised on the farm is not served in the school.)

RISE participants, and garden school pupils, can develop relationships of care and respect with animals that can then transfer to people. At difficult times things may get thrown around, but when there were eggs in an incubator at the centre of the school classroom nobody threw anything. Animals' emotions are honest and direct, and enable an easier reciprocation. Watching, and supporting, the whole cycle of life from birth can be transformative for people who have missed out on positive human relationships and allow them to form their own relationships with animals, experiencing empathy and attachment.

On a simpler level, when participants are overwhelmed, the barn can offer a safe place to chill out; the baled hay is stacked here, providing many opportunities for play. In return, the animals' manure is a major contributor to the fertility of the land. The combination of waterlogging and drought makes horticulture harder in this soil, but vegetables are grown commercially: strawberries, potatoes, cabbages, kale and leeks among others.

A lived landscape

A path follows the woodlands on the steep slopes above the banks of the Tees, where native hardwoods are being grown. If you walk through this area in spring or summer, you can taste many edible plants: sweet cicely, young beech leaves, wild garlic and garlic mustard. Even the gardener's bane of ground elder (leaves) is edible in season – this is why the Romans brought it. Walk down to the swampy ground and fallen willows where the Clow Beck enters the Tees and you can see the layers of glacial clay many feet deep. It becomes easier to imagine an older landscape: mammoth tusks have been found in nearby gravel pits.

The path between the top of the woods and the open fields may have been used since Roman times: the Brigantes' tribal centre at Stanwick is only a few miles away. The Angles came through at an early point, and metal detectorists now visit. Along with coins and brooches, many spindle whorls as well as harness fittings and pots have been found. Nearby is the lost medieval village of Jolby: the 12th and 13th centuries, before the Black Death, mark another high point of finds. Medieval fields were enclosed in the 16th and 17th centuries; a 19th-century packhorse bridge crosses the beck. From the 1970s farming became mechanised, reshaping the wider landscape: the contrast between the small-scale mixed farming here and the large-scale monocultures of its neighbours is immediately visible – hedges, trees, wildlife and observable natural diversity tell their own stories when they are present, and when they are not.

A new initiative

Ruskin Mill's presence at Clervaux took off from the Clow Beck Eco Centre, a 1999 initiative of local farmer and author Bill Chaytor geared to connecting young people with the natural world and low-impact technologies. Ruskin Mill was brought in a decade later when the centre faced funding problems, and started to work with young people who were not in education, employment or training (NEETS), in association with a local college. When children with learning difficulties arrived at the school, the older NEETS became very protective of them. Clervaux's mixed-use space, still changing today, has a track record as different kinds of funding have enabled the site to be used for different groups over the years. The Clervaux centre has always had a palette of new and old initiatives.

After some years, the local college ended the project, but Clervaux was still responsible for a small number of residential participants who had finished in other Ruskin Mill colleges. Staff developed a workable programme for them based around the farm, including further qualifications, and the current project emerged under the Trust's new concept of RISE, capable of supporting people into later life.

Participants live in ordinary houses in the town (see Chapter 5). Their days are spent not only on the farm but equally volunteering in the community – for example, in a local Oxfam shop, organising their own household tasks of shopping, washing, cooking, recycling and so on, gaining qualifications or engaging in local groups. Until recently, the Clervaux Café on Coniscliffe Road in Darlington town centre baked its own bread and cakes and served sandwiches, enabling young people to learn the principles of service and social enterprise. It is now planned to re-emerge as a facility for older pupils at the garden school where they can learn qualifications, sell their school produce and offer sandwiches and coffee for the public.

The RISE model of community, festivals and social enterprise answers a key question raised by many parents and guardians of older Ruskin Mill students: what is the future? Transformation takes many forms: staff tell the story of one young woman who arrived dressed up to the nines every day – until she discovered the joys of blacksmithing, lost the makeup and adopted tracksuit bottoms for the task. Meanwhile on Facebook, an ex-participant sends a photograph of his young family thanking staff for how the experience has changed his life.

An embodied connection to nature

"Nature connectedness" has become a flourishing area of research into the psychology of human happiness and in education (see, e.g., Louv, 2013; Richardson, 2023; Williams, 2017). This of course responds to what on any large scale is the very recent experience of *not* being in some meaningful sense connected to the natural world. We evolved as gatherers and hunters, our situation for the vast majority of our existence as a species; since the Neolithic almost all of us have been involved in direct food production through farming and fishing. For most parts of the world and most of our species, it is only very recently that this has changed; the United Nations Population Fund (2007)

Figure 3.3 Nature connectedness: Argent College student with seedlings

estimates that the first time a human majority lived in urban areas was in 2008, for example.

Even in these recent centuries – depending on where and who you are – the suburban garden or allotment, the connection to animals and the desire to spend leisure time out of doors are very widely felt needs, which we meet in a huge variety of ways, but direct experience of the natural or farmed world is no longer built into most people's daily lives as a matter of necessity.

Mainstream education is now so far away from the natural world that "forest schools" exist as a radical corrective to the norm. The lives represented on our screens as desirable are often almost entirely indoors, or at most in the built environments whose concreted ground is a significant factor in increasing flooding across the global North. It is not just the teenager whose life is spent on the phone; the clothing, hairstyles and footwear of many adults speak volumes about how little time in their day is spent outside of house, workplace or car – and how they access their food.

This is one thing when it represents an adult's lifestyle choice. It is something very different when someone is in significant psychological distress; and something else again when a young person has been brought up into an entirely artificial world. The very effectiveness of nature connection, in education and in mental health, is an indicator that a little goes a long way: even brief engagement with a world that is not entirely artificial can help to reset a better baseline and offer an opportunity to come down from the continual stress of the "attention economy".

Living in a natural world

For these reasons, the opportunity to engage with the natural world – to experience oneself as part of a wider ecology – is central to what Ruskin Mill offers young people, not only on its rural provisions but also in the form of the farms associated with each of its urban provisions; even, in Birmingham's Argent College, a rooftop microgarden.

For many young people, nature connectedness expresses itself initially in the sheer physicality of being outdoors. Not only outside buildings and cars but also outside the weather-shielding effects of cities, the weather hits harder: sun, rain or wind become much more powerful forces, and attention to what weather is coming your way becomes a far more urgent concern. How temperature and light change from morning to evening has immediate practical effects. The seasons are not just postcards but physical realities, with all their ups and downs; and the active body outdoors responds differently as we ask different things of it.

We experience ourselves in relation to a wider universe: as we have seen at Pishwanton and Clervaux, the sky, the wind and birds become a bigger part of our daily context. We come to know intimately how the sun moves across the sky – and what this means for where we plant crops. We might start to pay attention to the phases of the moon, or even notice shooting stars or planets.

The earth too – the rocks and soil of where we stand; the trees, hedges, crops and flowers; livestock and wild fauna – comes into focus much more clearly. *There* is a wasp interested in my food; those brambles are going to need careful handling; this mud is a pain to get off your shoes; this slope is hard to climb at the end of the day. What is safe and unsafe has a different kind of meaning.

The practical resistance involved in engaging with the natural world is a prerequisite for coming to inhabit it more fully, and coming to appreciate the kestrel or owl, the smell of gorse or wild garlic, the energy of the goat kid or the fluffiness of the duckling, the first shoots of plants or the ripeness of apples in the orchard. What Edward Wilson (1986) called biophilia, the urge to connect with other forms of life, can be awakened through contact, as our senses engage with everything that was already there to be noticed. Beyond this, for some people, the capacity to experience ourselves as being part of this ecology, and to experience the land or the world as alive, is an even more enriching and powerful experience – and one which distressed young people badly need.

The specifics of connection

Biodynamic ecology at Ruskin Mill starts from a close attention to the spirit of place (Chapter 1): what can we say about the soil and climate here, the flora and fauna they support, the different ways in which humans have inhabited and supported themselves from it? What French calls *terroir* – the way in which a unique and very local environment shapes particular crops – is now a well-known and directly tasteable aspect of this, often legally protected. Cheese, wine and tea are regularly described by locations, as are breeds of sheep, cow and so on developed for particular places and more or less suitable in others. A specific location affords its own raw materials: good clay for pottery, birch wood or willows, fleece, crops and so on that can be used for crafts or catering.

All of this then implies a connection across time, which young people gradually come to experience: the rhythm of the day, but also the rhythm of the year, as the soil that has been dug, planted and weeded becomes a crop to be harvested, stored or processed: served as food, sold in the shop, turned into preserves and so on. Ruskin Mill's seed to table curriculum is geared towards making this visible, not only in catering but equally where trees are felled to become charcoal or wooden stools, where sheep are sheared and the carded fleece becomes felt slippers, and so on.

Rhythm, and connection across time, are ensured by a practical *engagement* with the world mediated through a cycle of tasks through time. In this process, young people come to experience the effects of their own actions in a very powerful way: the food they are eating, perhaps the mug they are drinking from, is something they have *made* from the first bite of the spade in the ground. For many, it may be the first time they have had this experience of creating any part of their own world, rather than simply consuming something they are unable to create themselves.

This shift away from what used to be called "alienation" and is now simply taken as normality is a remarkable one; what we do changes our world. Experiencing this shift makes it possible to engage with the wider world in a positive and more responsible way: self-generated conscious action, what Ruskin Mill aims to enable young people to take part in, depends on realising that you can do something more than simply inhabit a world made by other people.

Figure 3.4 Understanding relationships: Brantwood pupil at work

Embodied connection

A "visceral" experience is one experienced in the gut, and nutrition is a central concern across Ruskin Mill. Wherever food is served – training kitchens, school canteens, residential homes, social enterprise cafés, at events – healthy nutrition and quality are central. Young people, along with staff and visitors, eat what they grow. Beyond this food is as far as possible organic or biodynamic, local or fair trade, and always good in both taste and nutrition. Just as experiencing the rhythm of the seasons comes through the feeling of wind, rain or sun on our skin, so too engagement with the natural world comes through the mouth, the stomach and the other senses.

It also comes through the direct and practical encounter with farm animals, birds, fish or bees as living beings who need many different kinds of practical care at different stages in the farm day, in the cycle of the year and in the rhythm of their own lives. As so often at Ruskin Mill, these tasks are not arbitrary ones, invented by therapists or educators; they stand outside those relationships and are given by the needs of the animal or the practicalities of a production cycle like fleece.

Young people whose experience with humans has often been difficult may find this situation an easier one to negotiate, in the development of emotions in relationships which are both safe and transparent. The specifics of particular animals and birds also matter: young people may find their own attributes or challenges mirrored by a particular animal, so that they are motivated to pay attention to its specific qualities and needs, listening more closely to what it is in itself. These kinds of relationships can be transformative, and staff pay careful attention to which animals a particular young person responds to.

At the origins of organic farming

Ruskin Mill practises biodynamic farming, the parent of today's organic farming. The term "organic farming" first appeared in a 1940 book by farmer Walter James, who had recently hosted England's first biodynamic conference on his Kent farm, and the two movements gradually moved further apart. Biodynamic agriculture had been founded as a movement in a 1924 lecture series given by Rudolf Steiner in what was then Prussia, a heartland of industrialised agriculture, with vast monocultural landholdings based on extensive use of chemical fertiliser.

Steiner's own background, however, was very different: the small farms of his youth in present-day Austria and Croatia had been largely self-sufficient, with a mix of crops and animals enabling both resilience and interconnection, notably around the use of manure and compost as fertilisers, and underpinning a more village-oriented community than the feudal militarism of early 20th-century Prussia.

Central to biodynamics at Ruskin Mill is the notion of the "farm as an organism": the farm is seen as a practically interconnected whole, not only across the seasons but also in the process of fertilising the soil. Rather than a process centred around the input of bags of "NPK" (nitrogen-phosphorus-potassium chemical fertiliser) and ever-larger petrol-burning machines, the ideal is that the farm is as far as possible self-sustaining, developing its own inputs – compost and manure – from within its own resources: regenerative rather than extractive agriculture. Steiner's biodynamic preparations are understood as further enhancing this process.

This model seeks to build resilience and adaptability into the life of the farm, rather than reducing the land to a single link of the agribusiness industry. Ideally, it is human intention and thought that are the key inputs. Each part of the farm plays a specific role, while connecting with and supporting the others. Over time students can come to see this more or less clearly: in Practical Skills Therapeutic Education, the farm is an *educational* organism. All Ruskin Mill land is biodynamically certified, and staff working the land are biodynamically trained.

This then means that the natural world is seen as a partner, and the farm seeks to operate in a way appropriate to its specific location: this is an intentional process, developing a particular history and identity. High standards in soil and compost are a natural result of this approach. The land, the plants and the animals are all valued as meaningful in themselves and treated well for this reason – for example, being kept in social groups of an appropriate size.

The pupil, the student or the RISE participant are then able to come into relationship with where they are at every level: the wider universe, the specifics of the place and the workings of the farm, the different crops and livestock, the staff and other students. Traditional farming is always also an activity that relies on and develops community, and Ruskin Mill's attention to seasonal festivals grows naturally out of this.

Conversation with Aonghus Gordon

Building relationships is transformative

When I started working with students, the first observation was the challenge of their not having a role model for building relationships. This goes right through many students' family background and surfaces in school very often, not understanding maybe even what teasing is: for example, challenging eye contact or a flippant comment from another pupil, attempting to build a relationship in an unhelpful way. That's a form of communication, but it ends up unwittingly as antagonism. There's not necessarily malice in it, though obviously there are many occasions where there is. So obviously the role modelling from staff is critical, and the context, and building de-escalation into design and timetabling, but that in itself doesn't actually do the work; it provides an opportunity for the work to happen.

And maybe what is core in a biodynamic entity is that it is an embodied entity and brings together relationships, for example, between the soil and the grass. If the grass isn't adequate, then the farmer doesn't have the provision for grazing, and the farmer talks about that as part of the farm experience for students.

Now students can see the effect of overgrazing, or that hay comes in at a certain time of year. And so they begin to see this relationship between something very simple, which is the grass, and the adequacy of the feed for the animals. That relationship is performed every day, looked at and talked about, and maybe once or twice a day the hay or the grass provides food for the animals. Their numbers reflect the amount of food reserves available.

And as the season goes on, you then get the cycle-of-life relationship where the students begin to see that there's an indispensable relationship between how you care for the animal and its well-being. They can see the life cycle of the animal with pregnancy, birth and aftercare, and they're in this very tender and vulnerable relationship with the organism of the farm – getting the grass right, the fertility right, the animal husbandry right and the human

Figure 3.5 Creating relationship: Brantwood pupil with lamb

relationships right. So they're in a relationship, and they begin to see that their conduct affects the whole being of the farm-cycle. And the farmer is offering thoughts that aid that relationship of what you could call health and life.

Our students find this a much more accessible relationship to enter into than a challenging domestic relationship which they might have memories of, which often let them down or which they didn't know how to manage.

They can transfer the health of the relationships on the farm – which they can often access directly – to other relationships.

For example, where students have picked up the goat kid and embraced it – and what emerges after a few weeks is that this is the first time that student ever embraced anything. We have photographs of this real bonding that takes place with the animals, and at times students and animals are inseparable.

But why is a biodynamic farm organism so different from an organic farm or a regular farm, or just giving people a pet? Very often the more regular farm isn't built on a relationship: it's built out of a different thought structure, about economic return. So relationships, which effectively cost money, have to be removed by necessity. They're just not affordable. And so you get this kind of monotony of action within the regular farm, which isn't very helpful for absorbing what is happening, never mind the difficulties our students have.

Biodynamic farming and making connections

Organic farming is based on an idea of *not* doing certain things. So it's as much a rejection of what's outside, to maintain the inside in a healthier state, as the central biodynamic concept of building the continuum of a line of understanding between the farmer, the animals, the plants and fertility.

The organic farm does do the first part of that fertility cycle, but in a biodynamic farm, the perception is that the more hands on deck, the richer the place. So it has a design process within it that can absorb as much human energy as possible, which is important to our work.

The other element is that as the cycle of the year goes on within the biodynamic farm, the students and some of the apprentices – who are role models for the young students – begin to understand this implication of what is performed and the relationship of pre-planning as a result of healthy performance of action.

That links up with Ruskin Mill Trust's strapline "universe, earth and people", in that the cycle of the year is directly linked with a cosmological idea, such as growing at a certain time and working with various seasonal constellations to help us relate to this. In a homoeopathic context, which is entirely based on relationship, the greater the understanding of the relationships between the universe, the earth and the consciousness of the farmer, the higher the level of return of fertility and productivity.

Now, do the students understand that? Not necessarily, but the biodynamic apprentices do, and they role model something that the students can catch, around understanding wholeness. And it's in this understanding of wholeness that some of the healing of the trauma of early childhood gets absorbed into an understanding of relationship: not only between animals, people and plants, soil and fertility, but also between person and person.

So there's a principle of care that gets taken into the timetable experience of students working on the farm. The intensity of those relationships is palpable, role modelled, evidential, and can be experienced by the students themselves.

Conversely, nurturing healthy, naturally reared livestock expresses the steps needed to engender basic well-being.

There's another relationship, which is that out of the farm comes food, and that food cycle can be challenging. So this is an elective experience for the students: collecting eggs, the vegetable box system or even going to the slaughterhouse.

So you build relationships from the centre of the farm, again in an ecologically informed cycle-of-life economics, where, unless the produce is consumed, you've lost opportunities. The discipline of timing, preparation and collaboration with the team on the farm comes through the "eye of the needle", because deadlines have to be met, even within their own canteen arrangements. What the students grow shows up as ingredients in what they eat at lunch time.

You then get this kind of second phase of relationships – which is not just within the organism of the farm, but how that is based on tangible relationships, such as handing the vegetable box over, writing the invoice or even collecting the cash. That is a consequence of getting the earlier dynamism of the farm in good health. So the food cycle is a further relationship, because it ends up on the table in such a way that you can track the origin of the food and the effort.

That curriculum in Ruskin Mill is "seed to table", and that's where it starts, whether it's animals or plants. And in that cycle from seed to table there is a timeline and imperative in which certain things have to happen. But there's a further relationship, which is that the plants, the animals and the soil are harvested, and that harvest can be the leather or the goatskin, the willows and possibly the trees, but also the clay from the land. So you get this kind of further harvesting of relationship.

In my experience, this connective quality of the direct material is entirely transformational and can have the greatest impact on the students, in that they discover that their entire shaping of an object can actually come from the very landscape that they don't necessarily see as productive. In fact, often it's thrown away. So we bring the hide, the willow or the clay into a hand-held relationship of productivity and service.

Bringing students into the world

This continuum is based not only on the relationship of the components of the farm but also on the relationships between people and of the people with the materials, and then you have a three-dimensional immersion in relationship building. And not just relationship in isolation, because it's about time-management, and what's truly remarkable in the farm is the discipline of consequences in not managing time relationships. It's not just relationships, but relationships in time. So you bring the students "into the world".

Prior to that, often they're not participating. They're observers, just looking at the phenomenon of relationships; now they have to step into those relationships. And the consequences of not getting the timing right are not someone else's judgement. They're a reality-check. And they have ownership over that reality-check, within time.

The acceptance of timing in relationship, which the farm and the materials of the craft in a certain sense create, means that interpersonal relationships that have often broken down, which are often experienced by children and students as judgemental and possibly subjective and incriminating, are removed.

So we rebuild their stepping into the world in a third-party context, because their first-party development and their interpersonal relationships, maybe with a second party like a tutor, are actually delegated to life cycles in time and consequences that don't make them a personalised issue.

Hence the importance of the biodynamic farm, if we get the intensity of relationships right. And in order to work this through, the other element is that the farm also has to be slowed down. The speed of a farm in a more commercial setting would bounce a lot of students out, and they wouldn't get access to what it offers. So the farming timeline is slowed down, and the intensification is designed so that there's maximum access at many different levels. This is a consciously redesigned farming cycle in which the cycle of time of the life of the farm is augmented with this capacity for the management of students' time capacities. And that is such an empathetic process that there is no rejection of the student.

That's exceptional. It's a very skilled process, and that's what we train our farmers in effect to do, which is why we have had to build our own biodynamic farm training, around our strapline of "Growing land, growing people". That requires a new perspective, opening up a process in time and space and enabling it to accept high levels of what you might call dissent and rejection, which are actually in the footprint of our students as unconsciously held experiences.

That dissent and rejection need to meet something that is compassionate but also uncompromising at a certain point. It's the bringing together of two educational processes, around the ability to self-realise in an external process in which they've elected to be in, so that it's a pull and not a push. Therefore, you have to draw forward the invitation and then this educational-therapeutic immersion starts to work.

I would be very precise about this and say that the trauma that was implicated in the muscle memory of our students, which is where it's largely held, can only be displaced if there's something new to replace it. So you can help them shed what was freezing their relationships and open up the opportunity of action and relationships based on a new objective context.

Working with the experience of violence

It's clear that there's something very transformative in helping lambing or growing plants, seeing new life come in, but our students have often experienced quite a bit of violence, physical or emotional. And on the farm there are different dimensions of killing, from the slaughterhouse to collecting eggs. I was once approached by a social worker who rightly had some questions about a student working on the farm and the description he gave her around the goatskins becoming drums, and the drums becoming percussion instruments in a music workshop.

Because the social worker was a vegetarian, she pricked her ears up and wanted a clear explanation as to exactly what the student had encountered. So I said, "Well, if I gave you one controversial thought, which is that it's my answer to one of the requirements of the Children's Education Act, which is that they had to have religious education, because I wanted to maybe confront some of those aspects in a experiential way".

So I disarmed her 100% and I said, "Maybe it's like this: what the student was giving you was his encounter with Death. And maybe how we confront it is that there was resurrection in the context of social interplay, creating something entirely new which wasn't possible without death; namely the skin".

That earned me at least another ten referrals. And I then took the student's biographic process and showed her that actually he also elected not to go to the slaughterhouse, because that was his free choice.

She then had a further question which was, "But what do you think would have happened if he had done it and hadn't got the insight out of it?" And I said, "Well, we would've dealt with it because in a farm, you need to know that animals die all the time". And that has to also be seen in the context of the utter abuse of animal husbandry in some large-scale commercial farming. So we talk about that.

And by the time the farmer has taken the students on the journey of the various ways in which the animals are treated well and not treated well, they have an entirely new relationship to what is an appropriate attitude if you have a farm: which is that it is also a place in which animals die. And the important thing is to have the right relationship, which is neither sentimental nor brutal. So from a farmer's perspective, that's one of the requirements.

Now, if you disagree with that, that's also fine because the student doesn't have to work with the animals. But these conversations are so transformative because they're based on the reality-check of how you handle that. Now, if we were to see any kind of cruelty as a transference from their own abuse onto the animals, that's our job to deal with that. But there is clearly cruelty in some of their own experience, and we have to deal with it. And it's in the farm structure that we do so. She was blown out of the water, basically.

And maybe the cruellest thing that you can ever perpetrate on a chicken – and we do discuss this – is the fact that the students believe that it's a construct of a supermarket. They have no prior understanding that the thing even lived until they came to Ruskin Mill. Through no fault of their own, they don't even know that it had wings, don't even know what it looked like. And that's the sort of level we're dealing with. So the fact that the animal is "re-dignified" prior to its death has a whole new relationship element built into it.

A deeper level of understanding

But I think it goes even deeper. The farm husbandry curriculum had one extraordinary moment of catharsis, with a father who wanted to place his son in Ruskin Mill and phoned me up. I knew that it was a long-distance call; he told me that he was in Latin America and that he'd looked at our information and that £40,000 was at that moment being wired to the Ruskin Mill bank account.

I asked, "How do you know about our bank account?" And he said, "Well, I just phoned up the office and asked for it because I wanted to make a donation". But I said, "Well, it doesn't quite work like that, we need an assessment". So I backed off and he pushed further.

I then saw the young man, but that wasn't before another telephone call with the father where he said that his son was the result of a dispute with his ex-wife, who had decided that she wanted to have a child with IVF treatment from a medical student, and basically judged him to be not intelligent enough. So the result was that he fled to Latin America and she stayed in China. And their son was born; he was on the autistic spectrum, and he was very bright.

I asked, "So what are his symptoms?" He said, "Well, he stands gazing at the sunrise and he names every star that has a name". And I said, "Hmm, that's a healthy habit. I can see enormous value for that skill on our biodynamic farms because he could be the local astronomer". And he couldn't quite believe it. But he said, "Well, that's why I want him to come to you, Aonghus". So he came.

Now, this is where it gets interesting. I gave a lot of thought to this. For me it was like a whole new beginning, and this young man was very unusual. He hardly wore clothes: a T-shirt and pantaloons basically, no pants, nothing, winter or summer. And I was looking at this young man and I knew that there was a script or something that I had to decode. I wasn't sure how to, but I knew that if I could decode it, a whole new pedagogy could open up.

And he actually gave me the clue in the end, because I couldn't get it, but I kept pushing my question and one day he asked if he could move out of his carer's house into a caravan. So I said, "Well, there are some legal problems". And he wanted to be in a wood and I said, "I'm going to have to find a wood". And that's quite difficult. But I did it, and I got legal compliance around that.

Then I said to him, "Well, if I'm doing this for you, you need to do something for me because I'm pushing the boat out in making this possible. And what I want you to do is to start keeping chickens". He said, "Oh, I should have stayed in my house!" But I said, "Why the caravan in the wood?" And he said, "I want to hear the woodland birds land on my roof and go pitter-patter, and I want to learn how to name the birds that land on my roof from their different pitter-patters".

I realised that this was utterly transformative because I'd got him from the stars, down onto the roof of this caravan. And I thought, "This is so incredible". Which is really why I did it, because he told me why he wanted it. So I said, "I need you to come into the world with practical things, and I'm going to ask you to look after birds, on the ground".

That's where the answer is, do you see? I said, "Chickens are woodland birds: they may not have come from England, but they're woodland birds". And he completely agreed and he then started making a chicken coop. And it was all going fine, and then one day he said, "I want to cook you an omelette, Aonghus". And that was well beyond anything I'd seen from him before. So I came along, and as I was arriving, I happened to see him take his hand and put it under the chicken and collect three eggs. And he brought them and he gave them to me. He said, "They're still warm. Have you ever felt a warm egg?"

So now that young man is a chicken farmer, and he often visits. And I've learned to use the farm, the biodynamic farming contexts as deep, totally transforming elements, not just of individuals but of whole situations. If you know how to open that canopy up, then you can drive much more than just collecting eggs.

The farm's potential for transformation

There are dozens of little examples like that. Now, this is difficult when you talk to people because I suppose they don't quite believe the thought processes that I go through. They stand outside of that and go, "How did you get there?"

And the answer is that it's just an utter focus on the situation with a student. You just drive it. And you've got this intuition "if I can crack this, I get a whole new paradigm". You've got to have that intuition to be able to have the confidence to keep driving it, to get to the jewel that's buried in there – because there are jewels all over the place, but finding them is pretty tricky.

And I have this private strapline that it's the farm and the animals that will actually carry humanity in its relational development. They have the power to exhibit certain types of syndromes that in the animal are brilliant and healthy but in humans are challenging and complex. So there is this kind of interesting correlation between the highest functioning aspect of students, and chickens and eggs. And I've seen it over and over again in this kind of connectivity and distance at the same time with the egg.

Students love counting eggs, and putting them in boxes, containing, and learning the first start of how to handle relationships. And there's no petting animals or anything like that yet. It's just the egg at this point, but it's coming into contact with the potential of life. So many students love egg-collecting. They've taught me how to look at different animal capacities and the distinctiveness and ingeniousness of different animals, which often have little streaks of qualities that the students have in themselves and they could use but don't quite know how to.

The more socially comfortable young people on the autistic spectrum don't come to Ruskin Mill because they've already learned how to use their skills in the world and are often rewarded for doing so, for example, people with extraordinary memory capacities. By contrast our students may not yet be able to use those capacities in the world; they are on a borderline.

Poetic and mythological thoughts

I think there are three different levels of Practical Skills Therapeutic Education. One level is what we're doing now, which is how you find the language to put something into a book that reflects what we're doing. Then there's the level of a working manual for the Trust, where we tell staff "You will need to do this because experience has shown that it works; and these are perhaps the reasons why". And after a few years of working with it, you could go and take a research question, together with the research team, and do some reflection on it.

And then there's another level, which is where my personal interest and biography kick into spiritual science and connect to a sense of cosmological order. That would probably only be of interest to those who may want to follow a Rudolf Steiner spiritual-scientific thought process, because there'd have to be some assumptions made when they pick up the book. A reader would have to accept some assumptions that I would be working from, which you couldn't prove on a regular scientific level: the base plan from which I developed my own ideas.

So discussing Field Three at that level, I would need to bring in Steiner's homeopathic principles, which do turn the world upside down and can't be understood in any other way than "It's an idea". But people who tend to read that and then develop a formulaic kind of dogma from it actually lose traction on one level, if they can't work it through into practical reality.

But what is interesting in that more cosmological idea is what you can also present as a poetic thought, that the human being exists as a potential within evolution from the very beginning, but that that human intention only manifests physically very recently. The non-specialised, generalist species of humans emerges in this symbolic language by letting go of all the attributes of the animal kingdom that are specialised and specific.

This human entity, which is managed by developing a self, is no longer impeded because the specific nature of gluttony, for example, has been released as "the pig", or terror has been released as, say, crocodiles. So the attributes of certain phantoms of excess are liberated from the human psyche and dropped into physical reality as the community of animals. When we see an animal, what we're actually awed by is the magnificence of human effort in shedding that attribute out of oneself and into the world. Hence the necessity for our loving relationship to what may have been once a quality inside us and is now outside, and the respect, reciprocity and goodwill that requires.

So that is one way in which Steiner describes the relationship of the animal world to the human being. And of course many ancient cultures were preoccupied with looking at the animal outside themselves. From the cave paintings on, they separated themselves from the animal, but not in a demonising way; it was always seen as sacred art. In ancient Egypt you can see animals represented as deities, with particular qualities relating to different human aspects. It appears in the animals in the apocalypse – the eagle and the head, the lion and breathing, rhythm and the bull's metabolism. And this carries on through Hieronymus Bosch or even into a modern painter like Chagall.

So this is a way of seeing the encounter between the student and the animal in all its richness and taking it as seriously as the student does when they make that connection with a specific animal, because they sense the potential for their own transformation within that. And that myth can be inspiring, just as great art is – but it would not be helpful to turn that into a formula.

Finding the right animal

You could say that all illness, in a certain sense, expresses the cluttering dimension of what is unfree in the human being. If we want to express independence and autonomy, we need to try and limit the impediments within ourselves that have animalistic characteristics, in the sense of not being fully chosen. So Steiner's fight for the philosophy of freedom is one way of saying that this is what the human being needs. That's how he sees it.

And if that is the case, then you can start to read the animal script in an entirely different way, which is what I've started to do, and to build an idea that seems to have some traction, which is that when a particular child or young person has a certain, let's say, oppositional-defiant quality, there may be some liberation in encountering an animal outside themselves which expresses this.

So you meet like for like, which is one of Steiner's pedagogical methods. For example, if you've had a history of abuse where you've been beaten – and unfortunately this is not yet uncommon – that young person or child might encounter an animal which for them expresses that history as medicine, in that they can build a relationship with it and work through it. And then in a certain sense the necessary handshake takes place, and the event of the trauma can potentially be relinquished.

So, for example, if we were to take a donkey in relationship to physical abuse, the donkey is projected as a beast of burden and there is often a legacy of abuse – which may account for the fact donkeys are probably the most looked-after species in the world. Some of the wealthiest charities in England are donkey sanctuaries. I think I understand why that greater compassion has been elicited more from the public, when you hear a description of what the donkey suffered from, being the butt of abuse in that way.

So having done this exercise with students and brought donkeys in from the sanctuary, we see the incredible compassion that students have for the donkey, to the point where it might take a week for the hand of the student to actually land on the back of the donkey and stroke it. And in doing so an irrevocable event has taken place, which is that the donkey has received the touch of a student who's been burdened by total fear themselves.

Even physiologically, that students actually bunched up into the kind of expectant posture of someone who is hit from behind. So the donkey has a similar posture; it puts his head down and with utter acceptance allows the student to put his hand on its back and stroke it. And that ends up in the posture of the student and the benign goodwill of the donkey, either accepting the beat or the stroke. The transformation of the student combing and brushing the donkey's back, and ensuring that its health is checked and its hooves are done, is one of rebuilding trust and relationship with another sentient being. So the animal arena is the first point of contact, not necessarily the human.

We do know that because pets perform that in a sense, and we also know that around horses. But what we haven't done is to consciously see these attributes in the animal world as being deeply therapeutic and reflective, mirroring, so that students can accelerate their understanding of a quality that is maybe not helpful.

To take us a step further, if you then take the goat and you ask, "Can the goat contribute to dealing with oppositional defiance?", the answer is that real transformational possibilities exist in that. We're doing it right now. But what's interesting with the goat, if it's correctly worked with pedagogically, are the horns that butt up against students' shins – nudging and pushing and in a way, being in the frontal plane – without particular overt aggression, but with a certain kind of kick and bolshieness.

And if you look at that part of the goat which describes a forward gesture, that is an attitude that some of our students come in with, in that they've had to fight for their lives on the streets, so their head's down and they're about to create the kind of left hook that they do as a matter of course.

Even their posture has this "down-up" in your face; the goat can take that posture and within its own being demand from the student a complete reversal of that, having acquiesced in that oppositional defiance. The goat then slows down and the student can take out the steel bucket, sit on a stool and start milking its udders. That is an incredible therapeutic moment within the same animal, in which the hands of the students have to sort of "become one" with the teat, and the empathy that's required will allow the goat to give its milk. That's pretty amazing to watch.

So to offer the student that range of transformational and emotional relationship is nearly impossible in the human domain. You could do it in a dramatic context if you knew how to do it, and we do have staff who do, because what we're after there is performative experiences, not didactic conversational experiences. But most of our students don't fully get that domain initially. They get it later on, when things have really gelled. And in the performative element of being able to go from oppositional defiance into compassion and giving – in which the student has to do a bit of a somersault – you have a kind of functional life-based interaction that exists in the real world. And our view is that no animals are harmed in this therapeutic process: it is through meeting and caring for them that the student can change.

Watching birds

Now I should warn readers that this next section may not be entirely pleasant, but it is a consistent experience. We've already discussed the chicken, in its distant, upturned crescent head and the slightly fretting, mechanical way in which it looks left and right. It never looks forward, and there's something in

Figure 3.6 The right animal: herding goats at Sunfield

the posturing of that – only left and right. Sometimes students on the spectrum disdain looking into the front, because it's too much and they'd rather look at what's not quite in front.

It's too overpowering, so they look sideways, and there's the same quality in the chicken's head, where their necks are slightly drawn up and not engaged with the other, but always sideways – in a very awkward and distant manner, but sometimes with the searing clarity of that eye that you sometimes see in the chicken.

Now if you then look at other animals that are predators, and you start to observe the way they function and you look at some of the conditions that students have suffered – such as sexual abuse – that is done predominantly through power and authority, and the hands are quite critical in that subjugation. So the question that I started to work with was "How do we get birds of prey to work very directly with students?" And it wasn't until I saw falconry that I became very interested in how the talons of the falcon fix on the hands of the student, and that gave me a picture of the unrelenting nature of the talon in relationship to the hands that may perpetrate.

The synergy of that moment gave me enough confidence to start introducing falconry. And then to my utter amazement, when I asked the falconry teacher "Do you know what these students' histories are?" she said, "No". I asked her, "How was it decided to offer falconry to those particular students?" And she said, "It's self-selecting; they have chosen to do it". So then I looked at their biographies and three out of four had had histories of sexual abuse. They themselves had come forward and selected falconry. And that was another very startling moment, of the kind of self-wisdom that exists in human beings when sometimes, out of their own deepest intuition, they know the medicine that they need.

But equally if their condition is highly defiant, they reject the very thing that could be helpful for them because they know it is the thing that can move them forward, but they're happy where they are, because it's safe. So that was quite a revelation.

Student and staff challenges

And understanding how different dysfunctions – in students and children – might start to show up and the different animal curriculum that could be developed, is an area of research that I think done in the right way, with the right ethical boundaries, could be transformational.

Different animals elicit different emotional responses from students, and we see these creating some of the deepest relationships that some young people have ever experienced to date, given their own past histories. This comes from their own responses and the connections they made, but we see this very widely and so we're carrying out research as to why certain student needs can sometimes be met by engaging with specific animals. If we are right, there is a high therapeutic potential here.

The ultimate goal that I would like to look at is to sit down with an unprejudiced biodynamic farmer and start by looking at all the constitutional aspects of children and young adults and seeing how they find themselves in the animal world and arranging an animal community, thinking of characteristics that are common in childhood and early adolescent development that could be supported by a farm community of life.

When somebody says, "Well what you're really talking about is a zoo, Aonghus", the answer is both yes and no, because this community of animals would exist not for entertainment or study but for remediation, in which the dysfunctional organ or the attribute that's gone off kilter can be met in such a way that it is partially healed by confronting that same attribute in the natural world. So this is the aspect of the zoo or the gallery in which somebody stops in front of a particular animal, has a relationship and moves into the relationship for a period of time.

In biodynamics, one of the challenges that I've met is that there are different streams: people who are interested as a model of food production, along with staff who are interested in the social idea of how to distribute healthy food. There are others who are quite interested in the educational idea, and there are those who want to demonstrate another aspect, even people who are interested in alchemy.

But in Ruskin Mill's case, we're interested in a therapeutic education of opening up the farm, not as an economic model, but as a therapeutic model. That means expanding the training of farmers, and for some farmers to get this deeper idea of a farm organism based on animal characteristics connected to human behaviour.

So how can we get more biodynamic staff to the level where they know whether a farm organism is working from that perspective? How can that level of understanding and skill be shared? Our growers and farmers have complex roles, working intuitively with students and training their colleagues at the same time as a developmental force within biodynamics in general and PSTE in particular.

Our overall goal is to use the world of nature so that students can move, responding to animals, in a way that they can liberate themselves in places where they have become fixated or traumatised. The renaissance of the Horsley Valley which we're now engaged in is part of that job.

William Morris and practical engagement

If John Ruskin sought to change how Victorians saw the world, his younger contemporary William Morris (1834–1896) sought to remake the world they saw (Thompson, 2011). As a central figure in the Arts and Crafts movement, his influence on how we live and what we use, in the global North in particular, has been immense, redesigning the entire aesthetic of the time with one drawn from nature and handwork.

In an 1880 lecture Morris told his audience "Have nothing in your houses that you do not know to be useful, or believe to be beautiful": a critique simultaneously of the fussiness and affectation of earlier design and the ugliness of mass-produced items which avoids the throw-away tone of Marie Kondo's "Discard anything that does not spark joy". Like Ruskin and Steiner, his life was marked by an extraordinary energy for transformation in many directions: his doctor diagnosed the cause of his death at 62 as "simply being William Morris and having done more work than most ten men".

Practical engagement, remaking the world, was fundamental to Morris' life, and in particular his contribution to remaking craft which is inspirational for Ruskin Mill. In a period when the wealthy practised conspicuous consumption and plundered the globe for high-status goods, while the urban poor were dependent on shoddy goods, produced from poor materials as fast and mechanically as possible to be sold (and degraded) fast, Morris reached back to the craft traditions and materials of the pre-industrial world as a way forward.

Central to this was a concern to reconnect the craftsperson with their activity and resist the reduction of human skill to machine-minding: a challenge that is now facing us in a new way today with the rise of artificial intelligence even in education, culture and the arts. Having started with an architectural apprenticeship, poetry and Pre-Raphaelite painting, he changed direction into design and craft, co-founding "The Firm" with others coming from the same arts. This made an influential contribution in many areas, from architecture, stonework, stained glass and murals to furniture, wall-paper, textiles and metalwork, writing at one point "The complete work of applied art … is a building with all its due ornament and furniture".

Like Ruskin, Morris personally committed himself to learning each craft that would be offered but went further in consciously recovering lost or dying crafts, exploring manuscripts and engaging in practical experimentation to work out how a particular craft could best be done: he spent a year working on traditional vegetable dyes, for example, regularly appearing with hands and arms stained blue from the vats, or gleefully telling his friends about his experience of boiling poplar twigs to dye a piece of wool "a very good yellow" (MacCarthy, 2010, p. 354). Dyeing, weaving and design were integrated in a body of textile work which remains influential to the present day.

In Morris' craft activity we find an enthusiastic practical engagement with every aspect of the material world: the resistance of particular materials, the long history of a particular technology, the combination of crafts into a finished item, the relationship between the craftsperson and the work, the commercial challenges of making an item available and the necessary argument about the importance and meaning of beauty.

At the same time Morris encountered challenges which could not be overcome, notably around the revival of medieval craft in an industrial age. The Firm was able to eventually become in part a social enterprise, but with profits only shared among its permanent staff – a limitation familiar from today's Mondragon cooperative experience. More broadly, the Firm set out to challenge elitism and produce goods for use that were affordable as well as beautiful and useful, but in practice the vast majority of the poor could never have afforded the results, which were attractive mostly to the Victorian middle class. For Ruskin Mill, of course, the revival of traditional crafts is re-imagined as an activity grounded in its therapeutic benefit for the producers, leading to a different kind of social enterprise.

This frustration, and a deep social concern, led the older Morris to become a leading figure in the birth of British socialism, to which he brought all his characteristic energy: between 1883 and 1890 he spoke to perhaps quarter of a million people in over a thousand public meetings, editing 400 issues of his newspaper *Commonweal* and in one year alone writing nearly 500 pieces. Organisationally, the attempt was unsuccessful and he increasingly withdrew from direct leadership; however, his vision of an ecological society that met human needs remains widely influential today.

In his final years Morris took up yet another craft, this time printing. For his Kelmscott Press Morris engaged with papermaking, font design and calligraphy, typography, hand printing, book-binding and engraving. The project gave a huge impetus to today's art of fine printing as well as publishing a remarkable range of books, notably a landmark edition of Chaucer.

Morris' concern for practical engagement with the world expressed itself strongly in his encounter with the stories of the Icelandic sagas, part of a long-term conversation with the North which has also been inspirational for Ruskin Mill in its own work with Norway and Iceland: the stark material realities of sea and ice, dark and fire shape the realities of farming and craft in these contexts.

Traditional Icelandic society in particular combined a down-to-earth realism, a close attention to place and a respect for myth and storytelling in a powerful way. The Norse word *gaumr*, surviving in Northern English "gormless", clueless, means care, attention, sense – qualities that are needed in each of the seven fields but equally add up to the qualities needed to handle the multiple realities of farming and fishing, relationships and lawsuits, travel and battle of the sagas' heroes and heroines. Together with his friend Eiríkr Magnússon, Morris translated more than 30 sagas into English.

These translations were just one part of a wide-ranging body of writing, from poetry to politics. In particular, he is often seen as a pioneer of fantasy novels (not least by JRR Tolkien), through books like *The Wood Beyond the World* and *The Sundering Flood*. His more science fiction novels, *A Dream of John Ball* and *News from Nowhere* (1993), anticipate Ursula Le Guin. Across his writing, he counterposes a sense of what the world *could* be with a confidence in the ability of human beings to shape it.

Whether engaging with dyeing or printing, with society or other languages, William Morris brought a nearly indefatigable energy to practical engagement with the world and the task of making. Influential from interior design to ecology and from fantasy to glass, this energy for transformation appears as an overflowing of enthusiasm driven by a deep concern for beauty, truth and goodness, and it is in this spirit that Ruskin Mill identifies him as an inspiration for Practical Skills Therapeutic Education.

Bibliography

Bateson, G. (2002). *Mind and nature: A necessary unity*. Hampton. (Original publication 1979.)

Fine, A. H. (Ed.). (2019). *Handbook on animal-assisted therapy: Theoretical foundations and guidelines for practice* (5th ed.). Academic Press.

Louv, R. (2013). *Last child in the woods: Saving our children from nature-deficit disorder*. Atlantic.

MacCarthy, F. (2010). *William Morris: A life for our time*. Faber & Faber.

Macdonald, H. (2015). *H is for hawk*. Vintage.

Mata, P., Gibons, K., & Mata, F. (2016). Woodland in practical skills therapeutic education. *Journal of Research in Special Educational Needs, 16*(1), 1108–1112. https://doi.org/10.1111/1471-3802.12258

Morris, W. (1993). *News from nowhere and other writings*. Penguin. (Original publication 1890.)

Richardson, M. (2023). *Reconnection: Fixing our broken relationship to nature*. Pelagic.

Steiner, R. (2003). *Agriculture: An introductory reader*. Rudolf Steiner Press.

Steiner, R. (2008). *Spiritual ecology: Reading the book of nature and reconnecting with the world*. Rudolf Steiner Press.

Storl, W. D. (2000). *Culture and horticulture: A philosophy of gardening*. Biodynamic Farming and Gardening Association.

Thompson, E. P. (2011). *William Morris* (2nd ed.). PM Press. (Original publication 1977.)

United Nations Population Fund. (2007). *State of world population 2007*. UN Population Fund. https://www.unfpa.org/sites/default/files/pub-pdf/695_filename_sowp2007_eng.pdf

Williams, F. (2017). *The nature fix: Why nature makes us happier, healthier and more creative*. W.W. Norton.

Wilson, E. O. (1986). *Biophilia*. Harvard University Press.

4 Therapeutic education

Visiting Grace Garden School

You enter Grace Garden School through a small laneway off a busy suburban road on the outskirts of Bristol. The traffic noise soon falls away as the lane winds down through oaks and poplars, sycamore and ash into the valley of the Trym stream and then steeply up the other side. Here, on a gently sloping bank, is a cluster of buildings, ranging from the Arts and Crafts style of the old Cherry Orchard house to the naturalistic wood shapes of contemporary Steiner architecture, something between a large farm complex and an Italian hilltop village in their interconnections: workshops, apple presses, running water, classrooms, a maze garden and therapy buildings organically interwoven with one another.

Walking left, along the slope that faces out to the Bristol Channel, you find sunflowers, orchards, polytunnels and vegetable gardens – kale, chard, runner beans, pumpkins, onions – and beyond these again the goats and the small kunekune pigs that the students work with. Higher up the slope is native wild-flower meadow – in summer there are bluebells and St John's wort, marjoram and wild strawberries – and the Bristol whitebeam, which only grows wild in these valleys. Towards the crest of the ridge is wilder woodland, with yews and holm oak, hazel and holly stretching up towards the crest of the ridge. Depending on when you arrive, you might see children playing on the festival field, picking vegetables for their lunch, cutting wood for craftwork, caring for goats or making pots from clay they have dug themselves.

Grace Garden School's young people – day students between 9 and 16 with complex social, emotional and behavioural difficulties, including autistic spectrum conditions – follow a contemporary outdoors curriculum, learning through gardening, crafts and the natural world. Their education, biodynamic farming and therapeutic experience is intertwined: if there are elements that are best delivered in a classroom or through one-to-one therapeutic work, this fits into a wider picture where the daily round consists of activities that come to have meaning through connection.

The seasons mark your senses when you spend your days outside: warm and cold, wet and dry, windy and still, dark and bright; flowers and harvest, green

DOI: 10.4324/9781003361541-4

Figure 4.1 "The principle of help" (John Ruskin): harvesting food at Grace Garden School

leaves and brown, the cycles of goats and sheep, the sight of a fox or a roe deer passing through, a buzzard overhead or a robin on the ground. Amidst all of this, farm animals are born and cared for and emotional connections grow. Eggs and honey are collected from hens and bees. Apples are picked and juice is pressed and drunk. Plants are sown, cared for, harvested and eaten every day in their midday meal – or sold to the wider community through a food box scheme. Wood, clay and wool are harvested and become items for daily use and wear. Music and drama fit within a cycle of seasonal festivals and deepen relationships.

In the process students work with hands, head and heart – developing physical skills they may struggle with more than others; coming to an understanding of number, quantity, time; learning to be with one another and with supportive adults; seeing the food and drama they create appreciated by the outside world. Maths, English, science, history and geography are learned through their practical activities as much as possible. Dyes, for example, are made from plants and used to colour the yarn they have spun, which is then woven into textiles: a process recapitulating William Morris' rediscovery of the techniques of medieval colour, but today used to help students understand the science of what they are doing. An Ofsted inspection noted that attendance is exceptionally high: students want to attend so they can care for the animals first thing in the morning.

In residential spaces the young people's health and well-being are cared for within a warm and supportive daily routine. They learn the skills needed to live independently: cooking and cleaning, shopping and budgeting, planning events and travelling. Individual therapies include speech and language therapy, movement, massage, occupational therapy and art. Over time pupils gain qualifications, engage with the wider community including through work experience placements and are offered support for transition to the next stage of their lives. They develop confidence in themselves through the material and meaningful products of their work, and through seeing others value these. As one said, he experienced pride for the first time in his life after just a few weeks of being at Grace Garden School.

The original Cherry Orchard house was an early Arts and Crafts building, still with studios and carvings from the period, designed by influential architect Edward William Godwin. It is said to have acquired the name when its owner fell in love with the leading lady in a performance of the Chekov play. Later, in the 1970s, it became the Cherry Orchards Camphill Community – a form of Steiner-inspired work where young people with learning differences were included within volunteer families on a long-term basis. Thus, the land was already farmed and the buildings shaped for these purposes.

Although this worldwide movement was founded in the UK (by Dr Karl König in Aberdeen in 1939), England's Camphill communities in particular are increasingly struggling in a world where regulatory demands seem to impact on the original social model of small, fundamentally voluntary organisations and where the pressures of an increasingly neoliberal world make long-term volunteers hard to find.

Ruskin Mill's model has always been placed within the village, town or city context, without separation from the wider world. It comes with an economy of scale that enables dedicated attention to demands ranging from Ofsted inspections to safeguarding requirements; the vast majority of young people attending are funded by local authorities on the basis of their individual Education, Health and Care plans.

Today's Grace Garden School curriculum is drawn from the work of the medical doctor and educator Eugen Kolisko (1893–1939). Having been the first doctor at the very first Waldorf school, Kolisko left Germany for England in the 1930s. Kolisko's vision advocated "a co-working of teachers, doctors and biodynamic practitioners". This interweaving of education, health and therapy built on the foundations of biodynamic ecology is central to the syllabus here, which braids the seven standards required of specialist schools in England with Practical Skills Therapeutic Education and inspiration from Steiner's understanding of the phases of human development.

Grace Garden School's multidisciplinary perspective, looking at and connecting all aspects of a student's needs, helps to provide an innovative and contemporary support to pupils' Education, Health and Care plans and a consistent and supportive space for their development within a largely outdoor curriculum.

Leaving the school, its physical situation – a warm and "held" space of young animals, growing plants, food and craft, from which you return to the busy road system around Bristol – stands as a symbol for the young people's experience, stretching their emotional and mental muscles as much as their physical ones in preparation for entry to a world that will ask so much of them.

Education as therapy

Visitors to Ruskin Mill's colleges for 16- to 25-year-olds sometimes worry that students are being taught forms of craft and farming that offer them little chance to make a living in the outside world. While a certain number do go on to work as craftspeople, in social enterprises and so on, this is not the purpose of a "Practical Skills *Therapeutic* Education".

Similarly, students definitely learn what educational managers call "transferable skills" of many kinds – whether developing their literacy and numeracy in café and shop work, or a real-world understanding of applied mathematics, geography or chemistry in craft and farming work; most leave with some formal qualifications. But this too is an additional benefit, not the main point.

What makes Ruskin Mill's education *therapeutic* is that in these practical and structured encounters with the world – from working with goats to shaping wood to meeting people – the student also meets themselves and in doing so confronts old wounds. The work that both children and students engage in brings new and powerful experiences, so that they can move on from earlier experiences that previously entrapped them.

The new muscle memories allow the old ones to dissipate: but this has to be performed physically, not simply in talk. In working with the material towards a real end – making a stool that someone can sit on, for example – the student needs to bring a new kind of understanding and focus to the task: over time this enables a self-transformation that is neither simply practical nor cognitive.

Ruskin Mill talks about the hands, the head and the heart: the physical activity (hands), oriented towards creating something that is meaningful and useful for others, and guided in a supportive environment, involves new learning and intellectual development (head), but the end goal is for the young person to be able to engage in "self-generated conscious action": to decide for themselves what they want to do in the world, to become able to do it, and to carry that out (heart).

Working towards this goal engages the students in self-driven forms of change that run up against, and start to overcome, some of the internal barriers they face. At a basic level, for some students it is an achievement simply to enter the woods – whether because they are unused to being in the natural world, watching and listening rather than talking or on a phone, or because for some the experience feels dangerously unstructured. For others, the achievement is to actually turn up, to learn how to trust a teacher who deserves it, or to overcome other barriers to learning. For others again, learning how not to

Figure 4.2 A practical challenge: cutting wool at Grace Garden School

give up and to see their initial efforts gain in strength and effectiveness as they carry out the same task over time is a crucial life skill.

A member of staff who had recently arrived at Ruskin Mill was offered accommodation in a building next to student residences. When their family managed to lock themselves out on a chilly autumn evening, staff asked one of their young neighbours if he'd mind driving five miles to pick up a spare key and let them in. He agreed cheerfully, and took a couple of his mates to make a road trip of it. The round trip might have taken a bit longer than a busy adult would have needed, but the key was presented within the hour to a very grateful family.

When they were commenting afterwards on how polite and helpful the young man was, and how unfazed at dealing with the situation, a staff member told them that when he'd arrived he had thrown stones at members of the public. Not every change is this dramatic, but it is this sort of transformation – in how a young person relates to themselves and others – that they (and their parents or guardians) value most, and that in turn enable them to go on to make a happier and more fulfilled life, giving back to others.

Taking a developmental approach

All serious educational and psychological research recognises the developmental nature of human existence, particularly for children and young people. It is not only our bodies that physically grow and develop; our ability to use them – from our first struggle to crawl to our capacity to ride a bicycle – constantly develops, and with physical skills like preparing food, playing a musical instrument or rock climbing it does not stop at age 18 or 25.

So too with our emotions and our cognitive skills. As a learning species, we have always had to find out from others how to become a fully functioning member of our own society and culture; what is expected of us, how to excel in what is valued and what we can give others. In contemporary societies, we are more likely to spend years in formal education systems than to learn through apprenticeship or from our elders: in a country like the UK, over half the population now goes on to some form of tertiary education, meaning that 15 years of schooling is now the norm rather than the exception. Meanwhile, all sorts of legal protections for children and prohibitions on what they can do indicate our recognition of their different capacities.

And yet, while research consistently recognises this fairly obvious point – that human beings are on a path of development – we increasingly treat the young as adults who simply don't know enough. They inhabit a testing-driven model of education that highlights only "what children know" as though everything else can be taken for granted, and all that is needed is to shovel ever more information into the child, in what Paulo Freire, over half a century ago, called "banking education" (2017, orig. 1971).

An extreme version of this can be seen all too frequently, with overstretched parents shouting at toddlers or even babies as though if they only understood some basic piece of information they would do as they were told. If we have passed that point in our own parenting years, we can often see that there is something happening with the child physically or emotionally – and that the apparently rational action of "talking at the child" is in fact deeply irrational, an expression of despair or exhaustion. Yet our education system increasingly does just this – in a model that serves a minority of children well, and many children extremely badly.

In Rudolf Steiner's philosophy of education, we need to start by trying to see the child or young person as they are at any given point in their development, with a very wide range of needs and capacities, entering new phases of development, driven by ever-wider goals – all expressed very differently depending on the individual. Then we need to shape education to this developmental reality, rather than try to force that complex and changing reality into the institutional requirements of formal education.

Steiner education generally tries to meet the young child – up to the age of perhaps 6 or 7 – where they are at, and in particular offering the love, security and attachment that is particularly needed in this period of life, and whose absence can be devastating. This is sometimes summarised as needing to see the world as *good*.

From then to perhaps ages 12–14, in this view, the child needs to see the world as *beautiful*: they need to be offered activities that speak to a sense of wonder and appreciation – in the natural world, in stories, in their developing formal understanding, in their surroundings. If the world they experience (starting from school buildings!) and are presented with is unremittingly ugly and instrumental, focussed perhaps only on money and fame, we can hardly be surprised if children are alienated from this.

At a later age, perhaps up to 18 or 21, young people come to care much more about what is *true* – as we can see in the global schoolchildren's demand to "listen to the science" on climate change and take the necessary steps but also in the huge gulfs between young and old around different forms of prejudice. These capacities too need to be met, not simply with an ever-increasing mountain of facts and prescribed answers, but with an education that genuinely offers a chance to exercise the mind.

Trauma and re-stepping

The young people who come to Ruskin Mill have rarely had a childhood full of the good, the beautiful and the true. If there is one common factor among so many different stories, it is rather trauma. For some, the experience has been one of direct abuse of many kinds; for others, of poverty or neglect leading to appalling experiences. Others may come from privileged backgrounds which did not contribute to building their own capacity. For others again, it has been an experience in which learning differences, parents' inability to care for them or behaviour that challenges have exposed them to inadequately resourced institutions and to methods which have compounded the problem.

Experiences are very varied and many parents make huge efforts, taking responsibility at a deep level to give their children opportunities that ameliorate some of the conditions they face, following their intuition and educating themselves.

Where parents, or local authorities, have exhausted other options and turn to Ruskin Mill, it is often because the young people are struggling in ways far beyond any easy fixes. Some may be unable to walk in a straight line, or keep moving all the time. A more dramatic case was that of a young man who would periodically take off for the 30-mile journey from Nailsworth to Bristol to visit his beloved aunt – on foot, and in a straight line, through hedgerows and across busy roads. How can they be helped?

A key answer in PSTE is "re-stepping", returning in a secure context to a developmental phase that was missed, or mislearned, at the appropriate age. Many of us have come across a milder version of this: an adult art or music class that helps us enter an area that was closed to us as children for whatever reason; overcoming a childhood phobia when it becomes important to us as adults; finding in DIY or cooking a way to engage with things we were discouraged from exploring; and so on.

Often re-stepping can take the form of "age-appropriate play": not playing a child's games, but engaging lightly with something that meets us where we are now, as adults, but helps us to explore the contours and challenges of something we were never able to fully engage with when we first needed to. Often we can see and welcome this in our friends, family or partner recovering from a bereavement or a breakup, on retirement or in other periods that have led them to want to re-imagine who they are in the world and inhabit their own hands, head and heart more fully – through play or leisure, to re-step and catch up with the person they are now.

In a meaningful practical activity with a trusted teacher – working with animals, producing food, making clothing, creating household items and so on – Ruskin Mill's young people can be brought to the same point and find the resources within themselves to overcome barriers that may have constrained them for many years. Of course the craft, or the animal, has to be well chosen, potentially meaningful to the student and capable of bringing them to the point of meeting and overcoming that barrier in themselves.

Can they learn, for example, to trust others in the intense environment of a forge or hot glass workshop, where they have to negotiate risk? Can they find a way to engage with an unpredictable animal? Can they master the tools and skills that can turn a piece of wood or a ball of clay into something recognisably useful? Can they get to the point of looking someone in the eye, asking what they want, serving them and handling the responsibility of using a till? Can they cope with spending a cold winter's day working outside in a muddy environment? What for more privileged youngsters might be a leisure activity, a Duke of Edinburgh task or a work experience requirement is often a far larger challenge for Ruskin's young people.

Figure 4.3 Contemporary apprenticeship: coppicing at Ruskin Mill College

Re-stepping recognises the importance of catching up with the points that are cardinal to every child's development: if these haven't been engaged,, that aspect of development will be obstructed. For example, someone may not have learned how to use left and right correctly. Depending on context, this may lead to humiliation and behaviours that hide this, or to fear of being found out. A craft curriculum such as green woodwork involves enhancing and exercising our use of left and right, so can be an age-appropriate re-stepping of a more general developmental need.

But what task should a young person be set, and what do they need to work on?

The senses as a diagnostic tool

Most of us learned a list of five senses – sight, sound, smell, taste and touch – in school. Beyond this, however, we routinely talk about our sense of balance or the sense of pain. We may also have heard, say, of proprioception – the sense of where different parts of our body are – we recognise spatial orientation, hunger and so on; we probably know that other species have different senses again, such as echo-location in bats; and we may use a more psychological terminology, as in "a sense of self".

Practical Skills Therapeutic Education works with a list of 12 senses, which can also be described as capacities or intelligences – not as a dogmatic proposition but as an effective diagnostic tool to assess where a particular student may be experiencing difficulties and where re-stepping might be effective. These 12 are divided into three sets of four, relating firstly to one's own body, then to the external world and lastly to understanding ourselves and other people.

Most commonly in human development, we start with foundational senses that enable us to experience and gradually coordinate our own bodies – touch, life (knowing whether we are healthy or unwell), movement and balance. As we do so, we also develop our bodily will to act and live. The "middle" senses that help us engage with the outer world are smell, taste, sight and warmth (temperature): these are also strongly associated with emotional/feeling capacity. Lastly the "higher" senses of hearing, speech, thought and sense of self and other are particularly connected to knowing and to our understanding of others.

As a diagnostic tool, staff collaborate around a student to see how well integrated or obstructed their foundational senses are. For example, can they wheel a barrow up a plank, or work with the sensations of how wet and soapy wool turns into felt? The middle, emotional senses might be observed as more or less well developed in a student's ability to draw a straight line when planning a task, or perhaps to taste whether food has been cooked enough. Staff might encounter students' higher senses in their interactions with them, and in watching how they are with each other, through craft observation and with animal husbandry skills.

These are just examples – and different staff, supporting young people through the day, running a residential home or teaching them practical skills, will encounter the same person in many different ways. Through the student study (Chapter 6), they pool their knowledge and understanding to see where a particular student most faces challenges and where they might best work on making changes for their development.

Imagine a young woman who for whatever reason – perhaps a combination of trauma, learning difficulties and poverty – has never fully learned to coordinate the different aspects of her body in skilled activity like riding a bike, which involves many different senses, such as balance and finely judged movement in the different planes of space, particularly of course the horizontal (leaning the bike to one side or the other) and the sagittal (moving to left or right) – even before we include noticing what's on the road or hearing traffic coming up behind.

If she comes to a woodworking shelter where her senses are already brought alive through the feel of the wind, the smell of the cut wood or the sound of the rain and where the combination of physical effort and adjusting to the temperature means that she has to be fully present in the space, she can learn to make the legs for a simple stool. The task is real and the wood has its own characteristics, including for this particular piece of wood. Perhaps she has helped to fell the tree before planning her stool and then selecting the right piece of wood and cutting it to length – it was not bought in a warehouse store already prepared – and she may have planted other similar trees which will mature after her time at Ruskin Mill.

She then works with her wood on a pole lathe, which requires her to stand and develop a rhythm with the foot on the treadle which propels the lathe, as well as moving her cutting tool very finely to left and right, deeper or more shallowly into the wood, and finding the right angle for engagement. All of this movement, in a body that is finely balanced – able to both rhythmically push the treadle that drives the lathe and to hold a very precise point with enough force to cut the wood – gives immediate and physical feedback: when I do *this* I prolong the shallow edge of a curve I am working on, when I do *this* I make a narrow decorative ring around the wood. The senses of balance and movement are engaged; she learns to master them and become a confident woodworker – and in the process she has started to take possession of her body.

Another way of telling this story is in terms of "focus, grasp and step" (Chapter 2): the craft calls for the eye to focus on a particular point, for the hand to grasp in a certain way and for the feet to take part – stand or move – in another way. Whether understood in these terms or those of the senses, there is a dialogue with the material which is initially physical but then always also cognitive – not on paper but the understanding that we all draw on to ride a bicycle – and then ultimately emotional, in the feelings that follow her return home from the work, the satisfaction of success or frustration of failure, and the confidence that comes from constructing a stool that is not just recognisably a stool but actually works.

Figure 4.4 Mastering the craft: making jewellery at Argent College

The "nine ancient crafts"

Steiner discusses childhood as a gradual "incarnation", coming into the body, which Ruskin Mill translates as "descent into matter" in order to underline the importance of genuinely being in the world. The growing child becomes increasingly present in their own body and in the material engagement with the physical world around them starts to shape. In the craft process, that engagement can be thought of as moving from the relatively simple processes of collecting raw materials, through the more complex work of processing them into something new and into the most developed practices of working with the refined or trans-formed material.

Re-stepping these processes, which of course most many young people, not just at Ruskin Mill, today have barely if ever experienced, can help them to come to exist more fully in the material and practical world around them –

not only on their phone screen or in intensely charged interactions with a very small number of others. These activities demand the cooperation and coordination of the different senses, providing an important experience of in-tegration through practical action.

Working through the whole of a single process – whether from lambing and caring for sheep through shearing, carding, dying, spinning to weaving; in the long sequence from planting trees to felling them and constructing the elements of a chair on a pole lathe; or in digging earth and refining it into clay, shaping it on a wheel, glazing, firing and putting the results on sale – gives a real and practical engagement with a world of matter from which students are often deeply alienated – at the same time of course as they depend on it for their everyday activities.

In the plant realm, leaving food aside, tending hedges and trees enables collecting willow rods for basket-weaving, planting trees for wood-carving and felling them for green woodwork. In the animal realm, sheep and cattle afford the possibilities of shearing, felt-making, spinning wool for weaving or tan-ning for leatherwork. In the mineral kingdom, the presence of clay and stone enables digging clay for pottery, extracting sand for glass and refining ore for metalwork. These nine crafts thus represent deepening engagements with the material world, drawing the student firstly into their own body and then into its skilled encounter with physical reality.

They also stand as archetypal symbols of the whole spectrum of ways in which human beings practically create the world we inhabit – even if today most of these are now produced in plastic, by machines, in sweatshops or on assembly lines. Glass (Chapter 2) is a powerful example: before working with glass, it is easy to take it for granted as a banal part of the environ-ment which the eye normally moves through. Having made a glass item, suddenly much of the everyday world appears as a *made* environment. A similar transformation can come with making your own food or learning DIY: things move from "just being there" to being actively produced by human skill.

The many different sets of concepts sketched out here – hands, head and heart; the phases of human development; re-stepping; the 12 senses; focus, grasp and step; the nine crafts and others – make up a toolbox that the therapeutic educator can draw on to understand and engage with the specific challenges faced by a particular young person and to help them move forward.

At Ruskin Mill, this takes place within a contemporary apprenticeship model: a new form of relationship between therapeutic educator and student which is neither about a pure transmission of technical knowledge or skill separate from human development, nor about a focus on the student's cognitive or emotional development cut off from engagement with the outside world. Apprenticeship is role-modelled so that there is no power over, but a transformative experience of co-learning in the craft context. The craftsperson has to learn how to reposition themselves so that the student's opportunity for learning is intensified, and to know when they are getting in the way of this. The teacher limits the self in relation to the other, pulling the student forward.

The strapline "hands, head and heart" indicates how practical activity leads to learning and so to change in the individual, whether that change is a greater control over fine motor skills, the ability to overcome the student's habit of rejecting difficult tasks and developing courage to take on new challenges, or the capacity to create something that responds to others' needs.

Conversation with Aonghus Gordon

The vision and the craft: a mythic approach

We can approach the world outside ourselves in two different ways. We can leave things as they are, but shepherd them; or we can take the material of the world and change it. There is an administrative, academic entry into vocation and a practical one. Of course we need both, so we have to find a way of healing this split between the researcher and the practitioner. At Ruskin Mill we draw on the myth of Solomon and Hiram, in the story of the building of the First Temple at Jerusalem.

In this story, Solomon had a vision for a temple containing the divine coordinates and asked Hiram to build it for him. Supposedly Solomon didn't have the practical skill to find the materials and build it, but he did know how to find someone who could. So there was an architect and a builder. Hiram could take Solomon's vision and make it real because he knew which materials were needed for different purposes – and he knew who could do the different tasks. Hiram had a practical understanding of the "genius loci" – he knew where to find cedars of Lebanon, or how to extract metal ores, and he could link the qualities of the material to different vocations and temperaments, or even generate new vocations in different people.

Field Four – therapeutic education – looks at this mythic story and asks "How was Hiram able to recruit the apprentices and the master craftspeople, and how did he know who to give different responsibilities to?" How much is truth and legend here is another thing, but a master craftsperson *did* have to be able to do this, at any time in history. So from one perspective you are simply working with a material, but you are doing it with a purpose of service to others, and that gives you a reason for developing all the skills that are needed to move from the tree and the temple – the skills of gathering the material, of working it and of working with the people you need.

In 1994 I met the educational consultant Vim Molleman who introduced me to this story, as he was part of a new stream in the Netherlands, called Hiram, focussing on vocational skills development. He reminded me that Dutch engineers, like German ones, are very highly paid. Vocational streams work in education there because there isn't such a big social or financial divide between practical and administrative skills. Meanwhile in England and Wales, where it is bureaucrats who are well paid, the split causes tremendous social unhappiness, so that vocational education is always a poor relation.

After seeing this in action in the Netherlands, I co-founded the Hiram Foundation, which helped me to become clearer about the sources of different modes of learning. I was directed to read Steiner's lectures on the Temple legend, which led me into a whole new cycle of research around understanding the medieval guilds. I saw how material can be shaped so that culture and economy fuse as they do in building of our cathedrals.

At that time Ruskin Mill had a stone mason, stained-glass window workers, carpenters and mosaic artists working at the Mill, and I realised that we actually had some of the key elements needed to build a medieval cathedral. I was very amused by this, and I realised that although we don't need to use those elements to build new cathedrals, we could take the concept of a cathedral community of practitioners. At the centre of that was not a building but enabling young people to rebuild themselves through a new understanding of the craft heritage, so I rewrote that myth centred on the student.

This is a humanistic way of thinking, very much in line with John Ruskin's work, where the real measure of a building, or a craft, is the effect that constructing a cathedral or learning stone masons' skills has on the people who undertake it. Ruskin's view was that the mechanisation of the industrial process, where artisanal workshops became replaced by the factory and later the assembly line, and the breakdown of direct relationships between producers, led to an impoverishment of our experience as human beings.

Hence like Ruskin we aim to put the arts and crafts directly in service for human transformation, rather than transforming the human being *after* they've been constructed, through entering the cathedral or appreciating the carving. It is the process of engaging the arts and crafts which is transformative. That's Field Two, practical skills, but now seen in terms of its purpose, not just working with material but also working with people through the lens of human sensory development and contributing to transformative learning.

Harvesting the materials

But we also have to harvest the materials we use, and that too is an educational experience, our Field Three. If you look at things like stripping willows, or even the dance "Strip the Willow", you start to see that in between growing your material and using it, there is a whole science of transforming it so it can be used to create something as a base material. That means that we can have a transformative science curriculum around harvesting willow, soaking, stripping, preparing and tanning it.

The same is true for collecting sand and making glass; for shearing sheep, carding wool and dyeing it; for felling wood and making charcoal for an Iron Age forge; or for digging and refining clay.

When we took students to northern Sweden to make knife blades from pondweed with Sámi teachers (Chapter 2), as well as antler or wooden handles and reindeer hide sheaths, that primary harnessing of material became a rite of passage for the students in the wilderness. They were undertaking a process of transforming the three kingdoms of animal, vegetable and mineral. This involved an inner ritual of transformation between what is given by nature and the intelligence involved in breaking nature open to reforge the precious materials, in a way that left no harm. That's characteristic of the Sámi culture, which is highly integrated and lives in cooperation with the environment, so it only touches it with a very light footprint.

Those knives bear the signatures of a three-stage process: the materials undergo change, the student undergoes change in this process and their communities undergo change, because those objects then serve the communities. This brings together the two sides of that divide, between Solomon's understanding of what exists and Hiram's skill in extracting it, in collaboration. At Ruskin Mill we have a long-standing interest in practitioners being highly attentive to how materials are harvested. That is one of the drivers for my own action research, which we later turned to the materials we used for building the Field Centre.

Developing a curriculum

What does this mean for our young people's educational development? In an ideal guild situation, the apprentice entered the workshop and they would quite organically become familiar with the materials given through nature. At Ruskin Mill we try to translate that into say a six-week block of three mornings a week, as a core curriculum. When we had small numbers of students, we could have a sequence of different entry points to learning – starting with minerals, or with plants, or from food. In each case you are taking from what is already given, entering a process of harvesting it – and then entering the material in a way that re-animates it in a transformed condition: a knife, a woollen item, a wooden stool, a coathook, food and so on.

If you add the human being to this image, you can expand the Hiram and Solomon story to bring in the Queen of Sheba working with them: Solomon in thought, Sheba in the heart and Hiram in the will, because the reconciliation between thinking and willing is shaped through the heart.

This offers us an imaginal context for the method. If you invite students into a position where they have to engage themselves in the process of the material, encountering resistance for the needs of the wider community, you replace one traumatic experience with a new, imaginal and transformative picture.

That means that you can bring knowledge and action into more conscious connection, which is therapeutic: what you create has to be of real service to the community, not just a decorative feature, and that brings knowledge and action together. We put a relational principle at the centre of things being made, helping the student make these connections through developing their connection to others. They understand how plants grow through the year, they know how to harvest them practically, they feed others – and others are happy to come and eat what the students cook; in our cafés strangers will pay for the results.

You could go back further and think about these myths in other ways. If you think of Adam and Eve after they were expelled from Paradise, Adam delved – he's represented as tilling the soil with a mattock – and Eve span. That's very intriguing, because it suggests that the archetype of intelligence, craftwork, is not male but female.

At one point we took students on art history trips and encountered the legend of Theseus and the Minotaur in Crete; on other occasions we performed the drama. Theseus is indignant that the Minotaur is consuming all these young Athenian men and women every year and volunteers to kill it – but it is Ariadne who offers him the thread of intelligence to get in and out of the labyrinth. We can work with this archetype, the connection between land- and craftwork, which is foundational to our method.

This can break down the indignation that some of our male students have around having to do what they might see as female work, like cooking or craft, especially working with fleece. On the other side, there are things that a lot of girls are resistant to, like going to the forge. Some of them are very keen to do hair-dressing, so maybe we need a parlour for animal care, a kind of practical hair-dressing – looking after the animals and caring for their coats. Hence the social enterprise centre at Plas Dwbl, which is one response within our curriculum to the thousands of years of discrimination between expectations of male and female.

This is a big deal, because part of the challenge for many of our students is to become less entrenched in the family situation they've inherited. Some of our students have never been exposed to a more cosmopolitan worldview. That is stronger where there are more isolated communities, but even in the industrial Midlands we had boys refusing to come to the Glasshouse because it was on the wrong side of the road, in terms of the territorial divides between communities or gangs. Until you start doing this work with young people, you don't realise the degree of separation and division, and the inability to cross boundaries into what they see as female or male work; but if you trace it back, you can see how it's happened and start to counter it.

Figure 4.5 Not "just for girls": learning to spin at Brantwood school

Focus, grasp and step

With our students, what delivers change is the land- and craftwork, but what underpins that and drives the specifics is therapeutic education. That is developed through the idea of physically re-stepping early developmental stages that may have been missed, such as the integration of focus, grasp and step

(Chapter 2). All craft involves focus, grasp and step, but for the tutor to understand these and the sensory development involved, there is a whole host of therapeutic understanding that's needed. So the conceptual lens is in Field Four, but it is performed in Field Two as practical skills. As our tutors move from being craftspeople to understanding more deeply how focus, grasp and step help young people, they reach out to become therapeutic educators.

In human development, focus is part of a process that starts with gaze – which is the first development in babies – to focus, and from focus to attention, and eventually from attention to meditation, which is more of a contemporary adult capacity. With gaze, we are only involved in the frontal plane. Focussing and grasp bring in right and left, the sagittal plane. Young children do this quite early on, and it's always a point of concern when children can't grasp things correctly. Some have delayed development in grasp; you could say that the rattle is a monitoring device to develop grip. Babies without grip can be identified as having potential challenges, just as if they don't move from gazing to being able to focus.

We can also ask at what stage they learn to walk, and about their step. Delayed crawling and walking can often be an area of concern. If you analyse step, grasp and focus, you will notice that many of our students have various challenges around those areas. But you have to observe, and check quite carefully.

Tasks, like pushing a wheelbarrow, walking in a straight line, crossing a plank bridge or being able to exercise judgement and focus between distance and the near field of vision, become developmental hallmarks, empathetic tests. So in craft or land work, students are performing focus, grasp and step, but from the point of view of therapeutic education, the question is how to understand that, and how it impacts on the sensory world of the student. This gives us some indications as how we can apply land- and craft-work where a normal developmental process has been obstructed in their past. Then, if we can find the right level of resistance in the materials involved in a task, we can enable the re-membering of particular kinds of movement. So we can actually claim the word "therapeutic", in that the student is re-stepping their lost developmental stages.

It's important that not only are they re-stepping into these foundational coordinates – focus, grasp and step – but we're also offering them the ability to engage and refurnish or polish their sensory integration. And the switch from thinking about 5 senses to 12 makes it possible to audit each practical activity in terms of its significance for those different senses, and we start to create a kind of toolkit of what we can offer students with different sensory and practical disorders.

The idea of human freedom

The drama of breaking open the earth appears in many mythological stories as a form of violation of the divine, and in those stories the interesting question is often what the consequences are. Of course we try to find narratives that we can corroborate with our experience, so for example to ask what the purpose of this violation is. In their lives, our students have also suffered a violation. Is it possible for one transgression to be helped by another? It couldn't be unless you had a concept of a direction that it might lead in.

If you don't have a human developmental model, you are simply cutting down trees, pulling up plants, digging earth and so on. You aren't transforming material, making things, cooking food or serving people, and it isn't transforming the people who do it. So we need at least an idea of human freedom and what that might look like, which is based around developing what could be called personal autonomy. Psychologists talk about executive functioning, and Ruskin Mill talks about self-generated conscious action.

From this point of view, we can think about personal autonomy as something we are working towards, and ask what attributes give us the capacity to make free and independent decisions, and to have the resilience to deal with the consequences when things are not okay. And what does that mean for the specific young people we're working with? Then it becomes clear that this has to be one of the ultimate goals behind our ideas around therapeutic education: we are not doing these things just for their own sake.

So the actions we ask young people to do are determined by a social end result, what we call the consensus of the community that's going to use the item. This generates a form of third-party endorsement: someone comes into the café and recognises what they are served as good food, or uses a tool that has been made for them, or appreciates a gift.

The reason craft becomes valuable as a tool in therapeutic education is that students are ultimately *not* doing it for themselves, but for somebody outside their self-interest. But from a developmental perspective, if you don't look after yourself first, you're probably not going to go any further. So first you make the item for yourself, then you make the item for your next of kin. Then in fact, you are ready to give it to the world. And better still, the world then purchases it, because that is how a stranger recognises that what you have made is socially meaningful.

Stepping into the world

Not all of our students can get to that stage, but our concept of social enterprise has many different entry points. For example, if a student isn't able to get up in the morning, you can start from that, because getting up in the morning can already mean recognising the fact that you're not just acting for yourself. Of course there are situations in which the tables are turned and where there may be nothing you can do, other than let the world do something for you.

But in terms of our client base at Ruskin Mill, one of our entry points is that the young people want to actually step into the world. That's true for most of them; there are very, very few who say, "Although I am in the world, I'm actually not going to participate in any way." And if they're still in that mode even after intensive work, it may be that that's not the right student for Ruskin Mill. There are other people who can understand that condition better than we do.

So for us to be able to help them, there needs to be that pull, visibly or potentially, towards self-generated conscious action in which they can take a tool – including their hands as in bread-making – to the material. But it takes a bit of imagination to start a programme in which social enterprise, contributing to the world, becomes the end process. If we go back to hands, head and heart, the heart is the catalyst for generating relationship and change. And that is full of vulnerability, with no guaranteed results.

If you organise your pedagogy around this trichotomy of hands, head and heart, then we're extending different educational leadership ideas into myths, legends and pictures. So you could say that a comprehensive school, which started as a model of social development replacing the past split between grammar and secondary modern schools, has a Sheba-esque element within it, in that collaboration is the organising principle between the practitioner and the academic student, and when it's done well, it's transformative for all concerned.

Curriculum models

There are elements of that model in the preconditions that Steiner insisted on when he was asked to set up the first Waldorf school in 1919. In that school, girls were expected to do blacksmithing and boys were expected to sew shirts, which caused some problems with the authorities. However, he failed to get shoe-making into the curriculum at all. They wouldn't allow it, because they saw it as work. So he could partially overcome the gender split in the curriculum, but not the split between academic and practitioner.

Steiner realised that there was a confusion in the minds of the educationalists who didn't realise that certain practical tasks were valuable in order to develop, for example, the integration of focus, grasp and step – and that those were preconditions for being able to develop concentration or to grasp an idea; grasping as an imaginative thought, not just a physical capacity. He linked focus to the precondition for concentration, physical grasping as the precondition for grasping a new imaginative idea, and learning to step physically as the precondition for self-initiative, where you step into the world.

Tragically, the comprehensive school idea in England and Wales was never fully implemented through the 1944 Education Act and never resourced properly. In a way, the polytechnics were developed on the basis of the comprehensive system and then they also failed to sustain their identity outside of academia. So the figure of Solomon's academic power is still dominant and it still subjugates Hiram's craftsmanship and working with the material world, and the attempt to find a middle way.

Metaphorically, that middle way is the binding capacity of goodwill to create an integrated model. In Ruskin Mill we see the development of thinking, feeling and willing as objectives for therapeutic education, or we can talk about focus, grasp and step. Sensory integration has three clear areas in the foundational, middle and higher senses. This trichotomy works at many different levels, moving from more polarised situations in which there's no middle space for conversation or development, and creating a third context. In a way, that model saturates everything we do.

What are we trying to achieve with all this? Craft and land work are curricular devices to develop a greater capacity for "being fully human". That means people becoming liberated from inherited obstacles that limit their capacity to be personally free. What does being free look like? The capacity to be creative; the capacity to be autonomous; the capacity to respond to the other. As we say in our vision statement, it is about being able to shape one's own future.

That word "shape" is important because it's performative and interactive. It suggests effort and action; it's not just choosing from a pre-given set of options. It's a participatory element, and the word "shape" was discussed around Ruskin Mill for months as to whether it was appropriate, yet it has stood the test of time.

The 12 senses

What this means is that there is no expectation that all our young people will go on to become craftspeople or farmers. Craftwork and biodynamic farming are vehicles for re-stepping, and for building the precursors for self-management and self-generated conscious action. We use the 12 senses as a way of assessing that.

Occupational therapists working in sensory integration who visit the Trust, particularly our schools, have a checklist of at least ten senses that they expect to look at in the development of young people with learning differences, so it is no longer particularly surprising to be working with 12 senses. Of these, the two senses that are probably key to developing a sense of autonomy and self-generated conscious action are the sense of touch and the sense of ego.

It is worth unpacking this a little bit: the hand is generally the instrument by which we touch the world, and it's through the sense of touch that we create our ability to become connected and separate. If you use clay, or shake the hand of another student, what becomes self-evident is that although we're very close to the material or to the person, there's a point which we can't go beyond. There's a self-limitation within the experience of touching, and therefore a boundary, of separation and the consciousness of something else.

Yet we have a yearning to be connected beyond the sense of touch, maybe an emotional sense of the other, or the divine, or something that we can't quite reach – but we have an inner knowledge that there's something beyond the limitation of the boundary that we experience as touch. I think this is a very important quality, because our students are consistently unable to monitor their spatial boundary situations. If they could, they wouldn't be at Ruskin Mill.

This area is so fundamental that if someone is managing it well, you know that many other senses will be in shape. In a way, the majority of those senses and capacities – or focus, grasp and step – are conditional on being able to actually understand the capacity to hold the right boundary in space and time.

So this really is a restructuring of the process of entering the world and entering the sense of self: where is my knowledge of myself, not intrusive to the other? As I move towards my colleagues, do I breach the tradition of space in my particular culture? Because this is different, and rightly so, in different cultures.

The human hand, touching the world

Human hands are extraordinary things. On their own, the neurologist Frank Wilson (2010) calls them "fish-heads"; just appendages. To get a hand working in a healthy state requires integrating the fingertip with the palm and the thumb. He describes the thumb as advancing human beings maybe another 16 million years, in that without it, we couldn't throw a stone and so on. The human hand can work with an idea, through focussing and unifying yourself and what is on the edge of your world into a relation-ship of targeting. That can be done consciously, and it's the thumb that is key to that.

Wilson shows us the Barbary ape's hand and the human hand and explains the significance of the muscular difference between them. He then describes the effect of the hand developing a thumb and its ability to focus on a grip or grasp that then can create a missile, and how we can say that the hand built the brain. In a way, the hand itself is the outer brain.

So when young people bring their hands to turn wool into felt – which involves a lot of rubbing warm, wet, soapy wool together until it mats into felt – it is a very challenging experience for this outer brain, and many really struggle.

When you work in felt, you encounter a very benign, forgiving, soft, ephemeral point of resistance. You're building up the hand's intelligence, to be capable of receptivity to something outside its comfort zone. A student's tentativeness or forcefulness shows up in the quality of what's left after a felt-ing exercise.

If students can only do this with a pair of gloves, that's surprising on one level, but it's also understandable because the sensations may be overwhelm-ing and they can't always integrate them. But even the action with a glove is helpful, because they're also working towards a result. Some of these results suggest an immense level of skill, pressing down and rotating so that the felt ends up like a piece of leather, whereas other students have their hands almost floating like an air bubble, where they can't exert pressure with their will, express intention through their hand and then physically rotate and compress the wool into felt.

I often use felting as an indicator of the relationship between the student and their engagement with the world. You tend to find that the students who are not well adjusted into focus and grip can't produce what you might call a normal piece of felt. And you could ask "how do we re-step the development of grip? How do we re-step grasp?"

First of all, coming into physical resistance with something warm and benign. If it has too much of an animal smell, that can produce an extra and unnecessary rejection from the student. But there are students who have no hesitation around that, in that they befriend the sheep and its smell. So we can analyse the student's interaction in compressing material like felt or clay and shaping it. These emotional, intellectual and practical qualities give very clear yardsticks for a student's capacity to work with their foundational senses: movement, balance, life and touch.

Self and other

In Steiner's educational theory, the senses of touch, life, balance and movement are linked to the development of what he sees as their corresponding higher senses – sense of self and other (ego), thought, speech and hearing. So if we're aware of this idea of the foundational senses helping to activate the higher ones, then we're not only re-stepping the primary elements, but we're also building the precursors for further sensory development. There's a very clear correlation between the investment involved in touching the world and creating separation and connection and the relationship of oneself with the Other, which Steiner calls the ego.

This is a different definition of ego from Freud's and Jung's, which causes some problems with translation. In Steiner's view of the sense of ego, its foundation connects I with You. That's the very essence of being able to meet the Other in such a way that you so to speak absorb the Other, pre-presencing, so that you can meet the encounter without power over the other. This isn't confrontation, which would be egotistical.

This sense requires learning and refining. So a craft activity builds connection and separation, with a sense of touch as the first entry to re-stepping. The materials test the particular capacity of the student to be in the world, and then to meet the world in the encounter between their own terms and the community's terms.

As a craftsperson I'm the maker, but not necessarily the designer; I take the design from the community's consensus about what constitutes a jug. This situation positions the students in effectively assimilating the other senses, because in order to take that first sense of meeting between myself and the other and translating that as a practical capacity, the craft curriculum actually has to find ways of enabling students to do that in a way which is both age- and design-appropriate.

Different students get to different points along this journey. They might, for example, take on a role model and aspire to the social capacity for doing all of this, but at the same time not necessarily own it fully. Positive social living is when you actually adopt good habits, even if you don't fully know how to create them for yourself. There's an aspiration to move into the world, as opposed to simply looking at it.

Coming back to sheep, if you look at the fleece, it is another skin, extended outside the actual physical skin. So it's a boundary, and in a sense what we do is to take that intermediate boundary and make it into a new kind of boundary by compressing it into felt. We form a new skin as a slipper, tea cosy or a hat. Personal slippers seem to be of great value. Some students can manage this as a collaborative exercise in which they feel the slipper on each other's foot, so that they shape it around the other person's foot while felting it. If they can undertake that, then you have a real dialogue with some physical good will forming the fitted slipper.

What is needed of the therapeutic educator

We have to look not just at the relationship between the students, or between the student and the wider community; there is also a relationship between the therapeutic educator and the student. Staff members' willingness to engage with what might be called a disability requires a capacity to absorb the reality of a student, to show sufficient interest that they can feel recognised, without crossing the boundary into sentimentality. That's actually a very complex professional boundary; everybody knows that thinking "poor Daniel" isn't helpful because it doesn't elicit the necessary self-understanding that the students have to become aware of themselves.

That means, for the staff member, being separate from the students so that you can guide a student into a reflective moment or process. In offering that as a therapeutic tutor, a craftsperson or journeyperson, your success is dependent on being connected and separate at the same time. This goes right back to touch and a healthy sense of ego, in which my empathy is with you – but my request for you to change is role-modelled, which is not straightforward.

The tutor sets up expectations; Vygotsky talks about knowing the gap between your student and yourself sufficiently well that you can pull the expectation appropriately towards a new step. And unless that therapeutic gap can be gradually bridged, neither the student nor the teacher is going to succeed. This means confronting an appreciation of the student's situation without harbouring sentiment or anxiety around the trauma or unpleasantness of their situation.

Sometimes a student might go as far as physical assault, and then the Trust enters a supervision process to offer therapeutic help, both for the students and the staff member.

The most helpful thing that I've been involved in with staff who are not sure how to move a situation on is to try and separate out the event not as a personal situation, but a constitutional situation. The student has had a history in which they're not in charge; they're still in a way victimised by past events. To see this objectively means not portraying it personally as a student assault on staff, but as a condition in which other adults may be the antagonists in the relationship. Then you don't need to personalise it, but to understand that this behaviour results from those conditions in childhood and adolescence.

That skill of being able to see objectively that it wasn't the student directly but the consequences of a particular history leads to a very positive and immediate clearing up of the situation. It's not that the students should just walk away, but the trickier part may not be so much the member of staff's capacity to process it, but rather how to actually generate a reflective situation within the students so that it is less likely to happen or be repeated. *That* is more complicated but can often be arrived at through new positive experiences of personal achievement.

The de-escalation that's needed for a healthy therapeutic approach lives in the right role-modelling and practical performance of work or therapeutic learning. So Ruskin Mill Trust seeks to be centres of de-escalation through the appropriate environment, in which students with high arousal limitations are not provoked into acting on them, because the therapeutic offer is transformative. A skilled therapeutic educationalist is by nature a de-escalator, who knows how to bring in craft and land work to help with high sensory overload.

Working with the pain of the other

In staff training, we aim to share the skill of our educational toolkit. This involves absorbing the pain of the other, actually taking it on and knowing your own boundary, so it becomes a set of bite-sized, digestible processes between you and the student. By saying "yes" to you, I immediately take something of yourself inside me. On your behalf, I will release some of that burden by taking it off you, by meeting you in an unconditional context. If I have a medium of craft or resistance where the conversation can take place, I can actually even accelerate that.

But if Fields Two or Three, craft and farming, aren't there, it won't be so effective in the form of a simple conversation, because the engagement process that's needed is embodied, muscular rather than sedentary. Many of our students are residential, and by transforming their engagement from sedentary to physically performing, they come to own an internal experience and not just a verbal conversation. Not that a conversation doesn't go in, but if it's not performed in a bodily way, it doesn't actually transform into muscle memory.

So the word "therapeutic" is really, in our case, a claim to performative transformation. The student can shed, in small bites, previous histories of negative experience and generate new histories of affirmation. That happens because you've shaped a world in which their performance of a different way of being has been appreciated by a third party, which is very powerful. It's not just interpersonal, but collaboratively interpersonal. So the staff member has a toolkit which opens up the possibility of undertaking that very complex work. I think this is more complex than most people can appreciate; that may be a good thing, because if they really understood it, very few people might want to do it. Still, people never fully understand what they're giving themselves over to in a learning situation, but they do give trust.

We can also think of this as spiritual digestion. That means that I am partly accelerating the student's journey by actually saying to the student, "Do you know what, Daniel, right now I can take that on?" That can create a little free space for the student to exercise a new skill. But if it's just a verbal dialogue, the student is probably going to have to take that moment back because they haven't performed the change and keep repeating it until they internalise it.

But with craft and farming, you may not need to start by doing something two or three times. Let's do it once. If you can do green woodwork while I say to you, "Well, give me that worry", it is more than likely that you will have forgotten it by the end of the process. Therefore it doesn't have to come back, and actually you've moved on because somebody said to you, "Do you know now that I know you can do that? Could you do this?" So it's over, gone. Therefore, it doesn't have to be returned to Daniel as part of his identity.

Beyond talk alone

This is why I can be impatient with psychotherapeutic approaches which move from cognition to the emotional life but avoid transformative physical action, because I think it's skills that we need to give our students, not insights. Skills generate insights, which is a different approach in therapeutic education. They're not incompatible; I would simply rearrange the order of priority and say, "In Ruskin, this is where we start, with practice. The conversation comes later". In other words, don't open the wound before it's actually been worked on, because the trauma and pain can be worked on and often shed quite early.

Our students often have long histories of failed or inadequate talking-based approaches. Where psychotherapeutic approaches have gone on for many, many years on a very regular basis under a kind of legalistic contract, the kids are severely damaged, in that they have learned pastiche answers which don't in any way relate to the world or the present context. In ABA (applied behaviour analysis), the student can be trained into giving the designed response in order to limit antisocial behaviour. That's a kind of incarceration through linguistics, with clever answers that they haven't arrived at out of their own volition. It's not self-generated.

Self-generation is absolutely crucial because it's such a different approach to ABA, which is the therapy often prescribed in the US for autistic people. When we set up a centre in California, a regular sentiment from parents was "Can you give me my daughter or son back?" Parents often throw ABA away after a while because they can't see the kid anymore, because they've been locked up and they have a kind of veneer of taught behaviour.

My response to the parents was "Yes, we can, but it may take two years". Having asked the parents what that might look like from their perspective, the response was "I would like them to have a friend". Through Practical Skills Therapeutic Education, we were able to achieve this in most cases within 12 months.

The need for indignation

This is linked to a certain degree to my own personal biography, and my indignation about the lack of choices that people have when they're doing this type of work. I believe it should be possible to do this work on the basis of spiritual-scientific insight into human developmental approaches, but that has been so squashed that it gives me the urge towards entrepreneurship to change it. And that's very powerful in my biography.

If that indignation wasn't there, I don't think Ruskin Mill or myself would move beyond a more normal therapeutic approach; but I don't think it's good enough for me to leave it there. So there's that tricky piece in my biography which is an unrelenting search for getting other perspectives into the economy, and it's the economy I'm interested in. Not just private life, which is like fiddling with cake decoration. I'm interested in re-baking the cake, and that's another thing driving me.

When you go to the US, people are as sincere as anywhere in the world, wanting to work with learning difficulties. Or take a brilliant woman like Zhu Jingzhi in Nanjing. If you shake hands with those people and you can role model another level of depth in "walking the talk," people do listen. But if you don't push on the border of conflict, you'll never get there, which is always a little bit of a tricky area for some people. That's personal biography.

The phases of human development

Ruskin Mill has developed a certain amount of practical knowledge and multiple different perspectives on how children develop in terms of age. In many ways we have brought Steiner into the arena of different forms of insight. The last hundred years since his work have spawned a whole kaleidoscope of approaches.

Steiner's perspective is not without its critics, as of course other classical psychological and educational perspectives have been. But what may be unique to Steiner's perspective is his particular way of correlating a child or young person's physiology to their emotional and intellectual development. It's a holistic approach. In Steiner's presentation of how children develop into adolescence, he describes physiological phases in which emotional soul qualities also start to open up, alongside stages of intellectual development, right up to the sense of self-identity. He applies specific curriculum experiences to aid those processes.

Over the last hundred years, research has increasingly agreed with Steiner that young people do develop intellectually and emotionally in a staged process, and that we need to understand that and work with it. That wasn't the case in 1923. Then it was unique.

Within this broad perspective, young people at Ruskin Mill present what we might call a "spiky profile", in that their physiological development may be relatively normal on initial observation. But when you speak to them you may discover that there's a delay in speech and language and listening, and in an assessment you might discover other challenges, some quite surprising. Those might include the lack of appreciation of the other as they sit down at the table and eat a meal; the inability to communicate other than what they want to say, often repeatedly; a lack of eye-contact; over time you may discover that the sense of self is absent or they are very vulnerable. And yet maybe they're also a very fine 16 year old with a well-developed physique.

On further investigation, it becomes very clear that the young person has a "spiky profile" in that there isn't a coherence between age-appropriate sensory integration, emotional integration and the ability to use their physical body. They have the strength to move a full wheelbarrow, but they can't understand the relationship of the request to do so to that ability. So our assessment process needs a template that can identify that spiky disparity between physical bodily development and a lack of ability to use that body, as well as emotional relationships, which might be considered infantile but could go along with quite a well-developed, silent intellect.

The intellect's internal capacity doesn't appear readily in outside communication or understanding. Likewise, emotional awareness of the other is limited. But the initial *perception* is that there is a regular, normal young adult. So Ruskin Mill's assessment of a specific person's profile is central to understanding the baseline from which we can then offer a Practical Skills Therapeutic Education curriculum offer. In the arrangement of the seven fields, this Field Four of therapeutic education is nothing other than a well-developed and fairly deep level of understanding of the specific constellation of someone's sensory challenges.

So our assessment is based on the integration of what we call functional/practical senses, such as the sense of life, which is very much connected to the student's energy level. There's the sense of touch, which is the ability to meet the world on a very practical level, say in a farmyard, and not recoil or not be so attached to it that you can't stop touching things. In the sense of balance, you've got, for example, the ability to actually carry a bucket of water. Many students can't carry a bucket of water without spilling it. They're not sure how to operate the internal tension that can compensate for the heaviness of the water carried by the right or left hand. And there's the sense of movement. So life, touch, balance and movement are part of the assessment process of how students are understood and enabled to work practically and in doing so make rapid development.

Steiner creates an interesting controversy around developing the physical body. He argues that the development of the bodily physical senses is a task that parents and teachers should cultivate prior to developing the more cognitive senses, such as sight, intellect and a sense of identity. So in these phases, physical development is correlated to those physical senses of space or touch and enables their later development into cognitive skills. And the more cognitive, intellectual senses such as sight, hearing or sense of self emerge out of the healthy functioning of foundational senses.

The order of development

When students come to us at 16 or when children come to our schools at 10, these processes have not developed in sequence. In some ways nobody develops their senses in an absolutely orderly fashion, but our students have typically developed their senses in a very disorderly fashion. That might be through obsessive capacities or obsessive obstructions, through parental interest and a focus on certain skills only, or inherited skills or challenges that may have been there from the beginning.

One good example is a young lady who came with immensely skilful eyesight. She was able to observe the ground from her normal height, about 5'10", as if she was wearing a magnifying glass. So her ability to find things was disproportionately greater than any other skills she had, and she became very interested in archaeological projects. That parallels Heinrich Schliemann, who discovered Troy and Mycenae; his eyesight was way off the scale. It was so fine that he could see things that others had no capacity to observe. That capacity to see enabled him to discover Mycenae, and I always recall meeting this young lady and letting her know that she needed to find a task to apply this brilliant skill to.

However, her first interest was in finding insects and investigating them without a microscope. She would describe them in great detail because she had high levels of verbal skill and an extremely good memory. So on a Monday morning, it was very important for her to tell the rest of the class about her investigations in the insect world using her extraordinary sight and fascination, and then she would calm down. That was also one of the finest pieces of cross-classroom development at the time; the other children would very often forgive her challenging behaviour because they did learn something unique from her.

So some of the higher senses often enable exceptional capacities to be found and appreciated. And the task is to help those gifted children or young adults to become more functional and sociable, particularly in the domestic realm. They need to learn to be appreciative of others, to have rhythm, to care for themselves, to cook and to be convivial so that their skills can be appreciated by others. We don't want them to be left alone as a strange phenomenon or a caricature which others are inhibited from contacting because of their lack of relationship skills by comparison with their special skills.

So that's our task at Ruskin Mill. And through our understanding of therapeutic education ideas, by harnessing insights around the 12 senses, we can then profile what areas might as yet be undeveloped but can also contribute in a social and intellectual context with practical skills. Or a student might have a strong emotional capacity but no interest in performing anything of value to others, and the craft curriculum might help to put into context that tension between their interest in sociability and their lack of action.

Some of these insights are drawn from Steiner's ingenuity in developing a sequence of learning programmes that were also connected to these developmental phases and encouraged the development of intellectual capacities *after* emotional capacities, so that the children's emotional and socialising process was not left out.

Rudolf Steiner's educational innovations

It's worth emphasising that Steiner's commitment to education was not at first with regular "neurotypical" kids, but with a young man who had a significant learning disability. He was invited to tutor this young man very intensively and developed a programme and teaching materials that brought him to the point where he could participate in life as a developmentally ordinary adult. The young man later became a doctor, which he would not normally have had a chance of doing given his initial profile. Starting from that extraordinary achievement and collaboration with the young man, Steiner could then see how to place a restorative process for all children through his curriculum innovation.

So Steiner's educational approach is based on the intellectual and emotional capacities are unified through physical development. His educational methods are now worldwide and are behind countless innovative projects. Ruskin Mill Trust owes a debt of gratitude to his pioneering and original thinking.

So this physiological capacity and intellectual-emotional capacity were situated in a very practical curriculum. If you couldn't actually get the body, the emotional life and the intellectual life ready to grow the next step, from the physical to emotional or from emotional to intellectual, he suggested that education was not being as efficient as it could be.

Working with spiky developmental profiles

The children and young adults who come to us at Ruskin Mill have these spiky profiles, and our task is to use the insights of the different fields to firstly carry out a baseline assessment and then propose a curriculum that offers restoration. Therefore, there is a re-stepping of some primordial elements, which we've researched intensively. We note – along with other researchers – that if we can step back into the early stages of physical coordination but undertaken in a way appropriate to the student's chronological age so there is no sense of humiliation or a feeling of failure, we can touch those stages of development and then accelerate quite rapidly, provided the motivation is also congruent with the young adult or child's.

At this point, staff training is often crucial, as staff need to be able to describe and situate the young person's emotional spiky development and understand that they need to orientate their physical skills into focus, grasp and step and in doing so contribute. One route into becoming skilful in the world is to find experiences in which you overcome barriers to learning. And the practical entry into learning is something that most students and children are willing to participate in, in spite of their often significant experience of past failure. These are very courageous children.

How we assess young people has a number of different facets. On the one hand, there is a practical investigative-assessment profile in which the functional physical senses in particular are assessed as we described. Language and verbal assessment is centred on what we might call the more cognitive senses, and there is a further assessment of the young people's social capacities.

There is an assessment of someone's practical skill sets, which could even come down to "how do you walk across the road in time to be able to cross, given the fact that it's not red when you arrive?" There's an assessment of how you might sit and negotiate with your peers at the dinner table, or how you participate in your relationships with the more cognitive skills, such as listening and communicating and being as clear as you can, recognising others in yourself. So those three aspects are functionalised in what Steiner calls the 12 senses.

The next part of the assessment would be residential if the student requires it. Some of our students live at home, some are with us during the week, and we care for some all year round. Here we're assessing them against some of the principles of the seven care qualities (Chapter 5). Very often in the residential assessment, you can find an arhythmical element of their lifestyles, where they've developed some quite challenging habits, which often excludes others. Or their rhythm of relationships might be disrupted, or their sleep patterns only start at 4 AM. Here we have to take great care, because the student's capacity to be independent later on in their journey depends on a curriculum that undertakes a restoration of those life processes.

If any two or three of these are disrupted, there might be a permanent requirement for additional adult support. And local authorities are keen on eventually being able to cost what the impact might be of a young person going through Ruskin Mill and how much support they would then need to provide after two or three years with us. What do they spend initially and what do they save in the long term? So in our methodology, we take the practical world as an entry point in this care delivery offer.

For example: can you make your bed, which in a certain sense is one of the crafts of domestic relationships? Can you learn to cook a meal? Can you undertake personal self-care? Can you maintain your sense of warmth? Can you actually support your sense of nutrition and nourishment? Can you functionalise your whole processes of secretion in a healthy way? Which means your whole toilet routines and your ability to sweat. Students need to actually become able to take self-responsibility after two years. So the students are in a bit of an incubation chamber, being helped and supported to overcome those challenges.

One of the first things we provide is a crossover between these educational activities and the practical work. For example, the whole food culture is now clearly correlated to being able to provide healthy emotional development. There is more intellectual facilitation when the right type of nutrition is provided, including the ability to actually sustain one's sense of purpose in a practical task. All this goes right down to developing a healthy sense of life, which connects not only to the practical functional senses but to the aesthetic or cognitive senses as well. So the routines and the life processes of the residential environment are supported by the daytime environment and very often in the practical entry points of learning; that 24-hour crossover is part of our offer.

Being robbed of childhood

One often unseen dimension of the manipulation of children is how they're exposed to adult attitudes inappropriately. From a certain perspective, child protection has not fully included the antisocial interface between some families and their social contexts. That lack of protection can often propel children into becoming young adults emotionally, but without a sense of identity to suit. This rupturing of childhood into a premature adoption of adult attitudes can be some of the most crippling, damaging experiences that some children have had before coming to Ruskin Mill Trust.

That robbing of childhood wonder and gaze has the effect of corrupting attitudes into quite a powerful, negative state of cynicism; children have lost their childhood but aren't able emotionally to deal with the adult world they are trapped in. Reversing this is probably one of our most challenging tasks. Often the intellectual capacities have found the language of cynicism as a defence, and therefore the emotional capacities can't really flourish, and as a result practical capacities are also often bereft. But we can work with that situation.

One of the tasks that comes from understanding the stages of development that Steiner and others have described is this: After maybe re-stepping some of the emotional stages of development, how can you move that towards a sense of purpose so that the child or young adult can actually have access to the sort of self-identity that Maslow might call their "self-actualization"? That correlates very well with Steiner's idea that the sense of self in its more developed state is also the ability to receive the other without coming under the coercive power of the other. You can withstand not only your own immediate impulses but also your tendency to give in to the other. You learn both to give from yourself to the other but also to receive so that it's reciprocal. And one of the tasks later on in the Trust's work is to bring students to that normal condition, to what can happen in a healthy development, and devise interventions which are often practical, not just emotional. Then the student arrives at a stage of development where you can withstand the encounter with the other alongside your own sense of self-identity, which can only really be developed as a result of the appreciation of others.

So you can claim your sense of identity from yourself, but it's usually insecure if it actually hasn't been endorsed by the other. And so craftwork and the service-orientated activities of the farm, work experience and the social enterprise are highly developed within the Trust. We audit them against the benchmark of how they facilitate that new capacity to accept appreciation from your peers and community around you – which normally takes place from 16 upwards in a regular development but may only be achieved nearer 21 in practice.

The contemporary apprenticeship model

We identify three stages in young people's learning journeys. The first is overcoming barriers to learning, simply becoming able to actually engage with a practical skill or activity. And those barriers may go back a long way and be very deep-seated. The second is becoming skilful, mastering a particular craft, learning to work with a particular animal and so on. The third is becoming able to give the results of your activity to the wider community in various ways – as a gift, through social enterprise and so on.

The first progression from overcoming barriers to learning to becoming skilful is a very personal journey. Some students can move through it quite fast, but others may take several years to do what another student could do in six months. It's a personal journey and we're never sure about it when a student arrives, because of the spiky profile that each of the students has, the interventions and the agencies they've encountered. So we put the various fields of practice in front of the student; at a certain point they need to be guided in their choice, but also it increasingly comes from them. And in a way the appropriateness of their choices does indicate the level of maturity and the speed at which they can move forward.

The role-modelling that the Trust provides is one in which the capacity of the tutor or teacher can draw out the student's objectives that need to be realised in that moment. The tutor's self-mastery lies in being able to recognise the gap between what the student knows they can do and the potential of what that student can become able to do. This is one of the more skilful things that the Trust is able to provide, and this drawing into that new grasping of their potential arises from the empathy of the tutor and the trust of the student. You move into becoming skilful because you've achieved the tutor's expectation around the opportunities they saw. The skill set that then often develops is one of an interest in providing services which have partly been developed through the goodwill of those who have been recipients of the student's private work.

For example, in the more practical catering areas, students know that they are appreciated for the tasks they've fulfilled and their ability to enter into the third stage, which is contributing to the world. The tutor's role-modelling and understanding, and their ability to bring out high levels of competence in these students, brings the student "flowing into the tutor's slipstream".

This ability to enter the world as it is, on the terms that the world requires, means the adaptation of a student who when they arrived may have spent 95% of their time in denial of the world and denial of themselves, because they had experienced so much failure. The rapidity with which they enter the world based on those relationships and tasks enables them to meet this third stage of giving back to the world.

In the Trust's term "contemporary apprenticeship", what we mean is that the old order of apprenticeship in which you were subjugated to the master's will, in no way describes the current practice. What "contemporary" means in the Ruskin Mill context is that the tutors' self-mastery has a new edge to it, in the ability to understand the context of the student as well as expecting them to meet the skill of the master. "Contemporary apprenticeship" is the tutor's capacity to become a co-learner with the student, so that we limit the sense of any rejection by the students.

Historically, any young person had to submit to the will of the workshop culture, which was often not necessarily the most therapeutic, especially if you had had a very damaged early life. The contemporary vision of that relationship is the new co-learning opportunities through a relationship of trust. The reason we sense that it's an appropriate form is that the students themselves find themselves learning in a healthy way by trusting another adult for the first time, not within a parental relationship, but in a relationship where the students see the teacher's mastery of the practical skills and understand that from a visual perspective.

The students learn by copying the visual movement of the master, following the slipstream of the movement. If the master can't address the needs of the student, it's an old form and not a contemporary form. And the training of tutors as therapeutic educators needs to be based principally on an increasingly conscious sense of the 12 senses that need refinement and development.

Rudolf Steiner as educational theorist

Rudolf Steiner (1861–1925) was many things, not least among them a classic educational theorist. Born the son of a railway telegrapher in what is now Croatia but was then the Austro-Hungarian Empire, he was a typical scholarship child, very bright but poor. Along with this, from an early age he had very unusual spiritual experiences.

He started his working life as the natural science editor of a new edition of Johann Wolfgang von Goethe's extensive scientific works, followed by a PhD that became his book *The Philosophy of Freedom*. To support himself as a student in Vienna, he worked as tutor and carer for the four children of the Specht family, in particular the 11-year-old Otto, who had social and learning difficulties and was considered ineducable. Steiner developed a careful programme that enabled Otto to enter a school and eventually become a doctor.

Moving to Weimar, Steiner became a literary figure and a popular lecturer to working-class audiences. In Berlin, he was invited to become the leader of the Theosophical Society in Germany and Austria-Hungary. This global movement sought to find the shared wisdom underlying the world's many religions, and was transformative in many areas of human culture, from western literature to Asian politics.

Steiner, however, rejected the Society's increasing focus on Eastern religions, particularly Hinduism, and highlighted western spiritual and esoteric traditions, leading to the foundation of the Anthroposophical Society in 1912. In this role he was an indefatigable organiser, moving the Society's base to Switzerland, designing and working on its Goetheanum building near Basel, and designing a second one after the first one fell prey to arson. He was also a massively popular public speaker, attracting huge crowds in the aftermath of the First World War and pursuing a punishing programme of lectures right up to his death.

As this sketch suggests, Steiner's legacy is very wide-ranging. It includes his contribution to the further development of Goethe's approach to science, which remained influential in the German-speaking world and contributes to present-day biologists like Stephen Jay Gould and what has been called the extended evolutionary synthesis.

Steiner is the founder of the biodynamic farming movement, from which contemporary organic farming broke off. Associated with this is a long tradition of therapeutic care, well-known through the Camphill communities. As a dramatist he had a major impact on what is known as Method acting via Konstantin Stanislavski and Michael Chekov. Other developments include the movement art eurythmy and anthroposophical medicine. Figures influenced by him include artists like Joseph Beuys, Wassily Kandinsky and director Andrei Tarkovsky and reformers such as Albert Schweitzer and Rachel Carson. Contemporary anthroposophical initiatives include the Triodos Bank (social finance) and the Weleda and Dr Hauschka skincare companies.

Steiner and education

However, one of his most enduring legacies is in education, best known via the Waldorf school movement he initiated, the largest independent school movement in the world with several thousand kindergartens, schools and other institutions. Initially developed for the children of employees at the Waldorf-Astoria cigarette factory in Stuttgart, the school was deeply radical in its day for being both co-educational and fully comprehensive, educating both the children of shopfloor workers and those of managers. The curriculum was deeply practical rather than based on rote learning. There is not surprisingly an extensive body of literature and practice associated with these schools (e.g. Stehlik, 2019).

Steiner's legacy as educational theorist is much wider than Waldorf schools alone; he was a very effective and popular adult educator for most of his working life. His talks on education run to at least 20 volumes, notably his final "Education Course", including his lectures and faculty work with the initial Waldorf school but addressing many other audiences throughout Britain, Germany, the Netherlands and Switzerland (see e.g. Steiner, 2003, 2013). Steiner's work has had a huge impact on other educational approaches, which have often belatedly caught up with the importance of practical activities, nature-based learning, comprehensive and co-educational approaches.

For Steiner, the goal of education is not a narrowly instrumental one of fitting young people into the immediate needs of the labour market. Instead it is centrally about human freedom, and how we can find our own place in the wider world – the natural world around us, the made-human world and the longer flow of history and culture.

This leads to a continuous concern for integration and connection in the content of education. Rather than separating study into different boxes to suit the needs of test structures and teacher allocation, the child needs to understand how *this* relates to *this* and helps us grasp, and act in, the world as a whole. But connection is not simply intellectual: it is practical and hence also emotional, connectedness. Thus, Steiner highlights the importance of routine and rhythm, emotional warmth and practical activities such as craft, making food, gardening, music and art: many of the things that make human life worthwhile.

A developmental approach to education

In Steiner's view the young child needs above all to experience the world as *good*; as they develop security, they need to be surrounded by *beauty*; the teenager who is securely grounded in this can develop a burning concern for *truth*. All of this enables the child to find the freedom to make themselves and contribute to the world around them: as we know, young people who have experienced the world as traumatic, who are alienated from the human world around them and who are immersed in the untruths of psychologically damaging environments struggle in very different ways.

This is one way into Steiner's most distinctive theoretical contribution, a genuinely developmental approach to human education, one in which young children are not simply incomplete adults to be filled up with content that is meaningful to adults but not to them. Hence the approach is not to start from developing intellectual concepts, but rather to build those on a foundation of healthy emotional development, which in turn is preceded by a practical capacity for healthy interactive play.

In theory this isn't very controversial: Montessori agrees with this position and even the English national curriculum, like many official systems, is supposed to start at a point where children have had a significant level of play. However in practice the tendency in the Anglophone world in particular is to encourage children to work on academic skills at a very early stage.

Steiner asks who the child is at each stage of its development. This can be readily seen in a Steiner kindergarten where play is central. In parallel with continental best practice – including in Finland, often held up as a model in terms of "results" – reading and writing aren't begun until the age of six or seven, by which time most children are ready for them and interested.

It should be no surprise if younger children, very many of whom don't yet have the capacities to learn reading easily and may only have limited interest in the content they are offered, often struggle with learning to read at three or four and sometimes build up strong resistance – but this of course underlines the value of a genuinely developmental approach which at every stage asks what is genuinely age-appropriate.

Young children *should* be playing in the mud; contrast this to the reality of so many young people's lives, from three or four to their mid-20s, of sitting at desks and engage in rote learning, being taught to the test and uninterested in the actual content except as a route to employment. Everyday "common sense" sees this as a good outcome, with those who are unwilling or unable to fit into this being the problem – and does not see education as having a role in supporting the child's actual development other than to provide bigger chairs to sit on.

Ruskin Mill works with young people who have been subjected to trauma and disadvantage, with educational differences and difficulties and behavioural challenges. Steiner's conceptualisation of the phases of human development invites staff to ask what developmental stages may have been missed, not only in formal education but also in their wider lives. How can these be approached again, in a different and age-appropriate way, what PSTE calls re-stepping?

Particular farm animals and specific crafts can prove really helpful for individual students (without excluding the possibility of relevant therapies and medicine) in engaging with these missed stages – whether learning to communicate with adults, managing to balance yourself in a physical task, integrating focus, gaze and step on the pole lathe, developing persistence in spoon-forging etc. While re-stepping is a specific need, it points to the wider need for developmentally appropriate education.

Beyond a normalising approach to the human being

Characteristic of Steiner's approach to education is a deep acceptance of the individuality of each person. The task of education, even therapeutic education, is not to bring someone in line with an imagined norm of how to be in the world, with success measured by a behaviourist mimicking of desired behaviours, as sometimes prescribed for autism, for example. As the term neurodiversity suggests, minds are *different*, existing on a wide spectrum; so too are personalities, bodies – and lives, as we start to shape our own.

In this approach, each individual develops in line with who they are. Ruskin Mill's goal of self-generated conscious action means enabling them to become genuinely free in determining this process. That may of course include re-stepping stages missed in childhood or working with behaviours that cause suffering to self or others; but it is never a question of there being an ideal human being that the young person with learning difficulties (or the "ordinary" child in a classroom) falls short of and has to be coaxed, punished or shamed into embodying better.

A better way of thinking about it is to say that the healer's (or teacher's) wound is not fundamentally different from the young person's wound. Like trauma, the wound cannot be unmade, but it can be healed and put in the context of the whole person. We aren't just trying, as in behaviourist approaches, to make someone into an unwilling imitation of an imagined norm: we ask what *this* child's gift to the world is. How can we bring it out and help them to express it in ways that can be authentically recognised and appreciated by others?

Thus, the Ruskin Mill approach – of growing and harvesting food in keeping with the seasons and as part of the whole farm, of preparing and serving it either for oneself and other students (at a college, in a student residence) or in a café, and of having it seen and appreciated by others as well as nourishing one's own body – is not about making the child "normal". It is about helping them to live in all aspects of their life in a way that they and others value.

Figure 4.6 Can you do this? A student-made stool at Ruskin Mill College

Bibliography

Biesta, G. (2014). *The beautiful risk of education.* Routledge.
Freire, P. (2017). *Pedagogy of the oppressed.* Penguin. (Original Portuguese publication 1971).
Kincheloe, J. L., & Cannella, G. S. (Eds.). *Kidworld: Childhood studies, global perspectives, and education.*: Ringgold.

Lachman, G. (2007). *Rudolf Steiner: An introduction to his life and work*. Floris.

Lindenberg, C. (2017). *Rudolf Steiner: A biography*. Rudolf Steiner Press.

Marchand, T. H. J. (Ed.). (2010). *Making knowledge: Explorations of the indissoluble relation between mind, body and environment*. Wiley-Blackwell.

Robinson, K. (2016). *Creative schools: Revolutionizing education from the ground up*. Penguin.

Stehlik, T. (2019). *Waldorf schools and the history of Steiner education*. Palgrave Macmillan.

Steiner, R. (2003). *Education: An introductory reader*. Rudolf Steiner Press.

Steiner, R. (2013). *Study of man: General education course*. Rudolf Steiner Press. (Original German publication 1913).

Tyson, R. (2017). *The rough ground: Narrative explorations of vocational Bildung and wisdom in practice*. Department of Education, Stockholm University., 2017

Wilson, F. R. (2010). *The hand: How its use shapes the brain, language and culture*. Vintage.

5 Holistic care

At home and at work

Upper Grange is a large 18th-century farmhouse on a hillside at the edge of town: walk out of the gate and up a muddy lane and you are walking across fields, rising gently to look over the hills, rivers, trees and houses that make up Stroud's five valleys. In the evening, you look out from the bedroom windows to see the lights of the town, and you might hear owls hooting.

The building is a warren of quirky but handsome rooms, furnished with warmth to create a welcoming place to stay. One half of the building is a student residence, where young people attending Ruskin Mill College live in a supported setting. The other half is a training centre, where staff from across the Trust themselves experience and learn to provide the kind of care that vulnerable young people need.

Upper Grange models with the visiting staff what Ruskin Mill wants them to create for students: a smoothly flowing rhythm that can welcome visitors, invite students to participate in household tasks and integrate the daily crises and ups-and-downs of a household. Visitors gradually notice a sense of calm and warmth, care and attention that is "more easily caught than taught", and a respect for the time needed for the different processes of a household: growing and preparing food, cleaning and washing up, laundry and bed-making, shared time together.

Probably this building has always housed a certain complexity in daily life: all these bedrooms, in a farmhouse this size, must represent not only multiple generations of a family but also apprentices and living-in employees. The larger spaces must have included not only a household kitchen but also space for preserving and processing food from the farm, spaces for business and spaces for visitors.

When you enter, the building might be filled with the smell of fresh bread being made by staff on a training course, sending a message of care and the promise of food through the corridors and keyholes. Craft items made by staff or students – pottery mugs, felt mats, glass vases, wooden stools – help underline the sense that homeliness is made, not bought. There are seasonal flowers from the garden in the rooms, and depending on the nearest festival

DOI: 10.4324/9781003361541-5

Figure 5.1 Baking skills for residential care: Upper Grange training

there might be branches with Easter eggs hanging from them, a Christmas tree or something else marking the rhythm of the year. The transition from outside to inside is marked by the offer of felt slippers to replace muddy boots and handmade hooks for dripping coats.

In the garden

Outside is a lawn with a pond supporting greater biodiversity, a pizza oven and spaces for craft like green woodworking and pottery. You follow the paved walkways between herbs, vegetable and flower beds in the main garden space, enclosed by espaliered apples and fan-trained pear trees. Here is a polytunnel, here a rose garden and a pergola with grapes good enough to make wine (wine from nearby Woodchester is sold commercially), and here are buildings used as a wormery, toolshed and potting shed. Against the hedge are compost bays, a hive and an underground watertank collecting rainwater for the garden. This close to open country, badgers and deer sometimes break in as well as other animals and many birds. The ecological context – and particularly the insects, rising from the pond or bees drawing nectar from flowers – is an important part of what the garden can teach.

The large garden is used both by residential students and by staff on training courses in Upper Grange, studying care, nutrition and biodynamic gardening. It offers many different learning opportunities: how to sow and plant garlic, potatoes, shallots or beans; how to care for plants through weeding and spreading compost; how to make the compost and time it; how to harvest plants. The soil here is not great, so much space is given over to flowers and herbs. Beside the house are holding areas for woodchips, farmyard manure and leaves that can be used in compost making.

Perhaps the most important learning that staff can bring back to the different residences where they work, as with the building itself, is the feel of the garden and the sense of life: *this* is what your garden could feel like for the young people you work with, and what you learn on the course is what they could learn too.

Learning to make a home

On the training side of the building, the main activity is home-making courses aimed primarily at Ruskin Mill's residential staff, part of their induction but also available at deeper levels within the Trust's extensive training offer. Participants come and stay from across Britain for several days at a time, an immersive experience that allows a more reflective learning. Often too older students join particular activities, gaining qualifications up to England and Wales' level 3 (school leaving) in the process.

Staff need to grasp the students' life processes and the care qualities needed to respond to them. They learn the basics of making a home, down to simple elements like setting a table and supporting students to do the same. They experience the "seed to table" curriculum that connects planting, gardening and harvesting food, making and eating group meals to composting food waste in the start of a new yearly cycle. They explore how to bring in festivals to help mark the rhythm of the year, and how to make homemade pizza outdoors with students for a special evening.

They learn how to engage in relevant crafts such as candle-making, felting Cotswold wool to make coasters or tablemats, or green woodworking to make handles for butter knives. They find out how craft items can be used to make a difference. In the widest sense, they learn how to create a supportive space for students, what it takes to make a home. Going back to their own provisions, staff have learned how to audit their residence against Ruskin Mill's list of care qualities: for example, what can we do for students with the garden we have? Can we grow food with them, will it provide flowers for the house, could we make an outdoors oven?

Being what we need

All this helps them to understand what students need, to grasp the vision and values of the overall student experience that Ruskin Mill residential care fits within, and to understand how their work in student residences contributes to the overall process of therapeutic education: "why do we do what we do?" Depending on staff's pre-existing experience, the course might serve to give them a flavour of what a student residence should be like, offer a refresher, give inspiration or help maintain a sense of purpose.

Trainees learn about key skills such as positive role-modelling and empathetic listening, and the importance of an unconditional positive regard that will enable them to be effective mentors. They come to understand how to find a balance so the home is neither too chaotic nor too formal for young people's needs: how to integrate the flow of events, crises and needs and respond well.

They also come to understand the difference between creating a warm environment and a finger-wagging prescriptiveness about how to live. While in Ruskin Mill Trust's care, young people are supported to make a further round of development. This takes place within a variety of relationships in which they rebuild their framework of perspectives, self-understanding and cognitive reasoning where possible. Nutrition is a key influence which may have further cycles of development throughout their later life once they have found an entry point.

Perhaps most importantly, staff learn how to step into their role rather than simply fulfil a job description. Genuinely helping others requires being authentic with yourself, and finding a good relationship with the vision and values that other staff in the Trust are also bringing to their encounter with pupils and students. It also requires taking the other deeply seriously: staff learn how to carry out a student study (Chapter 6) based on their observations of particular students.

Just like any young people learning how to live in and make a home, those in Ruskin Mill provisions benefit most from adults doing tasks *with* them – harvesting and preparing food, cleaning up afterwards, doing rooms and laundry, gardening – rather than having too much done *for* them. And like any young people, their capacities vary, and the task of the adult is to see this and offer them a way into the task so they can learn appropriately. After all, many of these tasks – cooking, gardening, craft, DIY – are things that adults also perform at radically different levels of skill, forming the basis for many a TV programme dramatising the fact and gripping large audiences finding new inspiration for their own daily lives.

On the residential side

A quick peek into the shared spaces of the student residence next door, while they are at college for the day, shows the training put into practice. There is a deep sense of warmth, from the colour scheme through the use of natural materials, to the comforting smell of a well-lived-in home. The living room is welcoming and relaxed.

Wood, wool and plants set the tone for the building, while the student voice is present everywhere – in their own art and craftwork; in larger craft pieces made in collaboration with students; literally, in the "Student Voice" newsletter that they produce; and in the choice of leisure materials.

The large kitchen and dining room is a convivial living area, entered from the living room on one side or from the garden on the other. There is good space for cooking together, and plenty of light. Just outside are the stairs up to the independence flat.

Sunfield

The holistic support and care training at Upper Grange has a sister training, Upper Grove, at Sunfield in Worcestershire's Clent Hills, for staff working with a diverse group of deeply challenged children with complex needs, which is being developed onsite where they live. All students enter the practical tasks of life according to their abilities. Some are still becoming familiar with the skills of hand dexterity, whilst others voluntarily support and care for their environment. The staff are trained in understanding very small, even micro-steps of development, where they then can appreciate and support the students no matter how apparently bite-size a particular step is. The residential offer for these children at Sunfield is an exceptional one, and is kept under constant innovation and review because of the range and depth of their needs and the changing student body from one year to the next.

The café

A short bus ride or drive away from Upper Grange – or, on a nice day, a 2-hour walk over Rodborough and Minchinhampton Common – you arrive at the entrance to Ruskin Mill once again. This time you go up the stairs into the café, where students supported by staff provide a full-day service from 10 to 4, including hot lunches and salads, hot and cold drinks and delicious cakes. The salads in particular are often fantastic, with food that may have been picked that day from a few hundred yards away. The café also caters professionally for many of the events and training courses at Ruskin Mill.

Where possible, Ruskin Mill colleges and even schools include cafés or shops that allow students to engage with the public and gain work experience in different settings. The functional skills involved are considerable – consider all the tasks needed to make a café work, and how students learn the connections between the different processes both within the café and on the farm. The public-facing engagement also builds confidence and helps students step more fully into the adult world: with suitable support and in an appropriate environment, they can go beyond the experience of only being looked after and move into greater autonomy. Perhaps most importantly, this independence can involve seeing and serving others and the wider community: it is not an isolated consumer experience.

The farm shop

On the ridge above the Horsley Valley are a collection of warm-coloured limestone buildings. Here are Gables Farmhouse and Tipputs Inn, both on the

Figure 5.2 Becoming a barista: working at Ruskin Mill café

Old Bath Road. Running steeply downwards, a trap for GPS-directed lorries and for anyone when icy is Hay Lane. In a courtyard, beside the willow basket workshop, is Ruskin Mill's farm shop.

As you come in, there are shelves of local and imported organic vegetables: all the produce of the farm together with more exotic fare from further afield. Onions and potatoes, apples and pears from the trees you can see across the gate sit beside oranges and avocadoes.

Inside, fridges hold farm-fresh salad, spinach, spring greens, parsley, celery or purple sprouting broccoli depending on season. Here too are trout from the fish farm, caught every Tuesday morning, along with biodynamic beef and pork. Farm-fresh eggs and in season amazing squashes sit on a table. Staples are sold loose to avoid packaging – sunflower seeds, oats, rice – and alongside products familiar from any health food store are other locally made and grown products like soaps.

In the entrance, sitting on handmade shelves, are student-made baskets and other craft items, cards for sale, biodynamic yearbooks and the Herbalists Without Borders handbook. This month, the farm newsletter highlights student Hattie's blackcurrant and apple jam, with a photo of her making it and discussion of how the farm's blackcurrants are frozen so jam and cordials can be made all year round. On the table are jars of the jam for sale, along with rhubarb and ginger jam, tomato sauce and chilli oil.

Students in the social enterprise

The farm shop is not only there to sell what students have grown, cooked and made. Like the café, it is also a space where students work, meet the public and learn, supported by staff. When students have become able to benefit from the experience, they can learn many different functional skills in a shop: taking in deliveries and restocking, processing and pricing – and battling to have the best pricing gun. Managing the till involves not only calculations, weighing purchases, handling cash or card payments, staff discounts and other complications; it means meeting people in a responsible role.

The clientele are mostly local and staff, familiar with the shop and the students and meeting them as they deserve. Stopping to chat with familiar faces is often a valued moment in everyone's day. There is a friendly buzz at busy times and the shop feels exactly like an old-fashioned neighbourhood health food shop – which of course it is.

In the process, students develop confidence; they know what is in the store and they come in as shoppers in turn. Through pricing and conversations, they also develop a lived sense of what things cost and what good food is like, necessary skills for independent living. They often like the realism of the shop situation: they are here as adults, serving other adults who do not buy food out of politeness or charity.

At the café and the farm shop, students not only experience a sense of warmth and care, but they also learn how to share this with others: welcome them, help them find what they want, serve or sell them nourishing food and drink. There is a clear rhythm to the working day and the week – the training day, the delivery. Students need to learn to embody constancy and become trustworthy, in serving the right portion or handling money in the intersection between the customer and the shop or café.

It can be powerful for young people to be on the other side of the counter for the first time. They come to speak more clearly and politely, adopting a more professional orientation. They are often proud of the products they sell and their knowledge of them – that bag of salad may be food they have grown or collected themselves, after all. At times they and their tutors will bring craft items or food, like Hattie's jam, to sell in the shop. In the exchange with the student, the customer's appreciation of what they have purchased is by extension an appreciation of the work they have done and of themselves as an individual. Feedback, positive and negative, is not directly personal as from a teacher, but rather facilitated through this real-world process as with craft or farming: it is no less meaningful and powerful for that.

Care to support autonomy

Chapters one to four lay out a valuable but potentially challenging learning journey. How can we really situate ourselves in the particularities of place? How can we learn to work with the resistance of the material world? How can we see all the interconnected relationships and rhythms of nourishment that support our physical life? How can we use whatever real-world tasks we face to overcome our own personal limitations and become more capable of acting autonomously, as genuinely free individuals in relationship with others?

These are lifelong tasks, which we encounter not only once but repeatedly as we mature and age, as our lives and circumstances change, and as the world asks different things of us. For young people who may already be struggling with learning differences and difficulties, carrying past wounds of many kinds and without the confidence that others in their age group may benefit from, this learning journey asks a lot. Of course transformation involves challenges which are big enough to be significant: but how does Ruskin Mill ensure that "big enough" does not become "too much" for the young people it works with?

Field Five, holistic support and care, is about providing a safe and nourishing environment within which young people are supported to flourish, with an appropriate balance of relaxation and positive challenges. "Holistic" here is not a code word for alternative; from the Greek, it literally means seeing, and integrating, the whole. Thus as we have seen, the seed-to-table curriculum connects the whole life cycle of a plant in students' own experience: from digging the ground to serving the food; or, in a Ruskin Mill shop, from cutting the willow to selling the basket, from the birth of the trout to selling it.

This is also part of the three-stage learning process (Chapter 4): overcoming the barriers keeping students from learning, then mastering the skill, then producing something that the wider community recognises as meaningful through eating, using or buying it. For Ruskin Mill students, the purchase of their items by a stranger is in some ways a more significant validation than the well-meaning response of a parent or carer, who they may feel would love it anyway. But when, in a residential provision, the food they have grown, harvested and prepared is willingly eaten by their peers, or craft items they have made are used by others, that is also a powerful sign that what they have done is genuinely good – they have mastered not just "how to do it" as a learning exercise but also how to produce something that others genuinely appreciate, something that is meaningful in the wider community.

The 24-hour curriculum

This personal learning journey, the seed-to-table curriculum or the cycle of the seasons on the farm all help to make connections that bring together a whole. But at an even more immediate level, the connection between the different parts of a young person's day or week is fundamental, and particularly when they have physical dis/abilities and health conditions of various kinds. Their needs and challenges do not go away with the transition between home, school or college and free time. How can they be supported with this?

Ruskin Mill's young people live in a variety of situations, depending on many different factors. Across the Trust, there are currently just under 400 young people, including both school pupils and college students (16–25). Some live with their families. Others live in residential provisions except for weekends, or all term, or in some cases all year round. Ideally these provisions have three students to a household: together with staff, this creates a social group with relevant dynamics. This situation creates a cultural identity of working in the world, and the houses can be distributed throughout the community.

Others again take part in Shared Lives schemes, in long-term placements within specially trained carers' own homes, short breaks and respite care. There is no one-size-fits-all model of care: Ruskin Mill accommodates according to need.

The 24-hour curriculum aims to bring consistency to pupils' and students' lives. As we have seen at Upper Grange, a key part of this is through the training of residential staff and ensuring that residential provisions have the same orientation to caring for young people that they find in their school or college and offer similar opportunities for less formal learning.

Cooking, washing up, laundry, cleaning and the other tasks of homemaking can all be undertaken with the same spirit that these or other work tasks are done in college or school. In the bigger picture, of course, the skills to live in a family, to develop friendships or to live with varying degrees of independence all take work and support. At the residential part of Upper Grange, the "independence flat" is lived in alone by a student finishing their time at Ruskin Mill and now able to live more autonomously – for many, a huge transformation of their capacities by comparison with when they arrived.

Connection through food and craft objects produced during their study time and used at home is another aspect of the 24-hour curriculum: wrought-iron coat hooks, felted coasters or slippers, glass vases, wooden stools, wicker baskets and pottery mugs or bowls are common sights in Ruskin Mill residential settings. A third dimension, when possible, is continuity of care, where the same support staff may be with a student in different parts of their lives, or at least where residential staff are familiar with what the study environment is like and vice versa. Integration of the outer world, then, is important in enabling the young person to develop a coherent sense of self.

The seven care qualities

For students, the overarching continuity between the different parts of their lives at Ruskin Mill comes from a consistent and shared approach to care, synthesised as the seven care qualities for day and residential students alike. These are developed out of Rudolf Steiner's (2002) list of seven life processes in his *Riddle of Humanity*. Similar to other lists, not least in the UK's national curriculum, he notes that already in the first few hours of human existence, we need to breathe, stay warm, be nourished and secrete, which over time includes excretion, tears, sweat and so on. As we grow, we need to maintain our health and well-being, we grow and we (sometimes) reproduce.

These may seem obvious, but each may be challenging in practice for some people. People with post-traumatic stress disorder may struggle to breathe out; teenagers with learning differences or mental health issues may refuse to wear more than a T-shirt even in winter winds; while issues around food and cleanliness are familiar to many parents. The list of seven care qualities works as a checklist, particularly but not only in residential care, for the different areas where young people may need support:

1 *Rhythm* – in the daily processes of eating, sleeping and working; in housework or the shared daily meal; across the week and the seasons of the year.
2 *Warmth* – in the home, in food and clothing, in welcome and generosity, in interactions with one another.
3 *Nourishment* – safe, healthy and good food; local and seasonal, organic or biodynamic; but also nourishment for the soul as well as the body.
4 *Trust* – adults role model and expect reliability and honesty, the capacity to take risks or respond to a crisis, recognising one another's strengths.
5 *Constancy* – young people need security, predictability and routine; they need to meet and learn to express measured responses, make informed choices and respond to change.
6 *Culture* – starting from students' own craftwork and the presence of natural materials; setting high standards and supporting students' own aspirations; a rich cultural programme including students in festivals and drama; education for a diverse world.
7 *Recreation* – students need play, space for vitality and for regeneration; they need the opportunity for service and giving back; they need the experience of community and living with others.

We may be lucky enough to have found ourselves in a life where these can be taken for granted and it seems unnecessary to state them, and of course there are different ways to develop any one of these qualities, while different young people may need different emphases. But if we think of their opposites – chaotic lives, physical and emotional coldness, eating disorders, being untrustworthy and unable to trust, a lack of constancy in oneself and others, alienation from human culture or a life without recreation – we can see that in whatever form, young people who all too often have experienced far too many of these need conscious help and support in providing, role modelling and encouraging these qualities.

A simple task like making bread can bring in all of these qualities when supported skilfully: for example, rhythm in kneading, warmth at every stage of the process, nourishment in the ingredients, trust in the process, constancy in the outcome, learning as an aspect of culture and re-creation in giving what one has baked to others.

Figure 5.3 From wool to felt at Ruskin Mill

Unconditional positive regard

Underlying all the different care qualities is the orientation popularised by humanistic psychologist Carl Rogers of "unconditional positive regard". At its simplest, this is a strong positive respect for the other – the therapist's client or, here, the young person – which is not conditional on their behaviour. To care for others, in this perspective, is not about their specific actions or words: it is to care for the whole human being, as we aim to do in parenting.

Of course that does not mean that we do not step in when they do things that hurt themselves or others, that we do not say or show that other things are possible. It means that we do not make our care, kindness and support *dependent* on them behaving well or doing what we want. We need to see and affirm the person who may be hidden behind many layers – of struggling to express themselves, finding a situation overwhelming, being overcome by emotion, acting out hurt or trauma and so on. This unconditional positive regard, not the to-and-fro of the learning space or quarrels in the home, is what is transformative and enables people to develop.

Underlying this – and holistic support and care in general – is an orientation to the whole person which sees their freedom and flourishing as inextricably bound up with healthy relationships with others (family and friends, other pupils and students, carers and teachers); with the food and materials they work with and eat or use; the place, landscape and buildings they move through; with the wider community and the wider universe.

Ruskin Mill's logo reflects this relationship between support and freedom: the central figure is not imprisoned within a circle of care but rather held on both sides, with an openness towards the wider world. Trust students are present by invitation, not incarcerated: they have the right to leave.

Unconditional positive regard, the seven care qualities and the 24-hour curriculum together represent the conditions within which young people can develop themselves to the fullest, surprising both themselves and others. To use a metaphor from gardening, the seed or seedling is capable of remarkable growth and transformation – but to do so it needs care and attention to provide the right conditions: soil and compost, sun and shade, water and drainage, weeding and protection from animals, and so on.

Conversation with Aonghus Gordon

Very early on in the history of the Trust, it became apparent when students arrived that you would notice differing levels of skill and understanding in the nature of care they had experienced. Each situation was different, and the point for us was not to judge but rather to understand what we were seeing in each specific case and what needed to be done.

In some cases, a student might have had an extended family structure which created a safety net for children, and very often a child that had challenges from birth would be supported by the extended family in that way. So they'd arrive having experienced high levels of care, marked by conscientiousness and competence, and in a way, the challenging issues didn't immediately show up. What was required was a more therapeutic approach to engender emotional and cognitive development.

Meanwhile in the experience of children that had fallen through the net away from care and love, you found a sense of injustice in the tone and posture of the students, and that would lead, with a bit of reflection, via the paperwork and the file, to discover a series of past experiences in which the youngster had been passed from pillar to post, very often experiencing multiple breakdowns of fostering relationships. Everybody was trying their best, but there was a kind of lack of new thinking and approaches to this recurrent problem.

So you'd have examples of students who would arrive from fostering situations whose bed had been a mat under the staircase. I would say that was unusual, but it wasn't exceptional; and you then have to ask yourself "How does that happen? What's taking place in the bonding and relationship between child and family?" You needed to ask yourself how that felt for the young person – they came at 16 in the early days – to have slept under the staircase on a mat.

Or perhaps the pressure in the family was such that everybody ate in their own rooms, on their own, because nobody knew how to actually conduct themselves at the table. So the management of that household was based on a principle of isolation, which in the end was voluntary. That's what people wanted to do, because they didn't have any other kinds of relationship and there wasn't anything cruel or unhappy about it. Nobody had the skill set to sit at the table, neither the children nor the parents. So everybody ate in front of the screen. That happens with parents who are actually very, very caring.

So over years you start to see different interventions in the relationship of bonding, caring and nurturing that either reflect a certain lack of skill or a lack of knowledge of how to move a situation on.

A spiky profile

And so the young people would show up with various profiles of a kind of *frozen* emotional development. You might have a profile of emotional development – age five. Intellectual development – 14. Physical development – 16, age appropriate. And you could conclude from that, that the young person would show signs of oppositional defiance and neglect, be attention-seeking and deeply needy, but have hidden this through skilful survival tactics.

So the question that came to the fore in our student reviews and student studies was "How do we meet that situation – of an emotional five-year old and a 14-year-old intellect with a physical capacity of 16 – well?" Their intellect and ability to be skilful would be very nearly normal, but the volatility that arose through the lack of emotional capacity to digest, let's say, a taunt, an obstreperous look from another student or an altercation meant that they were unable to see anything through, because they either felt that they'd been picked on or they didn't have the interiorisation to digest any kind of opposition.

Hidden anxiety

What was interesting in this context was to go back and find out the steps that human beings *need* to undertake in order to become more resilient. So what Ruskin Mill then did was to look around and in that process the seven life processes, or the seven care qualities became essential. And the first task actually in what we might call holistic care and support was the ability to provide students with experiences in which their anxiety was contained and supported.

Anxiousness was almost endemic, but it wasn't something that was initially noticeable. Very often there was gritting of teeth, flicking of fingers, habits of entwining fingers in the hair, picking the nose, scratching the left knee. You found, if you looked closely, very interesting little tics that alleviated a sense of anxiety. And what was clear is that craftwork absorbed not only anxiety

Figure 5.4 Learning responsibility: on the till at Ruskin Mill farm shop

but also relieved them of all sorts of little physical habits, so that smoother breathing and the ability to sustain and process became increasingly prevalent. They incorporated their adversities into the process of making. The craft items had a particular poignancy because they were connected to the domestic environment.

But what emerged was that practical engagement laid the foundations for a kind of personal renewal, decommissioning the self-deprecation which often accompanied anxiety and which was often fuelled by the sense that "I'm not capable" or "I'm incompetent" or "Something's going to happen and it's only a question of when." If that something didn't happen, there'd be a kind of flip backwards of needing it to happen, to sustain the older identity that the young person was now transforming; to precipitate a kind of event that had stopped happening because it wasn't necessary any longer, because craftwork had provided the right experience and relationship in context.

The anxiety was still there, but it had been subsumed into constructive activity. And I think from my own personal development, having watched that and realised the extraordinary speed at which anxiety could be de-escalated through practical, skilful work, this was one of the reasons why I became so focussed on creating new experiences that could alleviate the habituation and self-deprecation of one's own perception and offer something authentic to sustain a higher level of self-perception in relationships.

Constancy and trust

So the capacity to develop rhythm – which is one of the key things that we put into the households – a rhythm, that is regular, but it's not industrially managed. There is dinner, but it's not always on the dot at six. So you had a degree of what you might call constancy, but it was within a cycle of relationships where if dinner was late, that's also something we have to accept. We learn to trust that the dinner will arrive.

And qualities like the ability to form a rebonding relationship of trust, constancy, rhythm, warmth, nutrition, re-creation; those qualities came not only into the relationship with the household but also into the relationship with an active and guiding person, who at that time would be a personal tutor, a craftsperson who understood the additional significance behind being able to become skilful.

So the life qualities that sustain a student's sense of autonomy in which they have to learn to function out of their own resources make up the first part of rehabilitation from deprivation. That isn't just economic deprivation, but it's also intellectual deprivation, it's emotional deprivation and it's a skill-based deprivation. The culturally deprived experience of a child is multidimensional. It has an impact on how they not only see themselves but also their capacity to reimagine what they could possibly become and contribute.

What we call the seven care qualities are work that the Trust performs, drawing on Steiner's seven life processes. We've tried to translate how to sustain a life process as a curriculum context. So the care qualities become part of the guiding process of conscious caregiving. They explain, for example, what the objective is behind having a meal on time, that constancy is actually an important experience in the life of students when so many of them will have had very changeable relationships all around, so that they're not really secure about what to expect next. So the life processes are achievements in personal function. But to arrive at that point, you need a curriculum to feedback and enable the experience.

Working with parents

One challenge that emerged quite early on was a tension between the success of a caregiver and the sense of failure or guilt that that *might* engender in the parents. There was some skilful work to do around building a relationship with the parents in such a way that there was no way that parents could feel that their devotion to their own children was being negated by the success of an independent caregiver.

Our task was to collaborate with parents who were facing an extraordinarily difficult challenge – not to add any sense of judgement or criticism, but to try and develop a relationship based on a shared concern for the young person. And that was very tricky.

So there would be quite a complex route, maybe inviting parents to Saturday coffee mornings, or craft workshops, supporting the parents in their immense struggle in getting the student into a place like Ruskin, or into a more secure constant environment if for whatever reason we were not able to provide what that particular young person needed.

It's very difficult for the parents to trust another adult with a task that they feel they've failed at. The more skilful or manipulative young people would play on that to a degree with which you then had to find new guile, new learning experiences to ensure that that didn't become part of a new power relationship.

Now where this gets really interesting is that when the craft object that students had made during the day came into the relationship of the parent, the home of the student, their college home and their own life, then *that* conversation tended to dominate the exchange. This deflected from the possibility of the student seeing a chance to broker a highly manipulative relationship, either of projecting to their parents that they now had a new step-mother and father, or even of projecting to their parents that they'd failed them.

So the craft activity, and the objects of service produced in it, challenged the student to get into a particular state because they were being successful. The third-party appreciation that started around the craft blocked that potential area of interpersonal manipulation. And very often we would encourage – and this is where the curriculum came from – students, after having made something for themselves, to make it for their parents. That defused the regular situation, which was manipulation of the relationships between college, home and other students.

For more than 20 years I had a lot of direct contact with all this, and I was the responsible person for our residential work. I didn't manage the household, but I provided the therapeutic intervention for behaviour and supported the care managers in this. So that was one of my skills; looking at how to de-escalate and to tackle deeply challenging, ongoing breakdown.

Integrating craft, food and the household

For us, the qualities of the home, the ability for students and caregivers to ensure that the craft activities from the day-time curriculum become celebrated in the functioning of the household were always part of the vision. It's quite difficult to ensure, in that students sometimes do not want to do it. Perhaps they've sold the work. It takes training for carers to understand the value of craftwork being celebrated on the table.

So if we take the ideal, which was performed regularly but not all the time, then the items students had made (Field Two) created a 24-hour curriculum that could, from a sensory perspective (Field Four), be functionalised so the aesthetics would radiate back the genius loci of the place (Field One) within the bedrooms of the children and young people and the food from the valley or the market gardens (Field Three) would transform the understanding of healthy preparation cycles, foods, food, retail, etc.

So Field Five is the point at which young people could become fully immersed in the achievements of Fields One, Two and Three: genius loci, craft and farming. Staff's pedagogic understanding in Field Four of why this is so critical, and to be able to judge how to alter or change the curriculum and then (in Field Five, holistic support and care) to understand why it is necessary for the aesthetics and the higher senses to be rewarded through the craftwork, the nutrition and the civility around the table is probably one of the great achievements of Ruskin Mill Trust, when it can be integrated on a continuum. This work still continues in earnest today, because we have new staff coming in all the time.

Matching the needs of the child with the adult's capacity for role modelling

What was absolutely crucial in this context was being able to find the right student for the right adult personality, so the skill of locating the qualities of an adult's gifts so that they radiate without effort makes the job that much easier to sustain. If the student can follow in the slipstream of the adult's enthusiasm – let's say it's walking, and the student enjoys work walking – the degree of and the speed at which the transformation takes place is very evident.

So finding that magical match between the two is also part of the therapeutic approach. It's great to have a curriculum, but it's even more successful if you can match the curriculum interest of the adult with that of the student and then they enter it effortlessly and it becomes part of the life cycle of the household.

And we do a lot of very good matching! In fact, it's still one of the skills of the organisation: how to match qualities in adults with the qualities and needs that the students are also looking to do. That's not to say that you do that instead of professional training. The professional training that is essential in holistic care and support is the ability to handle the relationship between the adult and the young person in such a way that the adult isn't feeding off the limited emotional skills of the student, and that the adult can separate out their sympathy and antipathies in such a way that they don't end up as projections, which reinforce any cultural feeling of failure or vulnerability.

How to train staff

So the professional training includes the ability to differentiate out staff who actually have something to give, rather than those who are applying for a job because they need an attached relationship with vulnerable young people. That kind of relationship simply freezes and it doesn't allow for progression, because the student is caught in a form of emotional imprisonment, and the adult is really the one in need, rather than the student being given the pathway.

That's a challenging area, and the training that has been developed is one in which knowledge of self and other became critical, along with personal resilience and personal self-management and self-leadership – centred on an exercise of watching yourself in relationship to provocation. What happens when students make repetitive demands that wear you down? Do you give in? And how do you manage your sense of what you might experience as betrayal by the young person who you expected to honour your authority, if at some point they turn around to call you every name under the sun? Because you've built up that false trust, which was then broken in front of you and shattered.

The training that is in development will need to take account of how to empathise with the pain of that young person who is undergoing a transformative experience in a school or college. The gift to the adults is that they have to reposition themselves and change so that the student can be accessible, or the adults themselves accessible to the student. Deep in this understanding of working is an opportunity for the adult to change their context and relationship so that they access and hear what it is that the student needs. This should be seen as a gift given by the student to the adult, in that deeper levels of flexibility and empathy may be in the making.

So if you approach the student in an ordinary context, say a teacher-student or parent-child relationship, where in a certain sense a lot of children adhere to the custom and demands of adults, and the adults really set the tone of the interaction, you could argue that at this point the adult isn't really having to learn anything new. So a disruptive child could be understood – if it's possible – as asking something of the adult which is not entirely routine. What they're asking the adult for is to address themselves to the situation of the child's actual needs, which means changing the expectation. So we're asking adults to become flexible, responsive and capable of moving towards the child, rather than the child moving towards the authoritative parent or teacher.

Handling culture clashes

How does this work when there are culture clashes around things like nutrition, screen time, daily rhythm etc.? The greatest progress is made where the adult is role-modelling not institutional policy alone but a conviction-based attitude. The difficulty comes where the attitude is "It is what it is, that's the rules". That isn't effectively fulfilling the potential of bringing new and informed insights to students' daily lives.

Negotiating around their preferences without guided choice doesn't bring them forward to understand any of their less helpful habits. However, allowing students to make choices even if they might ultimately be unwise is part of the adolescent process of gaining insight towards self-leadership.

So it might happen that if I walk into a student residence on a Saturday night, the students might be eating fast food and playing PlayStations or whatever. That's fine if it's part of a structured, managed programme and there's a clear direction of travel. The priority might be to ensure that students don't stay out too late in unsafe situations at weekends, or even simply that they come back in, and then we can build from their sense of wanting to be at home.

We might also be helping them to develop guided choice, or listening to the student voice. So as with parenting, we are supporting them to move in a particular direction – a better overall relationship to food, a greater freedom in terms of culture – and that big picture and direction of travel is what matters most.

So in those situations it is the task of a director of care to slowly work their way through, and the expectations of parents can often be more impactful than the organisation itself. The conflicts that can arise in the way students use that sort of ammunition against the organisation are actually very helpful.

Now holistic care and support isn't only about caregiving: it's about the continuum of the relationship, when they start and when they go, so everybody's involved in it. There are certain functions that have to be addressed for the caregiving to be more conscious and directed. But in terms of the care curriculum resulting in opportunities for independence, there is a meta-curriculum: how do you metaphorically guide the student into relationships that are not based on negatives? Relationships based on courage; relationships based on "you actually need to handle this one, because this will give you access to a whole new kaleidoscope of possibilities".

The need for flexibility

So you have to be flexible, and the appointment of the caregiver is key. I've sometimes hired couples in which the food policy of Ruskin Mill would in no way be adhered to and the first thing I would say back was, "That's not a problem. What I'm asking you for here, with this particular student, is that you can help them not become addicted to being out after 11pm. So you will need to use every trick in the book, because actually they'll get into serious trouble. So you have jurisdiction to ensure that this one strategy is achieved. How you do it is your business."

And if you want to bring somebody in from the cold, and you're expecting them to eat a nutritious diet that they have never tasted before and that they're going to be safe after 11 o'clock in a household; that's so alien and foreign that anything else is a distraction from the main purpose which is, "You will be home by 11 pm. Because after that, I'm responsible for you and then I'm afraid it's the police who will need to be informed." So we don't want to go there. And if the caregiver tells me that that has been achieved after three months, that's a major achievement. The student is still here and they have managed to trust a new relationship. So the care qualities are also subject to the particular situation of the student and what's possible, given the habits of students and the contexts they've come from.

Their safety comes before the nutrition policy, but the objective is to slowly bring the nutrition policy in, ultimately to support their cognitive functioning.

Figure 5.5 The importance of good food: farming at High Riggs

Media, music and food

We are particularly up against three industries with our students: media, music and food. These are very powerful industries and have disproportionate influence in our cultural life. What's not always understood is how much of them preys on the vulnerability in society and creates addictions in certain vulnerable groups to enrich the industries. One is the visual world which has got access right into the interior of our cognitive stimulation. So the visual media world knows how to give a stimulant, and as we live in a world that is often bereft of cultural stimulation, it now has a monopoly. It doesn't necessarily impart nutrition to people's visual senses, only information. That creates a deficit that's then fed by a commercial imperative.

The art and design of the cultural world, going right through the higher senses, has become industrialised, so it becomes a technology which curtails a certain kind of intimate relationship to the senses. The senses get cut out to a certain extent and what was sensorially enriching is focussed, with an agenda. Obviously advertising is complicit in that. But some images are designed to stimulate gratification and if you are not able to have the discernment to screen that off – which many of us don't – then you become victim to the skill set of a whole visual world that is not based on a cultural imperative but is rather on a commercial underpinning.

So the media have found an entry point into the deeper recesses of psychological cognition and brain development and structure the audience to consume, to satisfy the demand in response to the decline in what you might call the stimulating and nourishing visual world. Nature has a task of stimulating that in human beings – nature deficit syndrome is only an example of how what is missing.

So if you remove children from their sensory potential of being in the naturally stimulating sensory environment, then you have the chance of constructing a new sensory world based on a manipulative design process. Our students are particularly susceptible to that visual world of stimulating. First of all they've been deprived, and secondly, they don't have the discernment because they haven't been given the tool-sets or skill sets, and therefore they find themselves being coerced. So, that's the visual world.

We then have the auditory world, and again there is a displaced relationship between musician and audience, where the intimacy between the craft of the musician and the audience is severed through recording as in the visual world, so the human relationship is not accounted for anymore. Hearing, as a higher sense, is saturated in commercialism.

So you can create a kind of heightened arousal through different levels of beat and intonation. And a student may use that to retreat from a world in which what they are hearing in their head is a voice saying "Well, Ruby, you are absolutely bloody useless", that sort of refrain year on year. They might then use music to anaesthetise themselves from the world that's creating their subjugation and retreat into a kind of bubble where they consume hours and hours of the beat or rhythm. So the music industry's got its various fingers into the vulnerability of the brain-screaming-sound relationship.

If you then go to food, you can again give instant gratification through certain types of food, that's based on specific tastes and predictability. If you disestablish discernment in consumption because it's purely pleasurable with no effort, then you can become a yet more effective consumer. So you can drown – in a metaphorical way – through the industry of food, the industry of sound and industrial sight. Taste, sight and sound are deeply addictive if they have a manipulative intention driven by commerce. And in a way, the kinds of vulnerable children we work with haven't a chance in the face of those immensely skilful configurations that are designed to prey on vulnerability. Nobody goes into those companies to say that's what their task is, but the design thinkers know the psychological basis of how to manipulate vulnerability.

Developing students' senses

So at Ruskin Mill, our cultural programme, our food programme and our aesthetics programme offer the renewal of sight, sound and taste in small doses. We give students the experience of good food that they have been involved in growing and preparing, plenty of drama and music, and creating art and craft from their own sense of initiative.

The problem is not that young people's sense of identity in the arts is expressed through music, or art, or drama. The difficulty is when these are turned into a technological dispensing machine, structured around the need to make money, in the film *industry* or the music *industry*. That situation does not have the same type of regenerative effect because the human relationship is no longer a personal one, and the student is simply a consumer of something they can't produce.

So every centre at Ruskin Mill, where possible, develops a cultural programme, by allowing students to play music, grow their own food and develop a primary drama or art curriculum. The cultural programme is to address particular certain qualities of the higher senses, sight and sound in particular. The relationship programme between human relationships and warmth and taste is critical to rehabilitating the sense of trust between people: hence food and relationship, which is the household meal and the seat at the table.

And then the foundational sense curriculum – which is movement, life, touch, balance – that is done through the land and craft curriculum. So in terms of therapeutic education, then you have one of the reasons why the curriculum is as it is: to develop those senses and give higher levels of discernment for the students so that they will be able to make their choices later on.

The good news is that when they do come back to Ruskin Mill after several years, they often give you interesting stories about what was transformational and very often it's little things. It has been food, it has been grace, it has been relationship, it was the log fire. They don't often have the sense that it's the big picture – they don't often have that language because also we don't often use that language with them, because that's method. We don't want to tell them about the method. We want to immerse them so that they wake up out of their own volition to their own insights.

Researching the method

As this book makes clear, Practical Skills Therapeutic Education emerged through a process of responding to the needs of particular groups of young people. While its core elements became clear early on and it draws on the work of Ruskin, Morris and Steiner, the method is constantly developing and being refined, as it responds to real needs in the world.

Reflective practice is central to this: all Trust staff are expected to practice "research with a small r" – that is, reflecting on what they are doing, noticing what happens when they do it, and changing or refining their practice along the way. The body of experienced staff who have been reflecting on their own practice over years or decades is fundamental to sustained and effective work with young people. In *Communities of Practice*, Wenger (1999) argues that practice which is not reflected on withers and dies; put another way, it is incumbent on practical people to renew their practice through research.

This cultural duty is a deep orientation within the Trust, whose charitable objectives mandate it to promote research in the areas of its work – not to rest on its laurels but to keep exploring and developing – and to disseminate its findings widely – not to keep what it learns to itself. Thus, Ruskin Mill has what for a medium-sized NGO is a very significant and expanding research, training, education and publishing offer, continually refining the method.

The method also underpins the effectiveness of the Trust's work with young people, generating the outcomes that motivate local authorities and tribunals to support students and pupils to attend its colleges and schools. It is clearly a major challenge to ensure that staff are capable of delivering this method effectively, and the Ruskin Mill Centre for Practice delivers a wide range of courses to staff, sometimes also to external participants.

To give an indication of this: staff's work at the Trust begins with two full weeks of induction in which they experience many of the activities that pupils and students do, discovering the impact of craft and landwork directly but also experiencing what it means to be a learner, seeing what it is like to face a real learning challenge, before they take up their role. Each year begins with a week of training, and each term starts with a training day. Staff are regularly supported to go on internal and external training, education and research events up to and including sponsored PhDs. After all, if staff are not themselves growing and developing, how can they help students to do so?

Depending on their role, staff working with vulnerable young people may be required to undertake a number of legally mandated trainings common across the sector. PSTE-related internal courses for 2022–23, for example, included accredited courses on teaching in specialist garden schools and on leadership in holistic support and care, as well as others on Steiner's educational insights and therapeutic music for special needs education.

Courses which are also available to external participants currently include a one-week course on the pedagogical potential of craftwork, a two-day course in holistic nutrition, a six-month course in biodynamic gardening, a two-year accredited training in biodynamic farming and education and various courses in Goethean science.

An action research element is present in many of these as an invitation to develop the habit of reflective practice. In action research, carrying out the research itself changes the situation: at Ruskin Mill Trust, an individual staff member or group of staff looks systematically at a particular element of their practice, perhaps carrying out interviews or observations across a range of cases to get a better overall understanding.

For over a decade and a half, the Trust has co-delivered or delivered Master's courses centred around PSTE: with the University of the West of England, with Inland Norway University, and now fully designed and delivered by Ruskin Mill but validated by the University of Huddersfield. These are part-time Master's for practitioners, studied over two or three years and concluding with a substantial dissertation focussed on researching an element of the Trust's work. These theses are made available to staff across the Trust and often form the basis of in-house presentations or articles in the *Field Centre Journal of Research and Practice*.

Alongside reflective practice and action research, the Trust currently sponsors eight staff members to carry out part-time doctoral research in different academic disciplines and departments – education (at the universities of Sheffield, Sheffield Hallam and Huddersfield); the Centre for AgroEcology, Water and Resilience (Coventry University); the Medical School of the University of Exeter; the Institute of Psychiatry, Psychology and Neuroscience at King's College London; and philosophy (Royal Holloway, University of London). Many of these practitioner-researchers are the internal leaders for particular themes within the Trust.

The Trust also sponsors external research, currently being carried out by academics at Coventry University, into its outcomes. This research draws on the Trust's extensive data collection on the progress students make with the goals they have set themselves and sits beside the more immediate inspection of such records by regulatory agencies asking similar questions. Finally, the Trust also supports research into the underpinnings of its method and has become a significant contributor to Goethean enquiry (Chapter 6) in the English-speaking world in particular (it is more developed in the German-speaking world and Scandinavia). A number of researchers are employed part-time by the Ruskin Mill

Centre for Research to carry out particular research projects, sharing the results with staff and the public through a range of courses and events.

Training and education, at many different levels, is thus an important means both for disseminating research results and for embedding new understanding in staff practice. Alongside these are publications, notably the *Field Centre Journal of Research and Practice*, already mentioned, which covers a wide range of research within and around the Trust, and the more tightly focussed *In Dialogue*, focussing on Goethean enquiry and holistic science. A number of one-off books, such as *Ruskin Today* (Cox et al., 2023), discussing his relevance for different areas of 21st-century life, *Experience Colour* (Vine et al., 2018), supporting an exhibition at the Glasshouse, or *Light, Warmth & Life* (Tennyson, 2022), exploring the work of textile artist Eta Ingham Laurie, based at Trigonos in North Wales, complement a series of smaller publications on topics such as the Trust's buildings and PSTE.

Finally, the Trust regularly hosts a wide range of events and exhibitions, both scientific and artistic in nature, bringing different aspects of its research to wider publics again. The different provisions all have their own programme of events which is well worth a look.

Figure 5.6 On top of the job: cooking at Freeman College's Fusion Café

Bibliography

Bell, G., & Valentine, G. (Eds.). (1997). *Consuming geographies: We are where we eat.* Routledge.

Brown, R. (2017). *A practical guide to curative education.* Lindisfarne.

Cox, L., Gordon, A., & Hewison, R. (Eds.). (2023). *Ruskin today: John Ruskin for the 21st century.* Ruskin Mill Trust.

Crawford, M. (2016). *The world beyond your head: How to flourish in an age of distraction.* Penguin.

Field Centre website: https://www.thefieldcentre.org.uk/

Rogers, C. (1995). *On becoming a person* (2nd edition). Houghton Mifflin.

Rolfe, G., Jasper, M., & Freshwater, D. (2010). *Critical reflection in practice: Generating knowledge for care* (2nd edition). Red Globe.

Sennett, R. (2004). *Respect: The formation of character in a world of inequality.* Penguin.

Steiner, R. (2002). Lecture VII – GA 170. The Riddle of Humanity [WWW Document]. https://rsarchive.org/Lectures/GA170/English/RSP1990/19160812p01.html. (Original lecture 1916).

Tennyson, R. (2022). *Light, warmth and life: Exploring the work of textile artist eta Ingham Lawrie.* Ruskin Mill and Trigonos.

Vine, T., Löbe, N., & Rang, M. (2018). *Experience colour.* Ruskin Mill Trust.

Wenger, E. (1999). *Communities of practice: Learning, meaning and identity.* Cambridge University Press.

Whittaker, J. K. et al. (2016). Therapeutic residential care for children and youth: A consensus statement of the international work group on therapeutic residential care. *Residential Care for Children and Youth, 33*(2), 89–106. DOI: https://doi.org/doi:10.1080/0886571X.2016.1215755

6 Health and the whole human being

Visiting Freeman College

Arundel Street in inner-city Sheffield can seem empty at some times of day, with high red-brick walls lining an old industrial street where little life can be seen. Pass through the right gateway, however, and you find yourself surrounded by activity on all sides. Here Ruskin Mill's Freeman College continues the city's tradition of metalwork, particularly cutlery, which stretches back before the Industrial Revolution that made it one of England's major cities. Sheffield silverware and Sheffield steel became famous around the world, using Peak District grit for grinding and power from the city's five rivers. While large-scale industrial production has largely left Sheffield, Ruskin Mill has physically reinhabited its spaces and processes as a therapeutic intervention, healing social wounds as well as psychological ones.

Begun in 1797, the Sterling Works cutlery factory was renovated and reconstructed in 2008, keeping its workshop layout but adding more social, eating and study space for students. Next door, Butcher Works is a listed building, a restored cutlery and grinding workshop space. An Academy of Makers was established here following discussions with local metalworkers, offering workshop spaces for independent master craftspeople who Freeman students can work with, as well as some of Freeman's internal workshops. Around the courtyard are spoon forging, letterpress printing, book binding, metal spinning, jewellery, an organic bakery as well as apartment living.

In both sites, you can physically feel the history of cutlery making and other metalwork: some of the rooms have kept their old purposes, equipment has been bought from old Sheffield workplaces, and some of the staff learned their trade from local metalworkers. Here are some of the grinding stones that were used for Bowie knives; as the stones were ground down, they were lifted up to progressively higher workshops for finer work. Facing the street, Fusion Café offers students the chance to learn catering and front of house skills, while a shop and gallery also connect the working and learning spaces to the wider world.

DOI: 10.4324/9781003361541-6

Figure 6.1 Making a copper spoon at Freeman College

Crafts and the student

Visiting Freeman's various workshops, the depth of knowledge that students enter into is visible in each room; opening different doors you enter into different worlds, each with their own characteristic look and smells, shaped around the needs of a particular material or task – even the cutlers' stools are designed for sitting on without wobbling when working with the characteristic movements of the trade.

The craft teacher's explanation is needed to understand what you are really looking at and how it all works as a process, both technically and in a student's experience. No surprise then that for many students, mastering this special knowledge which enables them to bring their visions into three dimensions is a source of great pride and confidence.

The dark history pointed to by Bowie knives is mirrored in many students' personal histories, so that knives and forks, tools for cutting and stabbing, are no longer a routine part of student production – except for butter knives, a perennial favourite and readily sold. Instead, students today follow a gentler course, starting with the challenges of beating out a small copper spoon. Depending on their interests and capacity to follow through, they may move towards a copper bowl, a larger copper spoon, a mug, a solid silver spoon, a dish and finish with something elaborate like a vase. The gesture of these vessels is one of holding and nurturing, but reached through highly skilled effort.

Spoon forging is a demanding art; it can take a whole term to make a spoon. As you work the metal, it becomes stiffer, echoing the student's resistance to completing a task which is far harder in practice than it seems in imagination. It can be annealed – heated to soften it again – with a blowtorch that reaches 700°C, a task which brings out a great sense of responsibility in the student. Danger and trust work together: the student has to trust their teacher, learn to trust their own capacities and trust the other students in the same space.

As the student shapes the spoon blank – the 70 g billet they start from – they also shape themselves. First the spoon is beaten into shape with hammers, but then it has to be polished: first with a coarse file, then with a smooth file, then

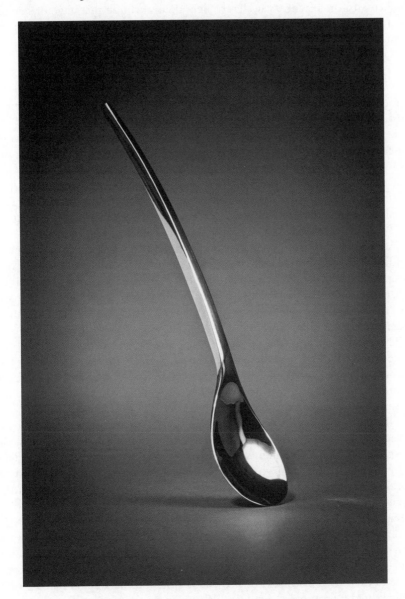

Figure 6.2 "As I began to polish my spoon, my picture of myself began to be reflected. It looked weird as it distorted my reflection. Sometimes I looked better than I thought, I felt, and sometimes I looked disturbed. My dislike for myself was tested because the spoon was beautiful."

sanded with coarser paper and finally with smooth paper. With a silver-plated spoon, the student sees their own reflection as the final product emerges.

The process of refining is a long and challenging one; students struggle with themselves about the length of the process, as they bring their willpower and skill into alignment with the qualities of the metal. Often this manifests in conflict with the teacher, who has to help them through this stage of struggle and rejection. Ruskin Mill's contemporary apprenticeship model uses this moment as a space of therapeutic education.

The plasticity of pewter

Students' encounter with metal recapitulates the whole history of humanity's encounter, from beating copper – a skill that precedes the Bronze Age – via silver and early modern materials like pewter to brasswork with industrial lathes. Of course students can rarely take part in contemporary mining – and ecological concerns mean that as much metal as possible is recycled – but they can follow the life cycle of their work through from the workshop to becoming a gift, part of an exhibition or an item for sale and then use. They are also able to take excursions to find Blue John stone on old slag heaps in the Peak, bring it back, polish it and set it in necklaces and bracelets.

In another workshop room, a tutor works with students putting pewter handles onto steel butter knife blades, carving their own moulds for the handles. Pewter is a very forgiving material, open to many uses. On one shelf is a coffee storage box in the shape of a London bus, made by a student fascinated with the capital. On another, a bowl with a lid for Turkish delight. On a third, chess pieces for student rooms.

The workshop is relatively small – because of the lathe, no more than three students can work there with the teacher at any one time. Pewter's history – heavy ceremonial mugs, familiar to some students from family memorabilia – sits side by side with plant containers around the walls, where cuttings are propagated.

The metal, too, is recycled – anything not used or not wanted can be easily remade. The material of pewter affords great freedom to turn vision into reality: as with the Turkish delight box or the London bus coffee holder, students can create "in their own voice". Nevertheless, bringing the vision into the world still demands perseverance and reflection and the capacity to accept that something needs to be done again. Without this resistance, it would have less therapeutic value.

Because of its plasticity, pewter is used to make leavers' medallions for Freeman students. The students in turn make gifts, every Christmas, for premature babies in the neonatal care unit at nearby Jessop's Hospital. This connects to some of their own histories but also enables them to make gifts that are often really valued by parents at a vulnerable time in their own lives.

Their own parents are often amazed to see photos and films of their children in the workshop, showing skills and capacities that they have not previously had the chance to develop or express. When they visit, students love to show off their knowledge of the materials and their tool-using skills: to become, for once, the experts in their own lives.

Outside the door

The surprising multiplicity of what lies just off the street in the old Sterling Works and Butcher Works is characteristic of the mixed uses of this Victorian industrial area today. Bracketed by busy roads, the quieter side streets include a silversmith and one of Sheffield Hallam University's many buildings; student accommodation and a parking lot; NHS offices and empty sites. Life comes and goes in and out of these old buildings as it has for centuries.

Freeman College's two buildings, too, form part of a wider ecosystem and a longer history. The college is named for Arnold Freeman, warden from 1918 to 1955 of the Sheffield Educational Settlement, a pre-welfare state attempt at responding to poverty and disadvantage which included activist Edward Carpenter and the Quaker Arnold Rowntree among its council and sought to establish "the Kingdom of God" in Sheffield:

> By the Kingdom of God we mean streets along which it is a pleasure to walk; homes worthy of those who live in them; workplaces in which people enjoy working; public-houses that are centres of social and educational life; kinemas that show elevating films; schools that would win the approval of Plato; churches made up of men and women indifferent to their own salvation; an environment in which people "may have life and have it abundantly".

Freeman was a Fabian, a conscientious objector, a Workers Educational Association lecturer and an anthroposophist. By the time of his retirement in 1955, the welfare state and urban development brought the Settlement to an end, but his successor Christopher Boulton bought Tintagel House and established the Merlin Theatre at Nether Edge. The theatre and arts centre has now been renovated and revived by Ruskin Mill as a venue for in-house theatre and local companies, with Freeman students using it as a site for work experience.

Also in Sheffield is Ruskin Mill's Brantwood Specialist School for children from 7 to 19, some of whom transition to Freeman College. Both Brantwood and Freeman have their own farming sites. Freeman students can work at High Riggs biodynamic market garden in Stannington on the outskirts of the Peak District, producing food for the Fusion Café as well as Freeman student meals and running a food box scheme. Meanwhile Brantwood children can look after chickens and goats, grow plants and work at the Iron Age forge at the outdoor classroom near the Peak's Eyam village, famous for the villagers' decision to isolate themselves and protect their neighbours from the plague of 1665–6.

This interconnection of farm and workshop, drama and work, across different sites, marks the richness of Ruskin Mill's offer, thoroughly in keeping with

Sheffield's character as an industrial city closely tied to the Pennines from early rural migration through to present-day leisure.

The student study and Goethean enquiry

Chapter 2 explored the direct benefits of craft and landwork for Ruskin Mill's young people, while Chapter 4 discussed the therapeutic education that its craftspeople bring to their work with young people. Working with metal or fleece, caring for animals or preparing food, the students are also shaping themselves. But people's needs are not identical: one of the long-standing Steiner critiques of mainstream education is precisely that it homogenises students and seeks to fit the student to the test rather than the education to the student. This is even more true for young people who face the level of challenge that leads their parents to Ruskin Mill and brings local authorities to fund the experience. How can staff know what young people need?

The short answer is that the 360-degree curriculum stretches young people in many dimensions. They develop physical skills, the practical understanding that underpins them, and the emotional maturity to meet the challenges of the world. In the process, many different specialist staff work with an individual young person in different capacities. They encounter them in residential and social settings as well as in the field, workshop or classroom, so they can learn better who they are and what can best help them.

Figure 6.3 Attention and appreciation at Grace Garden School

The underlying principle here, as with the genius loci survey encountered in Chapter 1, is that of JW von Goethe's appreciative enquiry (Chapter 7). Goethe's overall approach is an integrative one: empathically observing the person, living thing or other phenomenon of study in all its different modes of appearance rather than compartmentalising different dimensions – reading test results here, physical health issues there, mental health in a third place and social interaction ignored – but also seeing it in its "morphology", for example a young person as they develop over time. And, most crucially, appreciating and listening to what is being studied rather than treating it as a passive thing, an external object.

Watching the student study

A student or pupil study is a remarkable thing to watch. At some provisions there may be as many as 50 or even 90 staff who work with an individual student or know them in different capacities; in Freeman it might be only 12 or fewer. However many are involved, they all take the time at the end of an often challenging working day to bring a student into their collective awareness, share their observations and experiences of the student and try to come to a deeper appreciation of what that young person is working with and what might help them. From the Goethean point of view, everyone knows something, and knowledge becomes more objectively refined as it becomes less personalised, with diverse points of view brought together coherently between colleagues. At Freeman students are considered in turn, one a week so that each student is brought to the centre of staff attention regularly.

Different provisions have developed slightly different ways of carrying out the student study, but in each case there is a structure designed to enable a living picture of the student, in all their complexity, to be brought into the room. Drawing on the Parsifal myth, the underlying question is "What ails thee?", placing the student into the template of an archetypal human being in what Steiner calls the fourfold aspects of humanity, meaning that staff share what they have observed about the student in many different dimensions – without offering personal judgement.

They might begin with the student's physical ways of being: how they move, how they act, when they do particular things, and then move to what they notice about the student's life processes: for example, where are their rhythms broken, what happens when they are disrupted? What seem to be the big challenges?

The student's past school and family history might be brought in, in all its complexity – files can be contradictory for things as apparently straightforward as birthdays; the point is not to decide on a fixed truth but to bring all these different aspects into the room. Staff might move on to their own stories about the student. How do they perceive the student, how does the student perceive them? How do they see the world?

Watching a student study, what stands out is a feeling like watching good parents talking to one another: there is deep appreciation, a sense of what is loveable about a student, and honesty about what is challenging or perplexing with being around them. These feelings themselves are not taken as true but as information: if this student sometimes makes me feel scared, when does that happen and what can I name about that experience? And just like good parenting, there is a combination of real interest in who this young person is at present and what they might need and become.

As the student study comes towards its end, staff try to move towards a coherent overall picture of the young person, trying to understand more deeply what their way of being in the world expresses – not looking for an interpretation or analysis, but rather a deeper, empathetic rather than sympathetic, sense of them in all of their aspects. What is their story? How are they developing and growing?

There may be different kinds of visible outcome from a student study: perhaps a change in their craft or landwork curriculum, or a different approach in their residential care. Sometimes other therapeutic work may be called for, depending on the particular needs of the young person in question; or the relationship between Ruskin Mill's offer and their other medical supports may need refining.

Holistic health consists precisely in not separating these things out as entirely different, but seeing that the young person exists in all of these dimensions, while trying to find what kinds of intervention may be most needed.

Figure 6.4 The power of drama at Glasshouse College

Ruskin Mill offers a suite of Steiner-based interventions free of charge as additional accelerators for young people's development, supporting them to become more in control of their executive functions and arrive at a place where they have greater abilities to learn. Not all students will need these. They include eurythmy for spatial and movement dimensions alongside craftwork; massage to support sensory integration and the life processes (Chapter 5); and painting and colour therapy to provide a variety of cognitive and sensory opportunities. The student study group may also consider offering drama (Garnault, 2021, 2022a, 2022b), music or other developments, for example around nutrition.

All of these possibilities complement rather than contradict the conventional therapeutic activities, such as speech and language therapy, occupational therapy and functional skills, which are also offered at Ruskin Mill Trust along with medical prescriptions and of course Practical Skills Therapeutic Education more generally.

Perhaps the most important dimension, however, is the care and appreciation that the student study develops in the adults working with the young person: rather than shutting the door on the student and their problems at four o'clock, the student study centres the young person in all their complexity in the hearts and minds of the staff.

Conversation with Aonghus Gordon

When we were talking about the genius loci, we identified a fourfold aspect: the minerals, the plants, the animals and the human spirit – the individual human capacity people have to be able to rise above what might be more instinctual or habitual, to say no to themselves. We are always trying to be able to engender this in students, so that they can rise beyond their existing circumstances, with support and guidance. With students we call this "self-generated conscious action", where they can act in a way that does not simply reflect their conditioned cultural sense. Field Six recognises that this fourfoldness is not only within the landscape or in biodynamic ecology. Here, in the farm, it is stretched out horizontally, within the farmer, the animals, the plants and the soil. Similarly, it is also integrated vertically within the human being.

Here Ruskin Mill draws on the insights of Dr Ita Wegman, who inspired the foundation of Sunfield School in Clent, now a Ruskin Mill provision. Dr Wegman collaborated with Rudolf Steiner on the book *Extending Practical Medicine*, the only book he co-wrote (Steiner et al., 2013). Here she describes very beautifully the "like for like" process of working with a medicinal intervention by looking at the children's constitutional issues. She could diagnose those issues with Steiner's help as sometimes being internal, nearly invisible, but capable of manifesting physically to eyes that learned to see.

Dr Wegman, who co-founded Weleda, developed therapies and remedies that treated both the physical body with physical substances and the life body with additional exercises, for example with therapeutic remedies such as eurythmy, which she also saw as including the physical body. All these insights were to offer additional executive control in the process of adolescent development. This would also involve exercises in how to breathe correctly, how to move appropriately, how to retain your warmth and how to exercise your specific choices in a guided way.

At the same time she understood how those contributions could be given additional validity by the soul itself. So there is a collaboration of relationships, while we also have to understand the importance of what she described as the ego, in her terms our sense of identity in relationship to others.

The student study

Our own fourfold approach of understanding and diagnosis – if we are permitted to undertake it in understanding a student's journey in Ruskin Mill Trust – is centred in the student study. This is the opportunity for a student to be placed in the centre of a vision of appreciation. What the initiators of a student study present to the team looking at a student who is in distress, or simply needs additional support, is the question that Parsifal crucially fails to ask in the Arthurian legend: "What ails thee?"

In other words, "How is it that your journey has brought you to Ruskin Mill Trust? What is it that we might be able to contribute to your journey? How do we understand what besets you so that you find it necessary to continuously re-perform your behaviour?"

In the student study there is a strict protocol that starts by looking at the physical: observation, with no judgement. How do they walk? How do they push a wheelbarrow? How do they hold a tool? It could be how they actually manage their routines, how they fall asleep, how they wake, or how they don't always undertake systematic routines.

We might look at the colour of their complexion, their capacity to sustain their physical forces, along with their ability to absorb or reject appreciation, which we would call the soul of the student. And even better, we can ask how they rise to the occasion of being commended or supported, possibly by changing the direction of their conduct. We would call that the spirit or the individual kernel of that student, taking charge.

A student's vulnerability to coercion often arises when the sense of appreciation that they have for others and themselves isn't integrated, and from a whole host of disruptive situations that might arise from that, whether in the household, in their families or in their peer relationships. So the insights that staff can avail of in those student studies can be key to students' capacity to shift and take a step in a new direction. There are many anecdotes, stories and student journey profiles around how students often actually find new opportunities after a student study, due to the deeper sense of appreciation that staff can now give that student.

Therapeutic interventions

This is a holistic approach to medicine, where we can see how the land and craftwork, and the care situation, may from time to time require additional interventions. Here we can draw on a tradition of therapeutic interventions, including Steiner's and Wegman's, and other researchers.

To say that is not to dismiss anything else. Psychotherapy, for example, has its place within the Ruskin Mill offer, as does counselling, or specific movement interventions as a further way of working with spatial development. Eurythmy is another possibility, which very often has transformative effects on students' ability to gain greater consciousness and motivation around their physical bodies. Massage can also have this effect, sometimes responding to a sense of self-neglect or physical abuse.

Painting is another option, where the student's soul is potentially transported to new territories of experience: dealing with antipathy or loss, for example. We have some great examples of students collaborating in exercises where they have to bring colours together and form new relationships. The conversations they have around what they experience in bringing their specific colours into relationship are very often a transformative experience, through actually having new types of conversations.

All these therapies act in a certain sense as accelerators. They are to support the structures for self-regulation. This can also include working with the animals, with certain types of plants, and increasingly the Trust's ability to prescribe a craft as a helpful intervention, for example to manage the frontal plane: supporting the student in this instance not to over-stretch and invade the personal space of another.

Developing a sense of self

Often individual young people need very specific further development, and Field Six exists as that additional supporting power, including the student study. When a human being is given a concentrated sense of attention, or what you could even call a form of love for their situation, we often notice that they are supported on a non-physical level. It's difficult to quantify that, other than through our regular experience of realising that things have changed with a particular student. It's quite intangible or anecdotal, but experience has shown that becoming the focus of positive attention, and how we reconfigure a student's timetable or approach as a result of the student study, enables them to continue on what is sometimes a very challenging pathway.

My own experience after 30 years suggests that one of the key conditions is how the student is facilitated in developing their sense of self and purpose. Steiner and Wegman describe this as the ego organisation of the human being. The ego organisation isn't about the identity of self alone, but rather they define it as the sense of self in relationship to others, how someone mediates the interests of self with the ethics of being connected with others.

Egotism is then the fallout of that, as opposed to the ennobling effect of developing a sense of self and identity or ego in relationship to others. Steiner called this ethical individualism, which means that as someone develops a sense of identity, they actually experience it in relationship to how they grow, in being able to bring their faculties into play around their tasks and voluntary contributions, and ultimately to their own vocational initiative. You gain your validation from another, not through yourself.

The emergence of autonomy

A key part of Ruskin Mill's work is responding to the blockages that students experience to their sense of self and the capacity to find a fully facilitated identity. Even though we might support the life processes through high-quality nutrition and rhythms, develop the ability for the body to be effective and skilful, support the emergence of friendships and encourage their social relationships to be sustained – if we're not also building the capacity to take charge of the self and to endure difficulty, that doesn't allow full autonomy to emerge.

In the three years that we have with most students, their capacity to stand up at the end of their time at Ruskin Mill and give gratitude – which is a key marker of the ability to go out into the world – can often be considerably impaired if this is not addressed. Of course, for some people, it might be a lifelong task to be able to do that, but with less impacted profiles of development and challenge, it is something that you can expect to see within three years at Ruskin Mill. So that is the real challenge for us to undertake in that time.

The emergence of a sense of self-identity, being able to be effective, is in part the capacity to see oneself within a situation, to know that it is not necessarily of your making, but to nevertheless take on board the fact that these are the given situations. Then a student can realise, "From here on I can have a greater impact on my own experience of suffering, pleasure, success and acknowledgement."

You could say that where this becomes evident in the relationships of students to the work that they do, and the work experience that they choose, you begin to see them winning a sort of battle for themselves. One of the hallmarks of this is holding greater levels of power and autonomy, dealing with the levels of obstruction that some Ruskin Mill students have around that. So ego development, the ability to say "I got that wrong", represents the growth of self-generated conscious action – in staff as well as students.

The levels of development in everyday language

What concerns Ruskin Mill when a referral is made is the skill set of the student at that point. For example, are they road-aware? Are they aware of how to live in a shared household, or are they only really pleased when there's nobody else in the household, so that they have complete autonomy within that space? How they use space in relation to themselves is critical, and we call this the physical capacity.

Figure 6.5 Developing autonomy: making jewellery at Freeman College

Then we can look at the life capacity, which is their ability to eat, share and prepare food, to have an understanding of nutrition, an understanding of sleep and rhythm patterns, and an understanding of their own personal self-care, based within many of the ordinary life processes. Can they perform these functions? Can they actually wash? Can they breathe correctly? Can they actually maintain themselves physically, can they care for themselves? Those are all aspects of the life processes of their constitution.

Equally, how do they attend to themselves in relationship to others, with their relationships? So this audit of the physical capacities, the life capacities and the social capacities is needed as a benchmark. It enables Ruskin Mill to look at the additional journey that needs to be made, so that a student's independent living skills at the end of two to three years of work are enhanced and they make progress.

But equally we can ask, "What happens in the face of adversity? Does this young person run away? Do they run away from themselves? Do they run away from events that are adversarial?" The capacity to face up to a situation, whether it's one that they've created or a predicament that they've found themselves in, can also be an indication of their sense of autonomy and their ability to sustain challenge. This is one way of approaching that dimension.

The student study looks at these different aspects and then relates the challenges a particular student faces to new curriculum insights. Or it might be that a change of direction is needed in relationship to the external requirements of a local authority and in relation to our own vision of the ultimate purpose in the student's progress. Are they doing an academic training or a practical training or a combination of the two? Are they aiming for a qualification? What is their particular journey of self-direction, autonomy, self-generated conscious action? And that template is used to help design further progression of the student's timetable.

Different kinds of interventions

There are three core curriculums of our therapeutic intervention. One is practical skills, another is biodynamic ecology and the third is holistic support and care, for residential students (Chapters 2, 3 and 5). But even students who don't live with us still need the support and care of their Education, Health and Care manager. You could say the context that all this is presented in is Field One, their sense of identity in the community, the sense of them belonging to that community, the spirit of place. It includes very pragmatic things like knowing how to move around the place on the bus routes, as well as the magic of the place that might be found in the Millennium Gallery of a city, celebrating the craft of glass, or textiles, or agriculture, or spoon forging.

Field Six then brings in therapeutic contributions as accelerators for student progress, which from time to time can be blocked, so that it's not clear which direction the student wishes to take their next challenge in. In this sense, it is a point in the cycle of the year, the timetable or the student's biography when this kind of 360° review can take place.

Individual students often have what mainstream medicine calls multiple comorbidities, very strong medical issues which play a very marked role in their lives. These are highly complex, and it isn't the task of the student study to change the external medication or the diagnosis. Rather, we seek to understand why particular medication might be prescribed and to put that into context with the Trust's contribution for this journey.

From time to time there may be student requests to de-escalate their medication, which should only be done obviously through consultation with their

GP or pharmacological therapist, and the checking of those diagnoses is also done with another colleague within the Trust, who is a highly experienced child and adolescent consultant psychiatrist, specialising in mental health issues. So we need close attention to detail around some of the more complex student biographies, including those students who present as and wish to remain non-verbal. There need to be high levels of skill to be able to find new ways of communicating.

Field Six often also draws on areas such as sound therapy, music therapy or touch therapy. These start by facilitating a higher intensification of some primary sensory developments that enable, for example, touch and sound, or listening or hearing, to be integrated. The work of massage, painting, music and colour for those students who are sensorily more deeply impacted becomes their entry point of meeting the world, and the world meeting them.

So the range of facilities for Ruskin Mill students is very broad indeed. It's not that students are barred from any particular therapy, but it's clear that if you are physically and verbally deeply impacted, those therapeutic entry points become primary to your capacity to communicate. Then there's a shift for those students from craft and farming in particular to a focus on Field Six, to be able to meet and communicate with the world. That's an important detail.

Neurodiversity

There is an increasing awareness that if you fundamentally have capacity and you are on the autistic spectrum, you're very likely to be able to make a very major contribution, not only to society but also around yourself. The challenge for Ruskin Mill is that if your social capacities can be further developed, starting from the profile that many of our young people come to us with, then they too should have access to the social and skill set that many young people on the spectrum often show.

So whether you flourish in that situation is very dependent on whether your personal skill sets are in a relationship that can allow those more cognitive, creative and imaginative elements to flourish. Ruskin Mill is primarily interested in the social capacity of young people on the spectrum to be able to exercise what is very often their potential genius, or idiosyncrasy.

If I go back in time and look at the many young people who had the condition in the early 1980s, which hadn't yet been fully articulated at that point, I recall one remarkable girl who had an interest in Bolivian music from the ancient past, particularly the Inca period. She used to go down to Bath and busk and play and she'd come back with £50, which in those days was a lot of money. She eventually saved that up to go to Bolivia and meet Indigenous pan pipe groups.

Her eccentricities, however, were quite extreme, and her incapacity to live with anybody else was also extreme. So it may be that our contribution was to formalise her capacities, to socialise and give direction, and more meaning and purpose to her music, so that it found an interest in serving others.

She learned to busk, and we encouraged it, because she saw that when she didn't just act for herself but for other people, she had the reward of quite substantial financial returns from her skills, and that she was able to then reshape the direction of her travel. So I think Ruskin Mill's task in relation to neurodiversity is to recognise that the skill sets that are often hidden in conditions on the spectrum need an appropriate social platform in order to be able to be received and availed of.

Our task, then, is not one of defining, but one of enabling those young people on the spectrum to exhibit their capacities, because they've all got various skill sets. Those who can't communicate are obviously very vulnerable and are likely to need very long-term support. They too, if observed skilfully, will have very particular skills, very often mini-skills that need appreciation, and I think that can be easily overlooked when verbal communication is not their first skill.

In a neurodiverse world it should be clear that everybody's task, particularly with children and young people, is to ensure that the social autonomy and capacities that go along with a skill set, whether it's imaginative or practical, are enabled – so that the adult or young person isn't entirely dependent on a form of social support that potentially disadvantages them, because they haven't learned to become more autonomous, particularly if they are in a position to become so. That's where Ruskin Mill steps in.

We do need to bear in mind that while some of our neurodivergent students are already very skilful, others will not necessarily be seen that way unless we can enable that to come out. So I think we can talk about a journey of the emerging social ability to facilitate young people's sense of their skills and capacities.

Figure 6.6 Human flourishing at Sunfield

What we do at Ruskin Mill is to undertake the seven fields of practice in order to develop self-generated conscious action wherever possible. For adolescents that means an apprenticeship model of learning, while for children it means a therapeutic immersion into sensory development for children. So at every stage we have to see the needs of the specific young person we're working with. We call this guided choice.

Ruskin Mill in the wider world

Every two years, the International Festival of Glass takes place in venues across the historic Glass Quarter in Stourbridge and in Wolverhampton with exhibitions, masterclasses, demonstrations, workshops and tours; Ruskin Mill's Janine Christley is festival director. Its flagship exhibition, the British Glass Biennale, is held in Ruskin Mill's Glasshouse (Chapter 2). Studio glass – one-off or very small-scale production – was reborn as a craft in the post-war period, particularly as industrial factories closed and technology such as small furnaces moved from industry into the artist's workshop, so the full range of the material's possibilities for creativity could be explored. The 2022 Festival and Biennale also coincided with the UN's International Year of Glass to make the exhibition a particularly significant one.

At the opening night, the expert jury announced the winners among over 100 artists, designers, craftspeople and students chosen to exhibit their work, for prizes awarded by the Worshipful Company of Glass Sellers of London and others. A particular highlight at the Glasshouse was a major exhibition of Korean, Japanese and Chinese studio glass by 34 leading artists. The first International Bead Biennale, for the specialist craft of glass bead making, also took place at the Glasshouse. Collectors and connoisseurs, galleries and museums from around the world viewed an extraordinary range of beautiful and moving pieces of glass art – in an old glass factory, now a social enterprise serving young people with learning difficulties.

This interplay of industrial heritage, present-day needs and world-class art is no paradox but central to Ruskin Mill's vision. The Biennale is one example of Ruskin Mill's wider commitment to international engagement and collaboration, grounding its work in international best practice and sharing its experience and research around the world.

For the past seven years, the Trust co-delivered a Master's in Special Education: Practical Skills Transformative Learning with the Inland Norway University of Applied Sciences at Lillehammer, Norway's leading centre for training care workers, whose undergraduates do a term's work experience at Ruskin Mill. The former has now been superseded by the Trust's own fully delivered Master's, validated by the University of Huddersfield.

Also spanning the North Sea, the Erasmus+ Ecopreneurship project brings Ruskin Mill together with the Sogn School of Organic Agriculture and Horticulture (Norway), Nord University (Norway), the Norwegian University of Life Sciences, ALTA Consulting (Iceland) and Snæfellsnes Regional Park (Iceland) to develop models for cultural innovation in ecological entrepreneurship, focussing on place-based learning that brings together educational institutions, local communities and social and cultural entrepreneurs to explore what they can contribute to building sustainable societies. This builds on long-standing research collaborations with Norwegian colleagues in particular.

In continental Europe, the Revitalist Erasmus+ project is a collaboration with a series of Hungarian partners (Diversity Foundation, Tiszasas Municipality, WWOOF Hungary, Hungarian Quality Compost Association), the University of South Bohemia (Czechia) and Agricoltura Capodarco (Italy) that uses PSTE as a curriculum for social farming with disadvantaged groups (unemployed people, Roma and other ethnic minorities, people with learning differences and difficulties) in Hungary (Pereira, 2022). This builds on networks created during the earlier Ecomotive project.

The Goetheanum, founded by Rudolf Steiner in Dornach (Switzerland) and the largest Goethean Science research centre in the world, is a particular point of reference for Ruskin Mill and there are a wide range of relationships between the two, not least the presence of Dr Matthias Rang, Science section leader at the Goetheanum, who has joined as a trustee of the newly launched Ruskin Mill Centre for Research.

Leading educationalist Prof Gert Biesta is professor of public education at the National University of Ireland Maynooth, professor of educational theory at the University of Edinburgh and a member of the Dutch government and parliament's Education Council. He is also patron of the Ruskin Mill Centre for Practice.

On the other side of the world, Ruskin Mill has been running training courses for teachers in Nanjing (China) for several years and has signed memoranda of understanding with Nanjing Normal University and the Nanjing Disabled People's Federation towards possible teaching collaborations. It has signed a similar agreement with the India Autism Centre near Kolkata (India) who are exploring how to integrate research and education within staff training and development.

In the US, the Nature Institute in upstate New York has a long-term partnership with Ruskin Mill around staff training. In 2015, the Trust co-founded Meristem College in Sacramento for adults with autism spectrum conditions; Meristem is now fully independent. The Trust is currently collaborating with Temple-Wilton Community Farm, the oldest continually operating community supported agriculture (CSA) farm in the States and one of the oldest in the world.

These are just a few examples of Ruskin Mill's longer standing and more continuous engagements; it is of course constantly visited by and visiting peer institutions in its different fields around the world and has taken part in many one-off events and projects. Its founder, Aonghus Gordon, is regularly invited to give keynote addresses, presentations and trainings on three different continents. All these connections and collaborations show something of the international significance and quality of its work.

Bibliography

Cook, W. E. (2003). *Foodwise: Understanding what we eat and why*. Temple Lodge.

Garnault, P. (2021). Teaching acting. *Field Centre Journal of Research and Practice*, 6, 67–79.

Garnault, P. (2022a). Teaching Shakespeare. *Field Centre Journal of Research and Practice*, 7, 69–81.

Garnault, P. (2022b). "Tvorchestvo": The creative process. *Field Centre Journal of Research and Practice*, 8, 111–121.

James, L. (2018). *Odd girl out: An autistic woman in a neurotypical world*. Bluebird.

Nassar, D. (2022). Knowing well: Goethe, Bildung, and the ethics of scientific knowledge. *British Journal for the History of Philosophy*, 30(4), 646–665. https://doi.org/10.1080/09608788.2022.2075825.

Pereira, R. (2022). Can practical skills therapeutic education work as a social farming method in Hungary? *Field Centre Journal of Research and Practice*, 7, 26–31.

Reed, S., & Woods, J. (2022). An experiential journey through the principles of the student study. *Field Centre Journal of Research and Practice*, 8, 49–62.

Silberman, S. (2015). *Neurotribes: The legacy of autism and how to think smarter about people who think differently*. Allen and Unwin.

Steiner, R., Wegman, I., & Evans, M. (2013). *Extending practical medicine*. Rudolf Steiner Press, 5th edition. (Original German publication 1925.)

Wiechert, C. (2021). *Solving the riddle of the child: The art of the child study*. Verlag am Goetheanum.

7 Transformative leadership

Visiting the Field Centre

Back in Gloucestershire, the Field Centre sits in the middle of Gables Farm, at the top of the Horsley Valley and just under the old Bath road. To one side students work with sheep, cows, bees and donkeys and the track runs down towards the forest beside traditionally laid hedges. To the other side, a path across the fields of kale and cabbage leads to the horticulture buildings and the farm shop.

Here you are on top of the Cotswolds, on a dry limestone grassland plateau where people have lived and farmed since the Neolithic. It is a strange landscape: the flat and easily farmed ground is high up, one part cut off from another by steep-sided valleys as if by inlets of the sea. The next tops over, Minchinhampton and Rodborough Commons, are sites of Special Scientific Interest because their "unimproved" grasslands support over a hundred kinds of grasses and often rare wildflowers, 30 species of butterflies, adders and skylarks – along with the cattle that graze it in common and shape this ecosystem.

Southwards is the still impressive Iron Age hillfort of Old Sodbury. Westwards you look towards wind turbines and Neolithic barrows like Hetty Pegler's Tump. Northwards the valley runs down to Woodchester, with its buried Roman mosaic and contemporary vineyards, and the alternative delights of Stroud beyond. Up here the wind blows keenly, crows and buzzards catch the thermals and the trees stand stark against the sunset sky.

The Field Centre itself seems to have grown out of the landscape: wooden beams holding up a grass roof, clear columns collecting the rainwater, Cotswold stone entrance and a half-glass, half-copper dome letting in the light of the sun and the planets. Walk inside and you find yourself in an airy atrium with spiral paving and more wooden columns holding up the ring of wood that supports the dome, with the different rooms leading off: the sun room facing north, the library, the seminar room, researchers' offices and then the dining room and kitchen.

At most times of the year, this is an intensely convivial space, with a lot of chat as people come out of meetings and sessions and talk about what's happening with particular students and projects. The warmth is accentuated by

DOI: 10.4324/9781003361541-7

Figure 7.1 The Field Centre

the craft pieces on display or in use: felted slippers to borrow from a willow basket and items in clay, glass or wood, with flowers, plants and vegetables in the centre depending on the season – or sometimes the more mysterious items left from a research project or a weekend workshop.

As you walk around there is a sense of deepening: the rose gold colloid suspended from the dome in a glass sphere, or the different colours that shine through the head-sized pieces of dark glass if you hold them up to the light. In the Sun Room, along with artwork made by cooling wax in the eddies of a stream, there is a piece of glass, textured and coloured using medieval methods, from Steiner's first Goetheanum, burnt down on New Year's Eve 1922.

The rammed-earth inner walls have layers like a cliff face, because the earth comes from across the Trust's provisions, starting from the grey lias clay of the Horsley Valley bottom at ground level. Above this is a waving band of red clay from Stourbridge, yellow clay from Sheffield, light yellow clay from Darlington, golden clay from Clynderwen and on top the light limestone clay of the ridges where the Field Centre sits.

Unlock an unobtrusive door and you walk down a spiral staircase into the depths of the bedrock. Here, at the base of the staircase, is a cleft reaching into the dark, along the lines shaped by rainwater trickling through the limestone of this one-time seabed over the millennia. Facing the other way, you come into an octagonal cloister under the dome, surrounding the clints and grykes of the limestone. A beaten silver flowform sits in the centre of the space, beneath a glass oculus in the atrium floor above. At community events, the flowform runs with the rhythm of collected rainwater and the walls might echo the sound of stories or singing. At others, it is a quiet space in which to research the qualities of light, sound and listening.

Expressing and developing Ruskin Mill's ideas

The Field Centre emerged out of a community process of visioning, shaping a space that both expresses and develops the underlying ideas of the Trust. Echoing a thought expressed in Ruskin Mill's zodiac floor, its shape – with different themes and purposes all branching off a common centre – connects to the Trust's symbol in which the seven fields of practice all centre around the student. Or, more broadly, the human being in all their many aspects and depths (Ruskin Mill Trust 2020).

The Trust's senior leadership meet here, as do staff and outside students doing its Master's degree, connecting and disseminating the underlying principles and purpose of Ruskin Mill. Students sometimes wander in from the farm, and many evening and weekend lectures, workshops and courses bring in outsiders. The new Wool Barn adds space for these activities. Most crucially though, the Field Centre is a main location for the Trust's research, expressing a thought from biodynamic leader Manfred Klett that biodynamic farms may be the "universities of the future".

While Ruskin Mill Trust draws from 19th- and early 20th-century thinkers – Ruskin, Morris and Steiner – it does not imagine any more than they did that time should stand still. The Field Centre's strapline – "research enhanced practice, practice enhanced research" – speaks for itself: the Trust's practice needs to be kept alive through the encounter with many different forms of research, at the same time as it grounds that research in practice.

While all members of staff are encouraged to practice "research with a small r", to be reflective practitioners in their own fields, individual staff members are also supported to carry out action research on elements of their own practice (Reason & Bradbury, 2008), while the wide array of courses offered to staff and external students up to its Master's course involve lesser or greater dimensions of research into different aspects of Practical Skills Therapeutic Education.

Senior staff members are supported to carry out PhDs in leading universities to explore different dimensions of the seven fields in the light of a range of contemporary academic disciplines (see Chapter 5). The *Field Centre Journal* makes some of this available and accessible to wider audiences, and the Centre hosts a range of conferences and seminars. External researchers and – for now – Erasmus+ projects are also housed here.

Just as Ruskin Mill's young people are learning, growing and engaging with the wider world, so too are its staff, and the Field Centre symbolises this. The Centre – and the flowform – were made possible by gifts from Britain, Germany and the US, reflecting the wider conversations it is part of and its commitment to place its work into a broader world.

Figure 7.2 Inside the Field Centre

Goethean enquiry

Along with all of this, the Trust also invests – as part of its charitable objects – in research into the principles underpinning its method, within the tradition of Goethean enquiry. Johann Wolfgang von Goethe (1749–1832) is one of the central figures of German literature, not only best known in English as the author of *Faust* but also a significant natural scientist, making substantial contributions to botany, anatomy and the study of colour (Vine et al., 2018) as well as on method (Kühl & Rang, 2020).

Goethean enquiry is sometimes unhelpfully rendered "Goethean science", but *Wissenschaft* in German is not as narrowly bounded as "science" in English: any systematic body of knowledge, from literature to theology, can be *Wissenschaft*. Goethe's approach to *Wissenschaft* is very much that of a polymath: it is driven by a search for wholeness in the sense of interconnection, seeking to grasp with the mind's eye the principle that informs an empirical object. Before Darwin, he was fascinated by the family resemblances and specific differences of leaves and bones, and sought not so much a grand unified theory as a way of proceeding that would work equally well for all fields of knowledge.

Without going into technicalities, one key element of this is – as in Ruskin Mill's genius loci survey or a student study – to explore the subject from many different angles, and if possible with many different people. Rather than seeking a single narrowly defined type of data, a subject can be approached in many different ways. A Goethean session also has echoes of 18th- and early 19th-century science in the way many different people gather around the microscope or fossil, commenting and reflecting in a friendly way, arriving at a less subjective view not through the dehumanisation of the observer but through the multiplication of observers.

Goethean enquiry is not only this more rounded enquiry, though: it is also *appreciative* enquiry, involving the transformation of the researcher. Following this approach to the subject through many different empirical forms, the researcher themselves becomes an instrument of research, appreciating internally and consciously what they have experienced externally in dialogue with what is being researched and attempting to grasp its inner logic, its informing principle, as a whole. If this may seem hard to follow in relation to leaves or bones, its relevance to understanding a person is easier to understand.

The young person with learning differences and difficulties or behaviour that challenges does not exist on a single dimension, and what makes their lives hard can rarely be resolved in a single measured intervention. To really help them, we need to grasp the "complex co-morbidities" of physical health issues accompanying the learning differences of some of Ruskin Mill's young people, their "spiky profile" of adult language and childish behaviour, their layers of trauma and rejection – and all their strengths: perhaps their extraordinary memory, their wicked sense of humour or their ability to care for others.

We need to see them as a rich whole, made up equally of the gifts they bring to the world and the things that make their lives difficult, and meet them on that level with a real appreciation for who they are and what they need, not as a disembodied technician "applying" a single intervention in one part of their lives. Of course, this is also true for us even if we are not categorised in this way: to know another human being, or to be known, is a process of appreciative enquiry into their complexities and contradictions – as well as the dynamic change and development that is characteristic of life (Sassoon, 2022).

Unsurprisingly, Goethean enquiry is more fully developed in the German-speaking world, but the Field Centre and its network of sister research centres – the Colquhoun Centre at Pishwanton in Scotland, the emerging Castelliz Centre at Plas Dwbl in Wales and Sunfield in the English Midlands – has become the leading context for this perspective in these islands and a significant one in the English-speaking world (Franses et al., 2021; Reakes, 2022a, 2022b).

If Goethean science sees the human being as central, like the impulse behind the Field Centre, then the ultimate purpose of all this research and training, the meetings and the writing is to help young people develop, as the staff also develop themselves and their own work with pupils and students – generating warmth towards the human beings in their care while observing them in their totality.

Self-leadership

Taking courage for self and other

How do we become the kind of people who are able to support the process of transformation in others? If we want to act effectively as therapeutic educators, what does this ask of us? Ruskin Mill talks of the need to "take courage for yourself and others" in this context. Clearly, creating beautiful but carefully thought out settings for young people who are themselves also delightful, demanding and difficult at the same time requires courage in many ways. Courage is not something that exists in isolation – it is a quality we find in ourselves in relation to a task that has our name on it, to something the world needs us to do.

At the same time, since the Romantics this has been seen as the fullest way we can express ourselves – whether as artists, in the public world or in some other way. To identify a purpose for our life that goes beyond simply keeping going is both to ask a deep question about who we are individually and to set a high bar for what living up to ourselves might actually mean. In this sense, self-generated conscious action is not only a goal for young people in difficult situations; it is a goal for the adults who work with them as well as a method for enabling those adults to achieve that goal.

Self, other and world are not ultimately separate. As Steiner put it, "We have arisen from the world; we are a 'small world' in which, in a sense, everything contained in the visible, and a large part of the invisible world, has been compressed". We exist in relationship to one another and the wider world, but also to who we become as we act in these relationships, particularly the challenging ones: our self becomes embodied and enacted.

The seven fields and a fully human life

But what does this mean in practice? The seven fields of Practical Skills Therapeutic Education can be used to understand oneself: for example, I can look not just at the genius loci of a particular geographical location but also ask and seek to understand deeply what my own context – geographical, cultural, social, relational, biographical – means, or that of my organisation.

The seventh field, transformative (self-)leadership, is in part this ethically crucial consideration that what is sauce for the goose is sauce for the gander. If I consider that something is a key part of being human which can help the development of a young person who has experienced a developmental delay, then it is also a key part of being human for the rest of us.

This is, perhaps, the deeper meaning when visitors to Ruskin Mill often say: "I wish my children could come here" and "I wish I had gone here". All too many of us, after all, have been deprived of a rich sense of place(s), cut off from meaningful practical work, disconnected from the food we eat, alienated from experiencing ourselves as developmental beings, and so on. In some ways, the seven fields sketched in this book also mark out the development of a rich human life for anyone.

Figure 7.3 Bringing it all together: weaving at Ruskin Mill College

The need to change ourselves

More than this, however: those of us who find ourselves working with other people's suffering often do so out of a partial connection with our own. It is, after all, easier in some ways to recognise and name other people's wounds and harder to see our own challenges. But working out our own pain through the development of others has its own problems – not least, that damaged young people, who are often very acute people-watchers, will identify in us what we don't want to see in ourselves. Conversely, acknowledging who we are is a tool for self-leadership, for working with the "I" reflectively.

So identifying and naming our own barriers, difficulties and past experiences is a key part of honest and effective working with others. Our processes, unacknowledged, become a cyclical space of repetitive and often imprisoning habits; when named and worked on, they can become spaces of learning and transformation. The life processes (Chapter 5) are internal capacities for self-management. They can also become personal attributes, part of what people find distinctive about us.

Goethean enquiry is an important method for this: in exploring the outer world, we can also transform our understanding of ourselves, reflecting on our own process as we carry out research. Ruskin Mill staff are encouraged to see the self as something to engage with in a form of action research, developing themselves as reflective and reflexive practitioners, taking action to bring about change where needed.

In terms of the different fields, this involves finding a sense of orientation, inwardly navigating our engagement with the resistance of the world, seeing the outside as inside, seeing both connection and separation in our relationship to others, inner beholding, self-diagnosis and finally effort as a kind of grace.

Just as pupils and students are in a process of development, there is also a pathway for staff through the organisation, beginning with induction, moving onto review and supervision. A next step comes with college management – do they accept or reject it, or are they capable of moving towards taking joint ownership of what the college does? Beyond that are roles in the executive team, the initiation of cultural development and finally holding the meta-vision for the Trust as a whole. Each of these represents a transformation of who the staff member is in relation to the workplace.

If staff are learning and changing, this too is something that students perceive and respond to, just as they respond negatively to those whose bottom line is "do as I say, not as I do". Personal transformation is far more easily caught than taught, and role modelling is particularly necessary for many young people.

Setting aside time for this reflective work makes it possible to move from being simply a prisoner of a to-do list and a job description to fully taking ownership of a task and responding to the actual needs encountered. Ruskin Mill's staff are often extraordinarily impressive individuals, in part because of this: working in many different areas simultaneously but seeing the connections between them, flexible and humane in meeting others, acting in response to the particularities of a student or situation but against the background of the complex understandings gestured at in this book.

Figure 7.4 Mastering the crafts: Ruskin Mill College student exhibition

A recent set of reflections for senior staff sets them these questions as challenges arising from the different fields:

Field One (spirit of place) – Am I able to gain orientation, to know what is in front of me, behind, above and below?

Field Two (practical skills) – Am I able to become skilful with the materials and resistance of the earth?

Field Three (biodynamic ecology) – Am I able to cooperate with the being of the earth?

Field Four (therapeutic education) – Am I able to become skilful within myself?

Field Five (holistic support) – Am I able to source resilience within my own constitution?

Field Six (health and the whole human being) – Am I able to name what I still wish to achieve within myself?

Field Seven (transformative self-leadership) – Am I able to take courage for myself and others?

As a set of reflections, and the practical tasks that flow from them, these can of course be useful beyond the Trust itself.

Conversation with Aonghus Gordon

From the external to the internal

Looking at the seven fields of practice, I've done a summary of the leadership element in each (see above), thinking about the specific capacity for orientation it offers. So once we understand say Field One, the spirit of place, as an external practice, the question becomes "what could Field One enable as an internal practice for orientation?"

Leadership means having the capacity to know that this relationship exists, and act on it. A manager may not necessarily know that, which makes a huge difference between a manager and leadership. If you don't have that orientation, you wouldn't necessarily know that you have the possibility of taking a further step and being able to connect, which is where we get the possibility of inwardly navigating ourselves.

You might have a sense of being able to travel in a particular direction on a physical level, but if that's not backed up with something else, if you don't know that this external possibility is connected to a possibility of inner navigation, you will rely on other people. That could work, but if you don't have it yourself, you will stumble when the others don't know the solution. So if you have the external orientation without the internal orientation, and you have to go to your colleagues to ask, "What do you think?" when you really don't have an insight, you have a problem. You're something of a phantom leader.

Ruskin Mill's ultimate goal, of enabling people to become capable of self-generated conscious action, has several steps. One of the steps in developing that skill is to have an interior that can look at itself, a self-reflective consciousness. Actually making time for reflective practice is an important dimension of this.

There are a number of points in the daily cycle which can be optimum times to reflect on the events of the day and prepare for the day ahead. If you look at the sages of the past, and perhaps also those of the present, it is not uncommon to find them reflecting on the events of the day and bringing to light the issues that require resolution.

Practice has shown that if we do such a reflective cycle before sleep, we may find ourselves awakening with new insights in the morning. It is not necessarily that one awakens with an answer, but rather that during the first two or three hours of the day we can find insights, thoughts and imagination passing through us and jolting us into a new thought regarding the issue of the previous day. This is invaluable, and there is an accompanying level of courage needed to test the new understanding of the situation, or the perspective that has arisen.

We can also think of this in terms of the planes of space, of moving forward into an orientation and the ability to reflect. You can imagine those planes of space as being like three mirrors that literally reflect: as a leader, without some awareness of these mirrors you aren't going to handle things very well, and you would need a load of consultants around you.

If you had the orientation but didn't have the capacity to inwardly reflect and navigate, that would be like looking at the frontal plane mirror, the sagittal plane mirror and the horizontal mirror, like being lost in a hall of mirrors. But if you can place yourself in that hall of mirrors and act within it, you're observing yourself in the practical realm – which is being skilful – within Field Two, craftsmanship. How do you take the mirrors of the dimensions of space and convert them into mirrors, tools for self-reflection? That's the task in moving from self-management to self-leadership.

For example, if you were to make a beautiful stool but it didn't work as a stool, how would you understand that? It's beautiful but it doesn't function. So the item itself is the hall of mirrors here, and it's giving you something to reflect on yourself with. You could then picture yourself working on the pole lathe, moving in those different directions, and ask yourself, "What is this activity doing to me?"

Seeing people in the planes of space

Now you need the capacity to imagine for this. You have picturing processes, and the other qualities which you find in people who have an imagination connected to seeing. For example, "This person leans to the right. He walks in for his interview and he's leaning to the right. His head is on the right hand side". I've watched that very frequently and personally I don't like it. It's a kind of apology for their presence: "can you forgive me? Because I'm fine but I'm not. But, you know, please let me have the job". That's my reading of that. And then we move on to a second interview. I'm very interested in this gesturing against the planes of space and the ability to see a picture of a psychological type. I'd be careful with it, but it gives me an insight, which I would definitely want to check out.

In the same way, if somebody has breached the frontal plane and they're crushing my hand, saying, you know, "I'm a strong guy here, Aonghus, I'm right here", I might feel "Oh please go back into your own plane of space. Stop being so zealous". So I look at the psychological tie-in to the planes of space, how people hold themselves, the way they interact, but also how they use the space in the gestures of the body as an assessment tool for adults.

There is a signature of consciousness in how another adult shakes your hand. The gesture of the holding of another person's hand as a handshake is a significant encounter. A sense of the being of the other can be ascertained. It's not the primary decision maker, but it's significant.

Many of these gestures can be understood by thinking about acting. I'm using imagination, and my task is to be able to see things in taking responsibility for leadership. Like a mage: *imagine* is shorthand for that. A mage is a seer.

If you take the planes of space as a template to see through, you are operating from the outside in, into the condition of the picture. Or perhaps you're giving a health check to a particular condition. This exercise also needs to be done by staff with students, but as a skill in terms of bodily gestures as a health check. So inwardly navigating the three dimensions as a template for making an evaluation is part of their training.

"Do I feel comfortable with this gesture of this particular adult who's coming into the organization to teach or manage? Is the gesture the result of a hereditary tradition in a family of potters?" That happens very rarely now, but I have recognised the gesture of a potter in a family succession. And I have to distinguish between what might be a sort of expression of an apologetic character and the case of a potter, whose head is on the right-hand side, often nodding as they kick the wheel, because it becomes part of their character in the craft activity, being in tune with movement and the humility of the material.

The skills of interior navigation

Now if you look at the situation of an adult who's walking into the organisation or at someone who's been in the organisation and is stuck in a particular context or plane, your task is to go into the staff training process and look at the challenge. Depending on where they are, if they are anywhere past 35, you can usually have a very frank conversation. Because my experience shows me that their choices after that age have a different degree of personal freedom, often because their ego has been clarified. If you couldn't do that, because maybe that's not going to work or somebody is rejecting it, then they stay where they are, and that's okay. But I'm afraid that if they move into another role, they're going to be mauled unless they have the equanimity that goes along with it.

So to inwardly navigate is to be able to have picturing skills. In my view, it's about the planes of space in the practical realm of skill, which then become pictures that you can move about. It may even be possible to see future potential here. That means that the craft curriculum for students and the craft curriculum for staff training go beyond any single craft item, because you want them to become skilful in all aspects of movement. So maybe at one time, they're on the pole lathe and at another time they're hammering metal.

Those movements of left and right, forwards and backwards, up and down, in the three dimensions of space, are exercised in most craft work. Sometimes I might feel that a staff member has got stuck and can't actually translate the periphery of movement and bring them into a centre of attention to facilitate activities with students. If so, rather than tell them what is needed, it's characteristic in Practical Skills Therapeutic Education to go through a practical process. I might say: "Could you come in to the blacksmith's workshop and beat a flat piece of metal into a candlestick? And when you've finished it, light it, and reflect on the process". But the possibility for contemplating the centre with a candle would already have been performed in a healthy way by actually beating the metal on the anvil, so I'm working three-dimensionally in developing the syllabus.

That's my job. It's about being able to see and move the pictures, to see the outside as inside. A leader with therapeutic capacity has to be able to translate this seeing into a curriculum, and that's tricky. Meanwhile the leader-warrior's task is to see outsiders inside. If someone is just a warrior, that can be needed when dealing with adolescents. They are giving you a bunch of riddles to resolve, and most of those riddles are about movement.

If you don't have the right seeing capacity, you won't be able to unpack the riddles. So if you're a warrior that can only see inside, you'll stay still. And if you're a warrior that can only see the outside, you're probably going to get your head cut off. But even if you can do both at once, you will sometimes find that you then can't move because you don't feel you can get anything right.

Relating inner and outer

For example, in the definition of health, maybe you can't connect the unhealthy situation that a student presents with to the health of the biodynamic farm, or you can't see that internally the student's food decision-making process needs to change. But ideally you would go back to the farm and say, "For the next six months, with that box of fresh vegetables, let's make sure that the student's focus isn't just about the vitamins they're taking in, but that it's also about the relationships between outside and inside: what have you done during the day? How did you bring it into the home?"

If as an adult you can't see the value of that, then you won't really be able to help that student to see outside and inside herself. So there's this crossing of the boundary. And in the farm organism, which is Field Three, there is a connection between the inside of the student and the health of the outside, of the farm. So you're contributing to that.

There is both connection and separation. This is the bridge, the keystone in the arch of PSTE. What's outside comes in and what's inside comes out, so that the 12 senses kick in. And if a staff member isn't integrated in sensory terms, they won't be able to see both inside and outside in a way that supports executive functioning.

So if what you're seeing can't be digested, if what you're hearing can't be digested, if what you take in from the external world as taste, or the warmth that you generate, combusts inside because there's nowhere to go, because you need to find friendship, then you might end up with sweets rather than friends because you need a substitute for them. All those sorts of things happen: giving people unnecessary privilege because you're buying them into yourself. So you need to be independent in the relationship.

If you look at it on an emotional level: you might have enormous empathy for the student, their condition, their biography, the two-inch thick file of their student history, but then you might find yourself gravitating into a relationship that is not a healthy empathy, but sympathy. You're unwittingly supporting the student and you've entered into their life and you're not able to differentiate and separate out. It's not unusual for professionals to get involved in that very complex situation. So they become captured by the student and fall into the sentimentality of the situation the student finds themselves in, living in a projection.

This is easily avoided if you're on the autistic spectrum, because you stay outside the relationship anyway. And you could be delighted not to be even asked to make any connection. So where do connection or separation really kick in? Getting trapped in sympathy is a failure of self-leadership: you need to both separate from *and* be connected to the student. Goethe's concept is that you can be inside what you're considering and outside it at the same time.

You can see this in our diagram of the what, the how and the why of PSTE: all the points or fields on the left-hand side are external skill sets, and those on the right are internal. So the keystone, Field Four, is the crossing point between outside and inside.

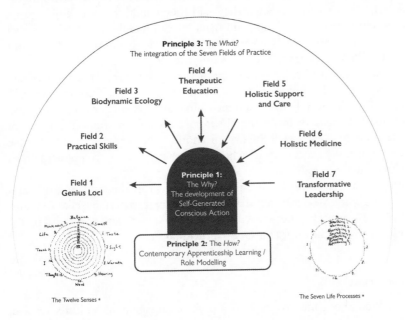

Figure 7.5 The what, the how and the why in PSTE

The importance of teamwork

I would say that any manager needs to have a certain degree of skill in this area, and most people can get as far as Field Four, therapeutic education. It's not difficult in our current education system, where if you work with our kind of students you will have been trained to keep yourself connected both to what's going on inside yourself and with the student in front of you. So the students are the trainers in this context to a certain extent, but unless this speaks fairly eloquently within your constitution, you're going to have problems further on, issues with your colleagues. If you're authoritarian, for example, you'll get rid of colleagues at that point. You won't bring them in much. You won't want anybody bringing the other elements towards you.

So inner beholding is centred on the skill of being able to see the activity of your life processes. For example: do I need a lot of effort to get up in the morning? Even though I might be exhausted from having had to carry too much, maybe I should still arrive at 7 am. I could make a phone call, but I could also take that time off somewhere else, because if I don't come in, then there's probably another set of consequences. So my judgement is that I am going to come in to work because I can see the wider context of my relationship with my colleagues and the action that I'm taking. So as a leader, I'm aware of a more 360-degree perspective.

That also means that I'm practicing the art of letting go, doing something with my feelings of indignation about what happened last night, with my colleagues who didn't turn up when they said they would, or just thinking of a situation where I was left alone. And maybe I can handle that if I know that somebody's observing, which means that I have a degree of trust, that it's not a situation where the organisation is taking the effort for granted.

If I observe my own process of inner picturing, I can see my own necessity for growth, just as I do with students. In other words, I can do my own self-diagnosis; I might be able to see a deficit but not be able to ask for assistance. Or perhaps I can ask for institutional support because my responsibilities are such that I need to. Now will the organisation's meta-vision be able to handle that, or will it just be a cost issue, where the other qualities are not actually in context and understood?

Without self-diagnosis, I don't think you can sit in the student study and take responsibility. So out of self-diagnosis, you create a certain sense of teamwork. We look at each other's strengths and weaknesses and recognise that it all works as a team, but not as a single individual.

From role to task

Steiner talked about life processes as a path of engagement: culture, resolve, exploring, an attitude of gratitude for all things in life. This is what in his philosophy is called a Rosicrucian path, of synergising. You feel connected to the whole of life; you have an attitude of gratitude for all things; you integrate all conditions and maintain your own integrity. This vision is vocation; you see why you're doing what you're doing.

So you move out of limiting yourself by an externally given role to a task you have taken on, which means that you have a degree of knowing why you're doing what you're doing. And you have a sense of the fact that you are responsible for yourself, because you've seen that you need to do some work on yourself, and then the role and the task come together.

For example, as a member of the Executive Team, I might have a sense of my responsibility for safeguarding, where I would feel "I've elected to do this, and as I undertake it, I can also see the gaps in my own capacity. So I will ask for an experience in which I can connect what the students are doing to my requirement of safeguarding and theirs." An example might be that a member of the Executive Team asks for more craftwork so they understand safeguarding, but also so they can link into what the journey of the student is.

One feature of Ruskin Mill is that when something needs to be done, people aren't prisoners of their own job descriptions. Field Seven involves an effortless grace, where people see the context of their own limitations and the colleagueship of others, so that the effort is actually a joy to give. You step into that place, because you're not actually here to fulfil your job description, you are here to change things. And you don't need a reward for the effort. That effortless grace means that you've accepted your karma: this is who I am, this is what I'm doing, this is why I'm here doing it.

Responding to a deeper sense of need

But the work needs to be done without an agenda, and that's tricky; otherwise we're back in desire. So in Ruskin Mill, we move to initiating cultural development, where we start to diagnose what's needed within the organisation, and we move from Field Six (health) into Field Seven, which is about acting not out of your own need but out of the organisation's need.

Within the life process, replication might simply mean inaugurating a healthy reproduction of oneself physically. But in an organisation, reproduction is not just replication, it's also a free gift: it's not subject to my image, but to the image of the meta-vision of the organisation.

If you're McDonald's, you might replicate things because you wanted 5,000 McDonald's: you would eradicate diversity in favour of quantitative replication. But for us there is also a process of discovery here, moving from the inside of the individual outwards as well as from the outside in: who is this person? This is closely connected to Field One, the spirit of place: the capacity to undertake Field Seven in replication, that dimension of leadership or meta-vision.

So we grow whatever the organisational initiative is through the different stages, and it takes on a life of its own. It *has* to be individuated. Otherwise it's an imperial imposition. So I plant these seeds in my flower bed, my veg garden or my herb garden, but then I actually need to see what happens when one bush thrives and something else doesn't really take in the same situation.

We have to accept the sense of place as an aspect of this. For example, when I was replicating Ruskin Mill in diversity at the Glasshouse in Stourbridge, in 2000, the first question I was asked by the staff was, "Will you tell us what to do, please?" and I said, "No." "Well, that's not leadership then is it?" "Yes, because I'm expecting you to discover the entry point of what a student needs. Otherwise, you're depending on me, which is a burden for creativity and future development. And you need to know that I'm not going to hover over you for more than three or four years".

So some people got terribly shocked and horrified, with feelings of abandonment, retribution and so on. Maybe I wasn't skilful enough in that place to actually find a functional leader who could help them understand what it meant to make the decision around when a particular student needs to be doing glass cutting and when they need glassblowing. How do we know that we've done a good lesson? Well, line up the seven cups they've made and see whether there's progress.

Seeing what you're doing

If you don't pay attention to the process of re-creation, you could become a blockage to the process. Then you might need to work with the crafts and observe yourself in the mirroring process. This is where replication is performed on a physical level, and it has some impact on liberating potential, because you're taking material and changing it, and you're also facilitating a mirroring of intention. But if you can't do that, you can't move away, because you can't see what's been achieved.

And people who observe leaders often get caught in projection, because they haven't got through the stage of meeting the image of what they've created. They still need to go through the process to own what it might be like if they did it themselves.

The problem with the practitioner is that they are in part a mage because they can create something out of nothing. The blacksmith was always seen in medieval times as close to the devil, because nobody else could work out how you create a lock in a door, because they had a kind of pictorial thinking in which they saw the practical world and how to resolve solutions. Practitioners may be seen as challenging, but that's why we work with them. They're not lacking in managerial skills just because they don't cohere to a linear structure, because they work in three dimensions.

As a leader, do you understand what it means to manage practitioners who have already described what it is they do, not in written form, but in three-dimensional form? If you ask them to reduce that down to two dimensions, you'll have difficulties. So you have to find a way of getting three-dimensional evidence of the skill-set that they have achieved, know how to interview them correctly and support them. And in fact moving away from the two-dimensional image towards a three-dimensional understanding is a key aspect of leadership.

Leadership and resilience in a changing organisation

The context of how leadership shows up in Ruskin Mill Trust is complex, in that it's an ever-changing organisation. So the moment you might think that you understand your role as Principal in relationship to your own team, the role of Head of Care, the Head of Learning, the Education and Learning Co-ordinators or your own deputy, something else will change. Not only do we work on ourselves as a process of self-leadership, but our "place" – geographical, organisational, interpersonal and so on – is also always changing, and we have to keep reassessing where we stand.

Managing yourself is central to creating confidence and consistency; and yet consistency is the very aspect that you can't rely on. The students bring a certain unpredictability. There's the vulnerability of the social arena from which they come and the complexity of the social layers that have given rise to the student profile. An auntie dies, emotional experience can't be digested, there's grief, anger, distress – and sometimes the parents might rely on the students more than the students can rely on the parents. So who's holding the grief for the parent whose child's auntie has died?

Over several years as Principal, you will see just about every social challenge that's available, so your internal resilience is greater than would otherwise be the case. And the resilience that has to emerge is very often located in a nonreactive form, which I would consider to be a trait of any senior leadership, but it needs to be consistent.

How do we create that resilience? In terms of self-leadership, we do have a very carefully honed and bespoke programme of resilience training, in which the emotional observation of the self is key to how one responds both to oneself or to the world. So holding oneself to account for the vision and the idea of what our students and staff require is an exceedingly important step to be achieved.

The training for self-leadership needs to be coordinated within a team context, researched through the current delivery of Ruskin Mill's Master's on Field Seven. This is not to say that leadership training does not exist: far from it. The key developers of self-leadership for the staff are the students themselves, as they stand in front of you expecting exquisite role modelling and self-leadership. We are trained inadvertently by those who require trust, consistency and self-knowledge.

Now if we ask what resilience training delivers in this situation, we've mentioned the emotional life, but that is to a certain extent a response to a constitutional quality. The constitutional qualities that give the capacity for resilience could be seen as what Steiner calls the life processes, or part of what we deliver to the students in their domestic environment, the seven care qualities.

So in self-leadership training, we're looking at the whole issue of care for others and self-care. How do we observe ourselves in relationship to certain personal qualities that may not be fully effective? The ability for self-leadership is more connected to whether one knows about one's weaknesses rather than one's strengths, in seeing the weaknesses, let's say, of your capacity to generate warmth. In my understanding, if you can't sustain your own warmth and you're pleading to others to be warmed in whatever way, as friendship or as coercing others to like you, you will not last very long as a principal or head teacher.

What is this quality of warmth? In our students, we're looking for an external quality, developing the ability to not go around like a scarecrow, shivering in a T-shirt in the first frost, which is not unusual at an early stage. How do we encourage students to take responsibility for the fact that the temperature has now dropped and that maybe a jacket is more appropriate?

That's self-care, to ensure warmth is the precursor for our own self-knowledge, to understand that situation of not being able to generate warmth, in a situation where emotional warmth is demanded, let's say a very unpleasant situation between students. A principal will have to handle a certain degree of adversity every day and your colleagues will expect to see warmth in dealing with that. So a leader needs the emotional capacity to make quite a vibrant offering of warmth.

Working with diversity and complexity

If we move to the third life process, nutrition, it's clear that if a student can't take in quality food, they're unlikely to be able to concentrate or even have the capacity to think coherently in a supported way, either about themselves or about a problem.

This is exemplified by not having breakfast in the morning. Those students who arrive without having eaten breakfast may bring high levels of anxiety and disturbance with them. And so not having nutrition is directly linked to their own turbulent conduct. But what does that look like in a leader?

Nutrition, by definition, would be something that a leader would be able to handle, that basic functionality. But in an adult, you're looking for more than physical nutrition. You're looking at how you can appreciate the diversity of the styles of tutor management, the styles of teaching, that quality that lives in an individual that can give enrichment to a very broad spectrum of students. You could call that "my way of entering the relationship of a student". And the constellation of tutors is very, very varied.

So if as a leader, you say "I only really want to be delivering chips as a methodology of nutrition", rather than making a balanced platter of skills available for the students, you have not recognised the importance of diversity, in how the students are going to draw their capacity to learn from this diverse group of people. So can a leader understand that maybe there may be a teacher – metaphorically – delivering coconut milk, whereas another one is delivering chips, or another member of staff might be creating a capacity out of the sense of place as a method of learning in which everything is cohesive? Nothing is imported here; it's all actually grown within the context of the culture. It's grown and delivered: the style of teaching within the method, within the vision, within the values. So can a leader cope with that degree of diversity?

Reflective practice

We could then move on to the next life process and say, "Well, how do those teachers reflect on what it is they've done? Are they able to articulate it or can they let it go? Can they reflect on it?" This is an important element, which in Steiner's seven life processes is called "secreting", the ability to produce out of yourself.

If as a competent teacher, you can't reflect on what has been given to you, and let it go as a gift, or go inside it and own it, then you're unlikely to be able to see how you can improve what's been reflected on. So you could say the gift of secretion is the ability to look back at what you've generated, given and reviewed again. Stephen Covey has researched the seven habits of highly effective people, and what he's found is that there is a whole process in leadership of how you yourself are the implement and the instrument for your own change, at the same time that you can change the context of the organisation you're leading.

So reflective practice around yourself and reflective practice around the organisation are inextricably linked. And the training that's emerging here is about being able to correlate, for example, those insights with the emerging self-leadership training and with the life process transformations that are deemed to be significant moments for reflection for senior leaders.

Part of this appears in the self-leadership training; but there are other aspects to it, in that the question that ultimately surfaces as an everyday factor for a senior leader in the Trust is whether you've got to grips with the very foundational issue which is that "I chose to be here".

And if you understand the implication of that choice, then on reflection you know that if something's not right, then you are jointly accountable for that. So to start projecting the incorrectness of a decision as an organisational issue rather than "I made that decision" does show up some fairly fundamental issues around the capacity for self-reflection.

What is interesting is that many staff will arrive with prior knowledge of the organisation: very often possibly rumours, or what's on the internet – and it can be challenging for them to get through the first test, which is "So you've heard the rumours. How are you going to handle those rumours so that they don't drive your questions or your judgments when you sit in the interview?"

My assumption when I actually interview prospective staff is that they will have heard all the rumours, and some are well rehearsed. So checking-in discreetly and indirectly as to how they handle those rumours is already a kind of test as to whether they're likely to be able to stand outside social pressures and make their own personal judgements, which they'll need to do to be a leader in Ruskin Mill Trust.

The other element in questioning is the degree to which they can answer a very important question, which is "Please describe a personal failure". That's a remarkable question, because mature adults understand the significance of the question while the less mature will go into a defensive mode: "Well, how can I possibly tell you about a failure, because that will be judged against me?"

But we're in an organisation where, very often, we're dealing with the past failures of countless decisions made by adults about the young people who come to us and we can't simply have retribution for that. We have to understand that that is the nature of the kind of culture that we're in, and then you've already got a major insight. So a defensive response to that question is not helpful. Of course possibly the most dangerous answer is, "Well, I don't know of any failures". That's my personal favourite, and it's not uncommon.

At the moment when the candidate can't actually digest the question fully, you can put on a scale of one to ten their capacity to describe whether it's personal; whether they've even listened to the question; whether it's professional; whether it's a family issue; whether it's something with their children; whether it's a regret, not even a failure.

Only very rarely can somebody give the question a really full answer. It involves quite a degree of reflective practice and insight, perhaps located in the context of a wider team, not only to describe but also to understand a personal failure. And at that point, of course, you are seeing an immense strength.

So it's not that we're not looking for failure. We're actually looking for the tone of the voice, the description, the choice of the personal failure without making any excuse, so that it just leaves a kind of legacy, "I was able to reflect in the process of its failure in such a way that it's clear to us that that of course it won't happen again".

Difficult questions

That's a distinctive leadership question, which is part of the interviewing process. There may be other questions, quite unexpected ones. For example, I've often asked people how they would wish to be buried, which HR directors have told me I can't ask any more. I've been told that I could be sued because it's an inappropriate question, and that it could be read as a religious question and hence discriminatory.

When I was allowed to ask that question, I was able to see into the line of an adult's capacity to have a way of seeing into the future, in their own personal pathway and relationship to the world, but also whether this is a deeply abstracted area of fear for them.

The word fear is really critical to me. Are the adults that I'm asking to take responsibility for young adults fear-full, or are they able to engage those areas of their own personal relationship to the world so that they can tackle some of the terror that their students may experience without feeling fearful themselves?

Or you could set up a question, in which you describe a dilemma, an emotional situation where the student either receives a sentimental reward or a developmental reward. And you need to be able to understand that in that particular situation a sanction as a developmental reward would be the right approach. A sentimental reaction might perpetuate a sense of apology to the person, but they need to understand that learning and development are not retributions or punishments, but an engagement into transformation. The answer that we're always looking for is the clear and firm response, rather than the sentimental response which ensures that the revolving door is never really challenged for those young people.

There are a few other key things that are important. Asking biographical questions of an adult is primary. Do they see themselves as being on a path of development, or is it a series of accidents that they really don't want to take responsibility for? And there's a question mark if they've found themselves moving in and out of other organisations. So we might ask, "Please, could you give me the last seven, eight years of your development curve in regards to your professional work? Because I see that you've had five different jobs. Is there a continuum in this or is this something very different going on?"

It is my view that we make those choices; they're not accidents. You cannot blame another company for your experience when you chose to apply for it. Did you find yourself discharging yourself? Not being able to face up to the same challenge? Are there the same challenges in how you actually move on? But the real question here is "Do you see yourself in a continuum of development or do you effectively see yourself as a victim of different work experiences and companies?"

If there's a tendency to see yourself as being constantly a victim in your biography or your work, it would be inappropriate to appoint you, because one of our key tenets is role modelling. We are working in our student profiles with the very situation of victimhood, and we need to have role models that can help them transform that.

Developing emotional depth

We've already talked about the degree to which somebody in a leadership position personally owns their path of development. For me, that is the number one thing. If you own your path of development, then you understand that in adversity and resilience, you can actually deal with the wave of challenges which you will inevitably meet. That could come from the authorities, from letting a student down, from a kind of mini-insurrection of students on the campus, from a group of staff who are consistently resistant, who may contribute to sabotaging decisions about method or policy: all those things are within your remit to slowly resolve.

You will need to have the reflective practice to understand how to develop emotional intelligence here. I think in *Emotional Intelligence*, Daniel Goleman (1996) observed that leadership is far more than just intelligence: it includes empathy and social skill, self-awareness, self-regulation and motivation. How do you put that emotional intelligence into relationships so that you can rise above adversity?

In Ruskin Mill, leadership is more about finding the right people in the first place, so a huge effort goes into initial staff interviews. By contrast, in many organisations what is key is manipulating the organisation's machinery once people have been appointed. So we still need to find a leadership profile in which the method has a high degree of congruence with their personality type; it's still a marriage of the two. We're now moving to a point where our training, in the Master's and elsewhere, can contribute to bringing people from the appointment process and match the personality with the method. We are still looking for human capacities to be able to transform themselves in line with what they will need to be able to do.

Incidentally the matching of the curriculum, the culture and the personality is still done as an art form, in a similar way that the timetable for students is still to some extent an art form, involving a high degree of intuition and sensing by senior leaders as to what would be helpful. But increasingly we bring in insight from various reflections, whether from the Education, Health and Care Coordinator, the senior tutor or the deputy of the college, with new information that can entail a change of timetable.

And it's the same with appointing a leader. In the past, where the Trust did try appointing people based on a list of competencies, we had some very strange appointments. It was quite embarrassing to see that the competencies listed on paper didn't match the abilities that were implicit in the reflection process, which was in turn embodied in the method itself that a leader had to ensure. We had a kind of breakdown in the relationship between, let's say, the emotional depth that's required to handle a curriculum based on Practical Skills Therapeutic Education, as against a list of competencies.

Going beyond

You're almost always looking for someone who can go beyond their existing context. You're looking for craftspeople who are capable of becoming educators; for people with an educational background who are able to engage with all the practical challenges we have; or for people from the mainstream who are open to doing something radically different. There is no pre-existing profile of somebody who can just step into a Ruskin Mill role.

However, the central challenge is the understanding in a leader that abstract reflection is not the starting point for learning. The starting point is to perform something with the student and *then* to reflect on it, which then can be vindicated by the practical item and the conversation and reflection about it.

This is quite opposite to traditional leadership training; but if you don't start there, you will have an "impositional" leadership model which will bounce someone out of Ruskin Mill pretty quick. There are several approaches to the situation – to request a personal development review, for example, or that they take on a course in which the choice of thinking is available, which may help to orient themselves to the deeper motivation of the Trust for the young people. They're obviously competent people, they're liked – however, what are their competencies? And so without seven fields training as a method of leadership in itself, you won't get the kind of congruence where particular fields relate to particular aptitudes and we see this as the method both for adult training and for student development.

We now have a constant process of trying to embed things, structure things, develop procedures and processes, appoint people, as a set of initiatives, but it doesn't *always* work. One of the challenges that partly divides me from some of my colleagues is that, if a leader doesn't hold the knowledge of the method in their psyche and doesn't understand that the detail of the method *is* the strategic direction itself, you then have to transcend that from simply creating the framework of policies, procedures, processes and so on. If they haven't had that training fully, you might consistently disrupt a leader's choice-making. That has been one of the kind of shadow aspects of Ruskin Mill.

On the other hand, there's a reason why it's still here, so it's a bit of a bone of contention for everybody. It's arisen like that partly because the PSTE method was historically seen to be supplementary to the outcome: up until about 14 years ago, PSTE wasn't seen as the thing in itself, just the icing on the cake. Most leaders didn't care. So what happened is that a few senior people would intervene – let's say in rescheduling priorities – so that the craft curriculum would be obstructed. And at Ruskin Mill College, it really was: we nearly lost craft as a whole. The refounding of the governance of the Trust then ensured an unencumbered strategic development in line with the method.

For that reason, I have this attitude of dropping in everywhere and connecting with the student profile and the curriculum delivery. If you know that background, you might understand why our meetings are still peppered with me saying "No, it's not like that. It's better that we do it like this". I hope this is nothing to do with "Aonghus's sense of not having involvement in everything". It's purely to do with the fact that this dimension – who our students are and the curriculum we offer them – is more strategic than anything else is, and that has three or four different other pedagogical attributes.

So that's a tricky face of the organisation, but it has a history. We don't want to be like that, but our goal is for our training to become such that people "get it" pretty quickly. So if we look at new appointments, there is an immediate appreciation there of the practical entry into learning, from the perspective that you need a whole variety of methods to be able to work with learning difficulties. So there are no barriers there. There's an immediate appreciation that this is healthy, and the only issue would be changing it and innovating it.

Help more, judge less

Trust is one of the key attributes of leadership. Trust can be thought of as confidence in the relationship with the unknown, being able to navigate the unknown. So speed can be the enemy of trust. You need to avoid the belief that you can control the unknown, and instead develop the capacity to navigate it confidently.

The antithesis of leadership is the statement "I don't care": the demand for more autonomy without requisite responsibility does not work. Autonomy means seeing more of the picture and acting accordingly. So if you want to train to be a leader: look for a problem, find a problem, solve a problem.

And one way of thinking about a healthy organisation is to say that it is constantly facing problems, challenges from the world. Like a person, it needs this resistance to identify the areas where it needs to grow and develop. For this reason, progress in solving problems is useful as a goal, but we shouldn't think of arriving at some perfect place where we are no longer changing, developing or learning.

Of course there are different kinds of problems. Some things simply require a bit of time and effort, but these are not necessarily those we learn most from. Research shows that the most significant problems can only be resolved by moving from an individualised response – everyone staying within their organisational job description – to collaboration, a purpose-driven organisational clarity. We can only solve those kinds of problems on a different level than the level at which we first encounter them.

At the end of the day, of course, this means people serving people, seeing that we are there to try and help others rather than just to do a job. People learn by stepping outside of their comfort zone, but on average only about 20% of people in any given organisation are willing to make the kinds of changes that are needed to resolve real problems, and they are matched by the 20% who will resist and obstruct.

This is true at every level. Managers are not typically problem solvers in this wider sense; they are people doing the best they can to operate within the constraints of particular conditions, so they are often invested in the way things are. Changing those conditions, reorganising the order of things within an organisation, is the role of leaders, which is something different.

But leaders also have to think about the problem of change: how can a leader negotiate their own blind spot? Because any leader will have one, and it may even be a consequence of their strengths. In particular, if you only appoint people who are like you in important ways, you diminish your ability to solve problems. Leadership is embedded in the possibility of seeing clearly.

Leaders change the order of things for the better, and this also needs to include horizontal networking, leadership by observing other people's practice in leading. Collaboration is really important here, and one thing that a leader can bring to this is the ability to nuance and be focussed when discussing solutions, distilling down the essence of what really matters.

Figure 7.6 Performing self-leadership: the Arthur play at Ruskin Mill College

A good leader's mantra should be: help more, judge less. Leaders add value and solve problems for others. The leader of the past knew how to tell, but the leader of the future knows how to ask. People close to the problem generally know, so you should always ask them.

Ultimately, the principal quality needed for leadership is courage, because setbacks are part of taking on leadership. So stamina is essential. In practice, leaders need to hold three different qualities when they are trying to solve problems. One is the understanding of culture, of how people work within the organisation. A second is what the organisational metrics are, what it is measuring itself against: how will we know if we are making progress? Thirdly, what is the process and structure needed to move things forward?

The key activities that leaders need to engage in when they are shaping the future are: ask, listen, think, thank, respond, involve, change, follow up. So ask other people; listen to what they say; think about the different things you've heard; thank everyone; respond to what's been said, involve people in what happens next; change things; and then follow up to really embed the change within the organisation.

Bibliography

Franses, P., Reakes, S., & Vine, T. (2021). *The legacy of Bortoft, Colquhoun and Goodwin*. Ruskin Mill Trust.

Goleman, D. (1996). *Emotional intelligence: Why it can matter more than IQ*. Bloomsbury.

Goodwin, B. (2001). *How the leopard changed its spots: The evolution of complexity*. Princeton University Press.

Kühl, J., & Rang, M. (2020). A model for scientific research. *In Dialogue, 1*, 60–71.

Reakes, S. (2022a). A morphology of Goethean science (part i). *Field Centre Journal of Research and Practice, 7*, 83–91.

Reakes, S. (2022b). A morphology of Goethean science part II. *Field Centre Journal of Research and Practice, 8*, 88–97.

Reason, P., & Bradbury, H. (2008). *The Sage handbook of action research* (2nd edition). London: Sage.

Ruskin Mill Trust. (2020). *The seventh anniversary of the field centre*. Ruskin Mill Trust.

Sassoon, J. (2022). Morphology and the dawn chorus. *Field Centre Journal of Research and Practice, 8*, 75–87.

Seamon, D., & Zajonc, A. (Eds.). (1988). *Goethe's way of science*. SUNY Press.

Vine, T., Löbe, N., & Rang, M. (2018). *Experience colour*. Nailsworth: Ruskin Mill Trust.

Conclusion

An inspiration for the modern world

Entering a Ruskin Mill provision and talking to staff and students for the first time, there is something in the air that is noticeably different from almost anywhere else: a distinctive aesthetic to the buildings and the craftwork, a smell of baking or of the land, a definite flavour to how people talk, a sense of purposeful activity and of course a sense of place. With longer acquaintance, the transformations in young people's lives become visible.

Most attempts to verbalise what Ruskin Mill does stutter to a halt, or make more sense in conversation than on the written page – precisely because its practice does not come in any simple way from a Theory or a Method. In the immediate, of course, it comes from the spirit of place, the practice of craft-work and farming, the orientation to a therapeutic education, holistic care and so on – a being and a doing which are hard to translate back into words.

This book has set out to explain the practices and ideas underpinning all of this, using the framework of Practical Skills Therapeutic Education. It is not always easy to do this, particularly since the inspirational figures who inspired the method, people like John Ruskin, William Morris or Rudolf Steiner – with their vast and sprawling writings, polymathic interests and gentle but radical questionings of the foundations of much of the modern world – are them-selves not always accessible.

However, Ruskin Mill is not a place where a branded, one-size-fits-all Method is imposed on hapless young people irrespective of their individual qualities and needs. Nor is it an attempt to turn ideologies into institutions. If it is a coherent, and largely consistent, encounter between ideas and practices, visions and challenges, the actual processes are much more complex; and that is one reason for this book.

That encounter is also a meeting between *people*, between students strug-gling with all sorts of difficulties and the staff who are trying to support their development. PSTE has developed out of this meeting, as an attempt to put into words what practitioners found to work for the young people they were teaching: it is not a ready-made ideology but a constantly developing way of describing best practice. The seven fields used to structure this book's chapters appeared as the result of an action learning thesis exploring Ruskin Mill's prac-tice. And the language of PSTE is still evolving, trying to capture its changing

DOI: 10.4324/9781003361541-8

Figure 8.1 Transforming material, transforming self: blowing hot glass at Glasshouse
        College

practice better and transmit it to incoming staff while engaging both with classic ideas and with contemporary research.

This book has tried to do three things in each chapter. Firstly, it has invited
you to visit some of Ruskin Mill Trust's many different provisions and engage
with these different post-industrial buildings and farming landscapes to see
how their potential is being re-imagined for the present day. It has then introduced each of the seven fields of practice that make up the method of PSTE:
the spirit of place, practical skills, the ecology of the farm, therapeutic education, holistic care, human health and transformative self-leadership. We have
tried to unpack some of the "why" and the "how" of each of these in turn in
an accessible and useful way. Finally, it has gone deeper into how the project
has emerged and developed over the years and some of the underpinning
thoughts that have accompanied it.

In the process, we have gone from some of the most basic and urgent
needs facing vulnerable young people to some of the greatest challenges facing any human being today. Education and social care are in crisis, not only
in Britain but globally: parents have to battle daily for their children; budg-
ets are squeezed; increasing regulation of all areas is both very necessary but
produces many unintended consequences. More broadly, the limitations of
existing models are becoming increasingly evident in many ways – a crisis of
ecology and food, a disconnect from place and the natural world, alienation
from our own bodies and practical capacities, and so on. We do not want to
claim that Ruskin Mill offers a complete solution to this crisis, but we do hope
that its experience can be helpful to those looking for ways out of the crisis

and an alternative strategy which places the whole human being at its heart – both who they are in all their fullness and the real potential they are capable of achieving.

Bloodless accounts of policy and best practice often take the very structures which are in crisis as the only possible framework to operate within – even when we know how different they are from one place to another, and how many times they have changed within recent history. The need to teach and learn, the need to care and be cared for, the need to make and grow our world – all of these are part and parcel of our species, not recent inventions. It would be more honest to say that there are often moments of great inspiration and innovation in response to crisis (Ruskin, Morris and Steiner represent examples of this) followed by periods of formalising and institutionalising. A continuous effort at renewal is needed to find a language to re-imagine how these kinds of inspiration can speak to the needs of a changing world.

Ruskin Mill, and this book, start from attempting to listen carefully to those needs as they are today: to the desperation of parents and guardians facing a seemingly incomprehensible system; to the frustrations, resignations, defiance and desperation of young people who have been repeatedly failed by the very institutions that were supposed to help them; to the specifics of different places and communities, what they make possible and what wounds they carry within them; to the practices of craft, landwork, therapeutic education and care as staff reflect on their own work; to the wider needs of the world we are in at every level. We do not claim that every answer here is the right one; but we are convinced that it is fundamental to listen to these deeper realities and try to make institutional structures adequate to them, rather than try to fit people into those structures.

This book is written in this spirit, of sharing a particular experience of people, places and practices. The aim is both to be helpful to people who are seeking immediate solutions and to offer inspiration to people who are thinking through for themselves how they can find a way to help others, to bring their skills into dialogue with the needs of the world and to contribute to cultural transformation.

The craft of writing from practice

This book captures a moment in time, but Ruskin Mill Trust is still evolving, as the method develops and is researched further and as the needs of the world change. The practice of the Trust involves creating forms like a potter: the material is shaped to what people require, in different ways. There are forms that represent stability where something has been shown to work, while others invite new social ideas. These forms are put into the world and different people – students and pupils, staff and parents, the wider community – "read" them in different ways.

The seven fields of Practical Skills Therapeutic Education, its shape as a method, became clear when Aonghus was doing the action research that eventually became his Master's thesis. This shape was then converted into the Trust's *Practitioner's Guide*, a staff training manual to hold the content generated by Aonghus and other practitioners over the years. At present the guide is being rewritten by senior staff practitioners, each holding a different field, as the basis for the Trust's Master's in PSTE: ideally, this is how the process of handing on works, from founder to practitioners, and from practitioners to new staff and others. As Laurence commented to Aonghus, Ruskin Mill Trust *is* his doctoral thesis.

The interviews in each chapter give a good sense of this process: how each aspect of Ruskin Mill's work came about and developed in response to a concrete situation presented by the world, and how that situation changed. What all of this means, of course, is that people – staff and students – are at the centre of PSTE. Aonghus as the founder has driven that process, with the very particular combination of vision, energy and skills that he has brought to the project and the long history of how he and his early colleagues responded to students' needs, a history which has then developed into the more formalised institutions of Ruskin Mill today.

If Ruskin Mill draws on many centuries of craft and farming skills and on multiple traditions of creative thought, these things still have to be embodied in actual people who bring their vision to bear on specific situations and real-world needs; otherwise, nothing will happen. That process is always continuing, and not only in Ruskin Mill. This book – which is not a thesis – is laid out so that people can explore and investigate different aspects of the Trust's

Figure 8.2 "I wish I could have gone here": on the pole lathe

work: we have not wanted to create a coffee table book, but rather one that people would become active with: to take the practical exploration further in their own lives and work.

What next?

We hope you have found this introduction to Ruskin Mill's method both hopeful and helpful. Hopeful, in that human lives, including those of young people with learning difficulties and our own, can be richer, can hold more meaning and purpose, and can support us to become more fully ourselves; and helpful, in that there are practical things that can be done to move in this direction.

If so, what can you do next?

You might of course wish to engage with Ruskin Mill itself. Potential students and pupils, their parents and guardians, are always welcome and the Admissions team will be happy to arrange a visit. Social enterprises – cafés, shops and heritage centres – offer an easy way to visit in many cases. Public events, festivals and conferences take place at different Ruskin Mill provisions, all of which are worth visiting in themselves. Many of our courses – in craft, biodynamics, Goethean science and the Master's in PSTE among others – are open to the public. There are also many opportunities for volunteering and employment.

If this book has whetted your appetite for reading more, you can find several Ruskin Mill books via the Field Centre website, along with the *Field Centre Journal of Research and Practice* and the holistic science journal *In Dialogue*. All are free to download and copies of recent publications can usually be picked up at Ruskin Mill provisions.

In writing this book, we have tried to speak to people in a very wide range of situations who feel that every human being deserves the chance to re-imagine their potential. We have tried to imagine parents and guardians of young people with complex additional needs, and indeed some potential students, some perhaps reading this book who might be able to seek admission to a Ruskin Mill provision in Britain, but many who for various reasons will not.

We have thought of people working in special needs education, in social care, in therapy or medicine for whom this book might be of immediate professional interest. However, we have also imagined a much wider range of craftspeople, farmers, educators and carers who might be looking for inspiration to take their own work deeper in some way, or thinking of new initiatives.

We are profoundly aware of the wide range of exceptional work being done in all of these areas, at the same time as we see the depth of needs and suffering to be met, and the limitations of many of attempts at responding to them. It is no criticism of the courageous and extraordinary efforts that are being made to say that we need many more people, around the world, to commit to such efforts, to create new initiatives and breathe new life into existing institutions.

Finally, this book has been written in the conviction that the seven fields sketched out here – a spectrum of fields of practical engagement with the world – can benefit not only young people with learning difficulties but also

Figure 8.3 "I can see a future for myself. I can do things that I never would have thought as being possible for me."

those who work with them, whether family members or carers, paid professionals or volunteers.

Beyond this again, Practical Skills Therapeutic Education systematises many years of experience in which these seven fields of engagement have proven transformative even in extraordinarily challenging circumstances. Ruskin Mill's charitable objectives mandate sharing this learning with the wider world so that others can also draw on this in ways appropriate to age, personality and circumstances. Our hope is that this book may help those who are wondering how they can become more fully themselves, and how they can contribute to the wider world more deeply.

Bibliography

Field Centre website https://www.thefieldcentre.org.uk/
Ruskin Mill Trust website https://rmt.org

Index

Note: *Italicized* and **bold italics** refer to figures and boxes.